SOUTHERN LITERARY STUDIES

Louis D. Rubin, Jr.
Editor

GRACE KING

The young Grace King, about 1880

Grace King

A SOUTHERN DESTINY

ROBERT BUSH

LOUISIANA STATE UNIVERSITY PRESS

BATON ROUGE AND LONDON

Copyright © 1983 by Louisiana State University Press
All rights reserved
Manufactured in the United States of America

Designer: Barbara Werden
Typeface: Linotron Perpetua
Typesetter: G & S Typesetters, Inc.

Library of Congress Cataloging in Publication Data

Bush, Robert, 1917–
Grace King: a southern destiny.
(Southern literary studies)
Includes index.
1. King, Grace Elizabeth, 1852–1932.   2. Authors,
American—19th century—Bibliography.   3. New Orleans (La.)
in literature.   I. Title.   II. Series.
PS2178.B87   1983   813'.4 [B]   83-9849
ISBN 0-8071-1111-2

To the memory of my parents
Wallace A. Bush and
Sara M. Bush

Contents

Illustrations

Acknowledgments

It is a pleasure to record my indebtedness to individuals and libraries incurred during the long task of preparing this book. First, I wish to thank John M. Coxe of New Orleans, who has given me permission to publish from the very large collection of Grace King Papers now deposited in the Department of Archives and Manuscripts at Louisiana State University, Baton Rouge. Many of the photographs are from the same collection, and they too are published with Mr. Coxe's consent. He has also kindly permitted me to publish from his own collection of letters of Charles Gayarré and has given me family permission to publish from Grace King's letters in other libraries. Mr. Coxe has answered many of my questions about family relationships within the King family and has generally cooperated enthusiastically as I have gathered research for this book.

Over a period of many years I have been given invaluable assistance by the staff of the Department of Archives and Manuscripts, Louisiana State University. My thanks go to M. Stone Miller, Jr., for the courtesies of the department he heads and for permission to publish the manuscript material I have quoted.

The sources of individual manuscripts are indicated in the notes. Among the numerous libraries whose holdings I have used in this book are the Beinecke Rare Book and Manuscript Library, Yale University, and William R. Perkins Library, Duke University. From my earlier volume, *Grace King of New Orleans* (Louisiana State University Press, 1973), I have reprinted selections from manuscripts acknowledged by me in that book. These include manuscripts from the University of California, Berkeley; the Louis Round Wilson Library, University of North Carolina; Manuscripts Division, New York Public Library; the Library, Pennsylvania State University; Academic Center Library, University of Texas; and Howard-Tilton Library, Tulane University.

I am grateful to the editors of the *Southern Literary Journal* for permission to publish substantial portions of my article "Charles Gayarré and Grace King: Letters of a Louisiana Friendship" (fall, 1974). I also thank the editors of the *Southern Review* for permission to use my article "Grace King: The Emergence of a Southern Intellectual Woman" (April, 1977) as the basis for Chapter Three of this book. I am grateful as well to the Duke University Press for permission to use in Chapter Four sections of my article "Grace King and Mark Twain," which appeared in *American Literature* (March, 1972).

I am indebted to the following for particular kindnesses: to Professor William W. Howells for permission to quote from a letter of William Dean Howells to Grace King; to Coralee Ankney, registrar of Trinity Church, New Orleans, for information about the baptism and confirmation of Grace King; to Audrey Vough, acquisitions librarian, Transylvania College, and to Helen H. Shelton, recorder, University of Virginia, for information about the education of William Woodson King. The photograph of Mark Twain on page 81 is reprinted by permission of the Mark Twain Foundation, c/o Edward J. Willi, 74 Trinity Place, New York, N.Y. 10006. The photograph of the portrait of Grace King by Wayman Adams on page 298 is reproduced through the courtesy of the New Orleans Museum of Art. My thanks go to William Fagaly, assistant director, for showing me the original painting. The drawing on page 299 satirizing Adams' portrait is by William Spratling from the book he created with William Faulkner, *Sherwood Anderson and Other Famous Creoles*. It is from the 1966 edition and is reproduced with the kind permission of the University of Texas Press.

I am grateful to Grace Hurst, a daughter of Will King, for granting me an interview and answering questions about her aunt, Grace King, and also to David C. Coxe for permission to publish his photograph of the Grace King house on Coliseum Street, New Orleans.

Of the various writings about Grace King that have been useful to me I would single out David Kirby's *Grace King* (Boston, 1980). Professor Kirby and I corresponded while we were preparing our books so that they would complement rather than excessively overlap each other. I also should mention the following unpublished dissertations that are important to my subject: Earl Noland Saucier, "Charles Gayarré, The Creole Historian" (George Peabody College for Teachers, 1933), and James R. Frisbie, "New Orleans Writers and the Negro . . . 1870–1900" (Emory University, 1972).

Finally, I am most grateful to the Department of English and the administration of Herbert H. Lehman College, City University of New York, for support of my scholarship and especially for a faculty fellowship which enabled me to hasten the conclusion of my project.

GRACE KING

One

Before Appomattox: The King Family History to 1865

I n 1896 Grace King wrote, "a woman is more truly made up of her past than a man. In truth, she may be said to be the accident or the miracle of her past." This principle, she believed, applied particularly to her own character and career, and she would have agreed with C. Vann Woodward's more recent observation that southern writing is characterized almost universally by the dominance of the influence of the past. But she was also aware that this dominance could be a weakness. In 1912 she warned her young friend Warrington Dawson: "Do not let your heart tie you too fast to the South. I realise that love of the past is a source of weakness, just as any other passion too fondly indulged. You live in the 'living present'—from which you must draw inspiration."[1]

As a child Grace King was exposed to the important events in American

1. Grace King, "Theo. Bentzon—Madame Th. Blanc," *Harper's Bazar*, XXIX (August 8, 1896), 666; reprint Robert Bush (ed.), *Grace King of New Orleans* (Baton Rouge, 1973), 348. See C. Vann Woodward, "The Historical Dimension," in *The Burden of Southern History* (Baton Rouge, 1960). Grace King to Warrington Dawson, Easter Monday, ca. 1912, in Dawson Papers, William R. Perkins Library, Duke University.

history which would determine the themes of the fiction she would later write. Her consciousness was dominated by the memory of civilian life during the Civil War and Reconstruction, and she felt deeply the impact of the conflict on the South. Her response was one of terror, humiliation, and bitterness, but accompanying these unpleasant emotions was an exalted pride in family and a deep loyalty to her country, which spiritually was always the South. In American fiction she was to become an honest interpreter of the effects of war and Reconstruction on everyday life, during the days of her own childhood and youth. But if her fiction was largely based on the experience of her own recent past, her writing of history came from her fascination with the remote past of her native city and state.

Whether a woman is more truly made up of her past than a man is a debatable point, but quite certainly Grace King, as much as any author, was the accident of her past. And depending on how one views the quality of her work, she might also be said to be the miracle of her past.

Grace Elizabeth King was born to William Woodson King and Sarah Ann Miller King on November 29, 1852, in a plain but substantial three-story town house in New Orleans at 936 Camp Street near the modern Lee Circle.[2] Her father was an important lawyer, her mother the daughter of the late Branch Miller, another important lawyer. The third child and the eldest daughter, she was reared with close relations to three sisters and three brothers. Her ancestry and parentage go far to explain her character and the drives of her life. William Woodson King (1813–1881) was born in rural Griffin County, Georgia, of a pioneer Baptist family whose ancestor is believed to be Michael King, an English settler who came to Virginia in the seventeenth century. Michael's sons, Michael, Jr., and William, were granted by the colony 340 acres of land in Nansemond County, Virginia, in 1694. Presumably it was William's descendants who settled in Georgia and then began their progress westward when the old Southwest became attractive to planters in the early nineteenth century. When Grace King's father was five years old the family migrated through the wilderness to the site of present day Montevallo, Alabama, guided in their journey by the famous Indian chief Red Eagle, or

2. Although the year of Grace King's birth has been published as 1851, 1852, and 1853, the correct year is probably 1852. A letter from Grace King to her sister May McDowell, November

William Weatherford, who had befriended the white settlers after the defeat of his nation in 1814.

As pioneer settler of the Montevallo area, Edmund King, Grace King's grandfather, acquired extensive lands for the production of cotton and corn. He built the first school in the area, and we may assume that he was a man to encourage his several sons to go wherever necessary to complete their educations. William Woodson King entered Transylvania College in Lexington, Kentucky, in his early teens, making the long journey across the mountains on horseback. He studied there at least until 1829. He then entered the first class of the new University of Alabama to take his B.A. degree in 1833 and his M.A. degree in 1836. During the 1834–1835 session he studied law at the University of Virginia at Charlottesville.[3] He visited Washington that year, where he met his kinsman William Rufus King, then U.S. senator, who would be elected vice-president of the United States in 1852. The visit to the larger center of politics may have spurred him to leave the limited realm of Montevallo and make his permanent residence in New Orleans in 1835. There, with Minor Elmore, he forged the partnership of Elmore and King, which became in time the oldest existing law firm in the nineteenth-century city.

William Woodson King had married for the first time in Montevallo and had fathered two sons. In New Orleans in 1848 Sarah Ann Miller (1820–1903) became his second wife. By this time he was already a successful and respected lawyer, who had served in the making of the state constitution of 1847. In 1848 he was appointed by the governor as one of a group of three persons "learned in the law, to consolidate and revise the Statutes and Codes." He was responsible for a third of *The Consolidation and Revisions of the Statutes and Codes of Louisiana*, published in 1852.[4] As a practicing lawyer he was a specialist in

---

29, 1885, is headed "My birthday—my 33rd birthday," Grace King Papers, Department of Archives and Manuscripts, Louisiana State University, Baton Rouge. Unless otherwise stated, all quoted manuscript material is in this collection.

3. Thomas McDory Owen, *History of Alabama and Dictionary of Alabama Biography* (6 vols.; Chicago, 1921), III, 983–84; Thomas Waverly Palmer (ed.), *A Register of the Officers and Students of the University of Alabama, 1831–1901* (Tuscaloosa, 1901); "King Family of Virginia," *William and Mary College Quarterly*, XVI (October, 1907), 105–10.

4. See L. Peirce, M. Taylor, W. W. King (eds.), *The Consolidation and Revision of the Statutes and Codes of Louisiana* (New Orleans, 1852).

litigation involving batture lands, a specialty that brought him both prestige and wealth.

The marriage of this ambitious newcomer to New Orleans to Sarah Ann Miller, daughter of an established family, was a successful one, marked by a traditional acquiescence on the part of the wife to the husband's wishes. Her family was Presbyterian, but she had been educated in a private Creole school for young ladies. Branch Miller, her father, was a sophisticated man who frequently took his daughter to the theater. He saw that she learned to speak French and had all the advantages that Catholic Creole education had to offer. This was the best kind of education to be had in the city in the early years of the century, and it established the tradition that Sarah Ann's children would be educated in a similar way. Such students grew up in full knowledge of the Catholic church and Creole ways, with few provincial prejudices to isolate them. They were able to mix with Creole society, which meant acquiring a cosmopolitan view not only of the city itself but of educated society in North America or western Europe as well. The acceptance by the Millers and Kings of Creole culture is indicative of the gradual melding of the two major groups that made up nineteenth-century New Orleans. After the Louisiana Purchase of 1803 the Americans tended to be despised by the Creoles in the old city, but the 1814 Battle of New Orleans, in which both groups shared the victory, signaled the beginning of good feeling and solidarity between the two cultures. By the end of the nineteenth century, in language and way of life, the Americans would have completely absorbed the French-speaking civilization. Grace King herself was to represent the new American intellectual drive that took Creole civilization within its embrace.

William Woodson King had been successful enough in his legal practice to retire from the profession in 1859 at the age of 46. At that time he had amassed a large fortune and with his brother Edmund Thomas had acquired a large tract of land for sugar planting in the south central part of the state, east of New Iberia. The original intention of the King brothers was that E. T. King would be the resident manager of the plantation; W. W. King would remain with his family in New Orleans. The King family seems never to have intended using L'Embarras Plantation as a country home, but it was a major source of income for the two brothers, and it was to play its role as an austere refuge for the family during the war years.

Grace King led the conventional life of a privileged child of the time. She attended the Sunday School of the Presbyterian church opposite Lafayette Square, where her father had purchased a pew. As a child she was more delicate than her brothers and sisters, and she was probably treated with greater care than they for fear of her health. Her grandmother, the widowed Mrs. Branch Miller, lived with the family and had as close a relationship with the children as the mother herself. Both women had much to do with their early education.

The grandmother, Eliza Annie Kirk Miller, was a woman of intense piety who wore out a series of Bibles by the constancy of her reading. She read "not by the hour but by hours." After the Bible her favorite study was the heavens, which to such a pious woman declared the glory of God. And she saw that declaration symbolically in the brilliance of the stars. When she could not read after dark she read the constellations from her window and explained them to her grandchildren. The coming into view of a new evening or morning star was an aesthetic event of the highest spiritual importance. The child "Sissie" King, as Grace was known, remembered her grandmother pointing out Sirius to her in a rhapsody which combined a love of beauty with a love of God as the creator of beauty.

Eliza Miller brought to the family an ancestry dominated by Alsacian Huguenot and Scottish stock. Her Huguenot mother, whose name was de Laybach, married a Scotsman, James Kirk; they migrated from Savannah, Georgia, to the settlement at Covington, Louisiana. The Kings thought of the town of Covington as an important ancestral center because the graves of their maternal great-grandparents were there. Frequently in later years they could escape from the pressures of the city and rest in the quiet town in the hot summer. They would rent a cottage near old live oak trees and raspberry-blossoming crepe myrtles, far from the social obligations of New Orleans.

Although the Kings had Huguenot ancestors, they never described their own forebears as Creoles. The name "Creole" in their eyes was thought of as specifically Franco-Spanish and Catholic. Several authors have said that Grace King was herself part Creole, but there is no evidence that her Continental ancestry was anything but Alsacian Huguenot, which would in no way be considered Creole. She was to become the Protestant American *par excellence* who championed the Creole in New Orleans, but she herself would never have said that she was Creole. Indeed, for all the affection she had for her Creole school friends and her admiration of the city's Creole culture, she sometimes had misgivings about the character of Creoles generally. When her cousin Annie Miller married a Creole doctor, in dismay and disapproval she allowed her Anglo-Saxon background to assert itself in private and spoke of the future bridegroom's manners and appearance as "Creolish," meaning Latin and inferior.[5]

*

During the decade before the war the King family traveled frequently for vacations and for health. They leased a house, for example, at Pass Christian on the Mississippi coast during the summer of 1854, and they visited the King relatives at Montevallo, Alabama, with some frequency. But there is no evidence that the women of the family ever visited L'Embarras Plantation before the war. The only accommodations there were a small farm house and a cottage.

In the summer of 1859 Grace King's father sailed for Europe for his health, visiting London, Paris, Switzerland, and Germany. He left no evidence of apprehension about the possibility of war, nor is it possible to determine his political views with accuracy. His brother Peyton was a delegate to the Democratic convention at Charleston in April, 1860, where he opposed secession before the election of Lincoln. He wrote W. W. King that "the great object for which I labored & talked, the preservation of the unity & harmony of the democracy having been hopelessly defeated by the extreme & impracticable position taken by our Southern delegations, I have concluded to await with resignation the fate that [illegible word] over us."[6] Since one brother expressed his opinions openly about such a sensitive subject, it may be that such a moderate stand was the prevailing attitude among other members of the King family before secession became a reality.

5. Grace King took Charles Dudley Warner to meet her Uncle Tom Miller in 1886. They discussed "Cable and Creoles and Creolisms." She later remarked in a letter to her mother, "I do not think any of Cable's creations ever made more grammatical mistakes and mispronunciations in the course of a half hour than de Roaldes [her cousin's fiancé] did." She criticized her cousin Annie as looking "about as dirty and Creolish as the Dr." Grace King to Sarah Ann King, April 17, 1886.

6. Peyton King to William Woodson King, undated.

The war did not vitally affect the King family until the spring of 1862, when Admiral Farragut's fleet sailed up the Mississippi to take the city of New Orleans, which meant that it would be occupied by Federal troops for the duration of the war. Grace King's own vivid recollections of the family's experience of that time are set forth at the beginning of her *Memories of a Southern Woman of Letters* (1932). Late in life she put together what she and her sisters remembered with what she had been told by her mother about the wartime events. At the age of ten, the sensitive girl saw from her third-story bedroom window the flames along the Mississippi levee, where great stores of cotton and other supplies were being destroyed by the Confederates lest they come into the hands of the enemy. The word "enemy" was used in the King family, suggesting to the child such biblical events as the slaughter of the innocents that she had seen darkly depicted in pictures. The Gustave Doré illustrations of the Bible were then popular and those engravings may have been the very pictures she associated with the terrors of war. The child feared that the entire family might be massacred. Had she been a little older, as George W. Cable was at the time, or as John W. DeForest was as a Federal officer landing with the occupation forces, she might have been able to absorb the events and consider them less emotionally in their historical context. But the occupation and the threat to the safety of her own family left an indelible impression on her as a child.[7]

William Woodson King had no intention of remaining in New Orleans while it was occupied. To continue his law practice or to live in any degree of comfort he would have had to sign an oath of loyalty to the Federal government. His immediate thought was of L'Embarras Plantation, that extensive and somewhat self-sustaining community remote from the war, where he might take his family and protect them from the dangers of the conflict. Another option was to send his family to Europe, which he could afford to do; but there was a decided onus that fell upon the families who lived in comfort in Europe while their country suffered the privations of war. He and his wife resigned themselves to suffer some of the rigors of life on a remote plantation

7. Grace King, *Memories of a Southern Woman of Letters* (New York, 1932), 4–5. See also George W. Cable, "New Orleans before the Capture," *Century*, XXIX (January, 1885), 922; John William DeForest, *A Volunteer's Adventure: A Union Captain's Record of the Civil War*, ed. James H. Croushore (New Haven, 1946), 18–19.

almost as a contribution to the war effort. Sometime after the occupation of the city had become an established fact, Federal officers arrived at the King house investigating W. W. King as a prominent citizen still maintaining a law office. Mrs. King sent her two small boys to his office to warn him. Before their father escaped that night into Confederate territory, he left instructions with his wife to bring the family and join him at L'Embarras Plantation. The execution of this difficult and even dangerous task required a series of heroic acts that reveal the stalwart character of Grace King's mother.

The first problem was to acquire a passport for the family to leave occupied New Orleans. Mrs. King was bold enough to go to the office of General Ben Butler to ask for one. He treated her with some contempt, criticized her husband for leaving the occupied city, and refused her application. Somehow the charming Mrs. King met another general as she was leaving and convinced him to send to her the papers that would assure the family's passage into the Confederacy.[8]

In later years the story of how the little group journeyed from New Orleans to L'Embarras was one of the best tales in Mrs. King's repertoire. The drama of the departure was genuine and memorable—the dark night, the two carriages waiting at the garden gate, and at a little distance the cart that carried the trunks; the climbing in of the children, the Negro nursemaids, the grandmother with the baby; then the incident of someone's thrusting into her hands an ugly rag doll for Grace to play with, which they later discovered was stuffed with Confederate money to be sent to a soldier in the north of Louisiana. Not all of the details were those a small girl would be likely to remember: "The house was left dark and gloomy, with the doors wide open. Nothing could be seen in the garden, but the perfume of the yellow jasmine came to us in farewell." They were leaving a house they would never occupy again, and they were abandoning most of its contents forever. Many years would pass before they would live in the affluent style they had enjoyed up to that moment of departure.

8. Permit, October 1, 1862, to Mrs. Wm. King, seven children and five servants and personal baggage to go to the Parish of Iberville and to take 2 lbs. Flour, Box soap, box candles, Box wine, Box sundries, Box containing Hams Tea Coffee / Approved, with permission for the necessary vehicle for transportation / By order Maj. Gen. Butler.

The steamboat on which the little group sailed was Union controlled, but when they were put ashore in the dark of the following morning, the captain whispered to Mrs. King that he was a Confederate. This explained why several barrels containing precious medicines were landed with the Kings' trunks. When she later discovered the supplies, including chloroform, Mrs. King had them sent to the nearest Confederate camp. The family was left in the rain on the levee bordering a sugar plantation. A field hand was induced to inform his master that they were there, and they soon enjoyed shelter and hospitality.

Sarah Ann King had only a vague idea of how to get to L'Embarras Plantation, though she knew they had first to go to Bayou Plaquemine, where they could hire a boat to take them the rest of the way. She borrowed a carriage and a cane cart from the planter who had fed them, and they journeyed that day in a northerly direction along the levee of the Mississippi. The rain had stopped and the children could walk along the levee or stop to gather pecans under the great trees. The day passed pleasantly, and at night they were again received hospitably at a large plantation house. On the following night, however, they arrived at a plantation that was deserted except for a Negro housekeeper. This time the Kings had to demand hospitality and settle for hominy and milk as the only fare available. In the cold of the early morning they set out again. At noon they reached a ferry crossing, but the barge, which had been partially burned, was not running. The ferryman didn't want to take the responsibility for the heavy load on the barge, but Sarah Ann King said she would risk it. The little party weighed down the good end of the barge, causing the burned end to rise above the waterline, and they crossed the river safely.

They arrived at a small town at the mouth of Bayou Plaquemine, where Mrs. King knew the name of a prominent lawyer who arranged all details for the completion of the journey. They spent another night at a local plantation house, this time the largest one in Louisiana, and in the morning two barges equipped with oarsmen were waiting for them on the little bayou. The route then led to Round Lake, where they encountered a steamboat bearing a scouting party of Confederate soldiers. The talkative Mrs. King entertained them with her account of what was happening in occupied New Orleans.

The next problem arose when the small skiff they were on ran aground. Fearing they might be forced to spend the night in the desolate place, the entire party called for help in unison. As it turned out they were quite close to their destination. Their shouts were heard by servants on L'Embarras Plantation, who came by boat to rescue them. William Woodson King had everything prepared for their arrival. He knew they were not far away when by chance he heard of a New Orleans lady and her children who had met a group of soldiers. The lady, according to reports, was full of stories about the city, and he knew it could be no one but his wife.[9]

"Bayou L'Ombre" (1887), one of Grace King's early stories, conveys the impression of what life was like on Bayou L'Embarras during the war. Like the King children, the young people of the story were imbued with an intense interest in the progress of the remote war; they were little heroes and heroines who felt patriotic about their cause but were frustrated in their wish to do something for it. They lived placid lives, waiting for the day when they would return to the city. Deprived of their accustomed comforts, they lived the rural life in which they had to make use of their ingenuity and their knowledge of nature. They learned to enjoy the pleasures of nature as well as to endure the hardships. Twice overflows inundated the swamp-surrounded plantation, at one point causing the water to rise over a foot within the small house. Raised flooring and planks had to be installed around the children's beds, and once a large snake entered the house with the flood waters.

The greatest danger of plantation life was illness, especially malarial fever, which both blacks and whites were subject to and for which there were only rudimentary medicines. There was no doctor near, but Mrs. King in emergencies consulted the family medicine book and played the role of doctor for her own family as well as the sixty some slaves the Kings owned. At one time her husband contracted typhoid and lay ill for weeks. Grace King remembered the chore of sitting by his bedside and fanning him to keep away the flies and mosquitoes, then giving her place to someone else. But in spite of such hardships her parents kept up their good spirits and never lost heart. Everyone on the plantation looked upon her father as a minor god who knew how to take care of his little realm in any emergency.

9. King, *Memories*, 9–21.

What kind of child was Grace King of L'Embarras Plantation from the age of ten to thirteen? A frail child who wore her hair in long ringlets on either side of her face, she was retired and shy, living much to herself and keeping to her books. Although she was later to become a woman of social power, she thought of herself as not at all gregarious and instinctively shunned the boys. Throughout these years of privation she was as conscious as anyone in the family that their life had to be one of endurance, but she remembered that her parents continued to kindle and nurture the bright light of ambition. "I cannot imagine a more miserable childhood than mine," she later wrote, "in all respects save one. I always had a glorious hope & ambition shining through it—and now I can truly say—I am thankful that I had the misery—for the hope. And whatever faults my parents may have shown in their family life . . . I count them now as the most precious of parents—in that they fed me on high ideals & purposes. They made me believe in the reality of the possibility of doing what I aspired to."

For three years the children had to be reared without the benefit of formal schools. Fortunately their grandmother, Annie Kirk Miller, and both parents were educated people who could teach the six children and oblige them to study with some degree of regularity. No Creole governess was in their employ here, but the three adults carried out their educational duties admirably. Mrs. Miller, in her sixties, lived with the boys in a small cottage near the main house. She had brought what books she could with her from the city and assumed the responsibility of the children's religious education, training them in reading the Bible, in learning their Presbyterian catechism, and in singing hymns. Mrs. King taught them handwriting and French, in which departments she was expert. Grace King recalled the joy of reading Fénelon's *Télémaque* aloud to her mother and the delight she took in the character of Mentor. Mrs. King had brought Grace to an advanced degree in reading French, and her pupil was responding to French literature with enthusiasm. To herself the young Grace read the adventure novels of Frederick Marryatt and the historical novels of G. P. R. James. Two of the family favorites of this period were Jane Porter's *The Scottish Chiefs* and Sir Walter Scott's *Tales of a Grandfather*. Although in after years Grace King tended to stress the hardships of the family's period of exile from New Orleans, there were of course many happy moments in which family affection and solidarity were strengthened by privation. The children had learned history from Porter and Scott. When fifty years later, in 1913, four of them toured Edinburgh together, Grace King's memory went back to a dark night at L'Embarras, when their father was away and their mother was apprehensive about the possibility of gunboats appearing on the bayou. Mrs. King brought the children into her own bedroom and arranged mattresses for them on the floor. How did they alleviate their fears except by reading books of Scottish history? "But what was the dark night, the lonely house to them? Or the fear of enemies?" Grace King wrote in 1913. "The logs in the open fireplace were burning bright. We lay on our beds delighted, while Branch [her brother], our best reader, from his mattress on the floor, with a candle propped on his pillow, read aloud to us about William Wallace and Robert Bruce. Even though we could hear at the same time the cannon booming at regular intervals at Vicksburg, we were in Scotland then."[10]

The constant exposure to good reading had its permanent effect on the ten-year-old girl. She remembered one particularly fine day when, as she walked alone along the levee of the plantation bayou, she first felt within her the urge to write. On the opposite bank was a cypress forest behind which the sun rose brilliantly and reflected on the bayou's black flowing water. She was excited by a book she had been reading and suddenly said to herself that she wanted to be a writer. The combination of the excitement of a book and the exhilaration from a brilliant natural setting that produces the child's vow to write is altogether understandable. Something similar happens to many a gifted child who has been fascinated by literature or has had a moving experience in the world of nature. Grace King recalled that this "aspiration became a command. It never left me. My heart seemed to be always waiting to execute it, and I grew weary for the occasion to come to do so."[11]

William Woodson King directed the education of his children with enthusiasm, and he stressed training for his daughters as much as for his sons. The girls were hardly to be educated as mere ornaments of society. Sitting in his arm chair in his homespun clothing, he taught arithmetic and grammar to

10. Grace King Journal, undated, c. 1904.
11. King, *Memories*, 48.

Fred, Branch, Grace, and May, who sat around him in their straight-back chairs. He was a patient teacher who gave clear explanations, but he was untiring and inflexible in making his pupils follow a problem through to the end. And when they succeeded in solving a difficult one, he registered a personal satisfaction, even a joy in their success. He was proud of his children with some reason: they were all bright and spirited. It was perhaps he who first introduced them to poetry and history, and he trained them in the spoken word. Because he liked Gray's "Elegy," the children learned it by heart, he taught them to recite the speeches of famous men like Patrick Henry, and as they grew older they also memorized the soliloquies from Shakespeare. The young Grace failed here, for her child's voice was thin and weak, and she had a shyness that kept her from excelling in the nineteenth-century skill of elocution.

The father took them on nature walks about the plantation, illustrating for them many phases of farm life they would never have known if they had remained in the city. They observed the world of the garden, the cows and chickens. He showed them the crafts of the slave population: spinning, weaving, shoemaking, and planting. These activities gave him joy that compensated for his financial ruin. His money and investments had already become worthless; he would lose his slaves; but he was a man of resilience who remained confident that he could regain his former affluence. And he believed his children would actually benefit from their years on the remote plantation. Grace King loved her father and saw him as the head of the family who knew exactly what to do on all occasions. "He was to me not human," she wrote, "but some superior being with which I could not compare other men. To be his child was to me a supreme distinction among other children."[12]

William Woodson King was beyond army age and had never known military experience. He knew the out-of-doors well, however, and knew the wilderness territory of southern Louisiana as well as a scout would know it. He did accompany Confederate troops on one occasion as far as the Sabine River on the Texas border; which may mean that he sometimes served as a

12. Grace King Journal, undated, c. 1904.

guide during troop movements. His brother, Edmund Thomas King, was an active guerrilla leader in the southern Louisiana waterways for the years of the war. William Woodson King ran the plantation for the greater part of that time, raising mainly sugar, which was distributed within the Confederacy and probably helped supply the army. The plantation also produced wool and vegetables, and later in the war years it supported a large herd of cattle. Edmund Thomas King, returning to L'Embarras at the time of an overflow, found the cattle standing in water and in danger of death. He immediately had them housed temporarily in the immense sugar house and spoke harshly of his brother's failure to accommodate them.[13] The incident may reveal that William Woodson King had little of the practical knowledge about farming that his brother had, even though his knowledge of politics and law was extensive.

After the fall of the Confederacy in the spring of 1865 the Kings began to make preparations to return to the life of the city, though it would be months before they could make that move. William Woodson King went to New Orleans to reestablish his law practice with his former partner Minor Elmore. On June 16, 1865, he took the oath of loyalty to the Constitution of the United States, a necessary step for anyone in a public profession. His wife shipped quantities of cotton to him in the hope of his being able to sell it, and she may also have sent wool, which could be sold in the North. On August 1, 1865, he described to her the conditions of the city: "It is at present impossible to form any idea of future prospects. Everything seems unsettled, & a restless uneasy spirit pervades every quarter. Negroes will not work. House servants cannot be obtained & all creation seems turned upside down." Even at that late date when his slaves were legally free, he held on to them, as they were all the wealth he had left besides his land. On August 20 he wrote, "The State Convention in Mississippi have abolished slavery. The truckling scoundrels!—This is ominous for us."[14] The comment suggests that he thought he still had some chance of keeping his slaves.

13. Edmund Thomas King to the editor, New Orleans *Times-Democrat*, June 27, 1910, p. 19.
14. In the official document, N. 393, signed by Wm. W. King, June 16, 1865, he not only affirms his loyalty to the Union and to the Constitution, but swears that he will "abide by and faithfully support all laws and proclamations which have been made during the existing rebellion with reference to the emancipation of slaves." William Woodson King to his wife, August 1 and 20, 1865.

An incident of the fall of 1865 indicates that the King slaves, probably aware that they were legally free, resisted their continued enslavement. W. W. King may have either taken or sent a group of his male Negroes to Texas, possibly to lease them to another planter. The Texas experience was a disagreeable one for the men, and they returned unexpectedly to L'Embarras Plantation, full of resentment for their master. King was in New Orleans at the time, and Mrs. King, alarmed by the Negroes' abuse of him and their threats toward her, moved her household to the distant house of a neighbor at Bayou La Rompe. She stayed there with the Tally family until the resentment subsided and the men went back to work. Fred, Grace King's oldest brother, wrote his father that "those miserable negroes arrived very unexpectedly from Texas, and I think if you or Uncle Tom had been there, some one or two would have been in the other world." Mrs. King was later visited by one of the blacks, who asked her to return. She wrote her husband that the blacks feared she would complain to the authorities about their behavior. The petty rebellion seems to have subsided without further trouble, but the last paragraph of Mrs. King's letter is of considerable interest as she describes the response of her fourteen-year-old daughter Grace: "Sissy has made you an undershirt, poor child; she was so indignant at hearing you abused that she almost got a fever—her eyes almost flashed out of her head.—May [Grace's younger sister] was for fighting."[15] The future author never recorded the incident in her writings, but her response to it is typical of her character. Although we can only reconstruct the complaints of the blacks against her father by conjecture, the fact that they dared threaten her mother and abuse a master whom she considered ideal was to her an outrage.

In October, 1865, William Woodson King was living in a rooming house in the city, having borrowed money for food and clothing. He wrote his wife that he had been disappointed in not getting a house for them on Canal Street, which would have been within the central area of the city. But he had rented a house "below the city, near the Barracks." The house would have to be

---

15. Edmund Thomas King to William Woodson King, December 16, 1865; Frederick D. King to William Woodson King, November 17, 1865; Sarah Ann King to her husband, November 17, 1865.

renovated and it would not be ready before the twentieth of December. If the lessor should do everything he promised for them, King wrote, "we shall have the most agreeable residence we ever had in the city—all for $35 per month." He added that "the horse cars run to the place every few minutes." He probably gave his wife a more impressive picture of the house than it deserved.

The return trip to New Orleans was an exciting experience, especially for the children. It occurred no earlier than late December, 1865, but may have taken place several months later—in 1866. In October, 1866, Grace King's brother Branch wrote a brief essay about the trip probably as an academic exercise at the Jesuit college in which he was enrolled. The family had made their way with their baggage to a point on the Atchafalaya River, where a steamboat was scheduled to pick them up. When the steamboat failed to arrive, they "danced and frolicked until near 11 o'clock." Then everyone went to bed only to be wakened a few minutes later by the sound of the steamboat's whistle. Branch, who had not seen so spectacular a sight as a river steamer for three years, was thrilled by the boat's magnificence as it came "puffing and blowing up the river" with all its windows lighted. He could not sleep for excitement that night, and by morning they had already sailed fifty miles up the Atchafalaya on their three-day journey. He thought the scenery was "magnificent"; alligators were plentiful along the bank, and the gentlemen enjoyed themselves shooting them. Branch sat up until midnight on the third night of the voyage to see the lights of the crescent city as they approached it. "There like a beautiful panorama stretched out before me was New Orleans," he wrote—"myriads of lights from masts, towers, and steeples shown in the clear still atmosphere. . . . The morning came and with it the lumbering of numerous vehicles all along the levee." Soon they were all in a carriage driving to the new home his father had rented.[16]

It was a five-room house for a family of ten with probably two servants they had planned to bring from L'Embarras. Located at the very southern boundary of the city directly opposite the Federal barracks—the address was the corner of Delery and Chartres streets—the house was not far from the

16. King to his wife, October 29, 1865; Branch King to the Rev. Father Regley, October 5, 1866.

levee of the Mississippi, where the family might stroll on a Sunday afternoon. Nothing was wrong with the area except that it was anything but fashionable. There were few shade trees, the houses were commonplace, and the barracks with their blue-coated soldiers were ever-present sights—symbols themselves of the South's humiliation and defeat. It was a very long ride by slow horsecar to the center of the city, and after their three-year exile the Kings must have felt that they were still in exile from the city itself. Certainly neither the neighborhood nor the house compared at all favorably with the home they had left three years before. And after her husband's enthusiastic description of it, Mrs. King and the children were probably faced with deep disillusion and with the feeling that they had descended to a lower-class neighborhood.

The family lived at Delery and Chartres until 1869 or 1870, then in 1870 lived briefly at the corner of Moreau and Delery streets in the same neighborhood. In 1870 or 1871 they moved again, to Erato Street, a little closer to the center of the city.[17] All of these addresses became symbols to Grace King of the years of financial struggle for her family and the hope of returning to the Garden District to associate with people who counted both socially and intellectually.

There is no evidence that the King family were oppressed by the presence of Federal troops in their immediate neighborhood. Indeed, two letters in the Grace King Papers indicate that the daughters were paid visits by army personnel. One letter from A. D. Nelson in Indian Territory, July, 1870, was probably written to Grace King's sister Annie (Nan). Assuming that he was either a Federal soldier or officer, his remarks indicate that all was not misery and despair during the Delery Street years: "And how are the 'dear girls.' Are they at school yet, or have Grace and May won their diplomas. . . . Delicious wasn't it? Sitting on your portico of a warm summer evening, fighting mosquitoes, scolding the children, cracking jokes and pouring down the cherry bounce."[18]

---

17. *Garner's New Orleans Directory* lists the residence of W. W. King as Delery, corner of Chartres Street, 3rd district, for the years 1867, 1868, and 1869; Moreau, corner of Delery Street for the year 1870. *Edwards' New Orleans Directory* lists King's residence as 169 Erato Street for 1871.

18. A. D. Nelson probably to Annie Ragan King, July, 1870; a second letter from W. N.

The suffering of the Kings was thus both relative and symbolic. They were loyal enough to the old cause of the Confederacy to resent the very presence of Federal troops. Their neighbors did not suffer from poverty because they were used to it and had never known another state. But the Kings had been rich and now had to suffer the humiliation of being poor. And their status during Reconstruction was really worse than during the war itself. Before Appomattox they could steel themselves with the satisfaction that they were heroic in enduring privation and exile for the cause. Their hope then was that once the war was over they would soon regain their former prosperity. They could not predict that the process would take more years than the war itself. And during those years their circumstances allowed no feeling of heroism at all, only despair and endurance of an ordinary neighborhood. It was easy to blame all their misfortunes on the Federal occupation forces so in evidence across the street—a resentment they felt keenly when the family went for Sunday afternoon walks on the levee and heard the evening gun fired at the barracks.[19] They had been beaten: the little world of their family was painfully representative of the larger world of the fallen Confederacy.

Many of their former friends avoided this humiliation when they recovered their fortunes. The Kings could not avoid envying such relatives as Thomas Depassau Miller, Mrs. King's brother, who remained wealthy during Reconstruction. For although he was generous to his sister's family from time to time, he was sometimes resented when he was not quite generous enough at the right time.[20]

Life on Delery Street was an experience that came for Grace King as she passed from the ages of fourteen to twenty. These were the formative years of her mind and heart that generated within her the drive that would in time produce literature. Much of her fiction would depict the life of New Orleans during Reconstruction. The Delery Street period of her family provided the material on which her novel *The Pleasant Ways of St. Médard* (1916) is based. After

---

Amory to Mrs. W. W. King, March 8, 1880, suggests that Annie (Nan) was engaged to a military man whom she may have met in New Orleans and who was transferred to Fort Benton, Montana.

19. See the fictional account of this in Grace King, *The Pleasant Ways of St. Médard* (New York, 1916), 144.

20. Comments by Grace King in several letters to her sister May McDowell suggest this.

the book was published she said it was taken from life, but she never called it autobiography, nor should it be read as anything but fiction based on family experience. We have relatively little documentation of the Kings during these years, and Grace King has little to say about them in her memoirs. So the book remains the primary source for our knowledge of the tone of life of the period—the struggle, the endurance, the shame, the irony of the topsy-turvy world. How much of the book is really true? The setting is quite authentic—a five-room, single story house in a working-class district inhabited largely by French-speaking Creoles or "Gascons," a neighborhood where Protestant families of the professional class were rarities. The prevailing images are the river, the levee, the Federal barracks, and the presence of large numbers of blue-coated soldiers. The Talbot parents of the novel are closely drawn after Grace King's parents. Grace King herself is Cicily, the delicate child subject to chills, but the children of the fiction tend to be much younger than the King children actually were. The long monologues in which Mrs. Talbot recollects the bitter experience of the plantation are fictionalized but possible thought sequences for Grace King's mother. For the Negro family attached to the Kings (their former slaves), the author used the names of Jerry and Matilda, an actual couple who had worked at L'Embarras Plantation. They may or may not have come with the family to New Orleans, where, in the fiction, they endure a painful separation and achieve their independence.

When in later years Grace King blamed the Federal government and the "Yankees" for the family losses and suffering, she must have been aware that both the losses and the suffering were the elements that determined the fabric of her own character. Without the pain of poverty and the bitter indignation that followed it, she might never have written anything. She would not have developed the sense of irony that would frequently give power to her writing. Her irony is not that of a Swift, but it might be comparable to Ellen Glasgow's or Mark Twain's. By 1870 the Grace King die was permanently cast; what followed was the question of whether the early experience was to be used at all and if it was to be used, how her formal education would embellish it and give it permanent meaning. Her education was to equip her for competition with dozens of competent American authors of the 1880s and 1890s, and for a scholarly career comparable to that of any southern woman of her time. Her

special powers were to be in English, American, French, and German literature; in the French language for her future role as a non-Creole championing
the old Creole culture; and especially in the history of Louisiana. Indignation
entered her heart with the recent history of war and Reconstruction, but for
the older history—from Bienville to Andrew Jackson—for this she would
develop only the objective scholar's passion for an extraordinarily rich past.

Two

The Preparatory Years: Education, Society, and Travel, 1865–1884

After the three years of education the King children were given by their parents and their grandmother on the plantation, they were eager to enter schools on their return to the city. The state of education in New Orleans in 1865 was chaotic. Grace King was later to describe it in her memoirs and in two articles, one on Mary Humphreys Stamps (1909), a leader in public education in the Deep South after the war, and the other on Madame Girard (1922), a private French teacher. "It is in the memory of some of us, children of the war," she wrote, "what importance our education assumed after defeat. . . . Private schools sprang up . . . all over the South—those wonderful schools that some of us knew, filled with scholars who could not pay, provided with books picked up in old garrets . . . and taught by women in mourning, pale, thin, sad, gentle, but inflexible in the enforcement of an ideal of 'principle,' which we were taught to look upon as the Holy Grail, which would transfuse even poverty with heavenly radiance and elevate suffering into a sacrament of sacrifice."[1]

1. Grace King, "A Southern Educator: Mrs. Mary Humphreys Stamps," *Century*, VXXVIII (June, 1909), 271.

But alongside such new schools were the established schools—the best in New Orleans—and it was to these that the King children were sent. The boys went to the Jesuit schools, the girls to Creole schools for young women, directed usually by Paris-educated lay women with religious instruction given by the clergy. These schools for girls were modeled on the famous Ursuline convent school, which was directed entirely by nuns. Because Grace King's mother had attended such a school, respect for that education was well established in the King family. These private schools were exclusively for white girls, but Protestant Americans were welcome among the overwhelming number of French-speaking Catholics. The older King sisters were sent to a school of this sort, the Institut St. Louis on Dauphiné Street between Ursuline and Hôpital. The school was conducted by Mme. E. Deron "from the Imperial House of St. Denis." It was a fairly large establishment, occupying five buildings, class halls, exhibition hall, auditorium, and dormitory, all surrounded by a beautiful garden.[2] An oasis in the city, it was like the traditional American private school. Young women were accepted as boarding students or as day students. Grace King and her sisters were day students because they lived near enough to make the long daily ride by mulecar or horsecar, along one of the streets that ran parallel to the river, through the entire length of the French Quarter.

How was the impoverished William Woodson King able to send his daughters to such an exclusive seminary? The tuition for day students was actually relatively inexpensive, though even so the Kings probably found it difficult to raise money to pay the school bills on time. Mrs. King's brother Tom may have helped, but there is no evidence that he did.

One of the striking qualities of the Institut St. Louis and other schools like it in New Orleans is the phrase with which Mme. Deron, the directress, advertised herself: "from the Imperial House of St. Denis." She had been educated in Paris, and her school thus encompassed the full tradition of French education. This is important to note because the French notion of educating young women has never been that they be trained exclusively and solely as ornaments of society. Acquiring social graces was a secondary matter. This is not to say that education was modern or progressive, for much of the

2. See *Gardner's New Orleans Directory*, 1860–68; New Orleans *Picayune*, October 24, 1865, p. 2.

discipline involved learning facts by heart, writing synopses of historical events—the kind of inflexible nineteenth-century methods in which the student was not stimulated to think independently. But serious work was expected of students and a genuine love of learning was the primary aim. The combination of intellectual training in the family, the practice of reading aloud together, and the encouragement of intellectual parents made all four of the King sisters excellent students. With the discipline of good Creole schools they were prepared to be intellectually curious for life.

The Institut St. Louis stressed ancient and modern history and modern languages. Both disciplines left their mark on Grace King. The study of history prepared her for the time in the 1890s when she would start historical research in earnest. As for languages, she had the opportunity to learn French under the guidance of instructors who had studied in France. She particularly admired a Professor Rouen, "the typical, learned professor, with sensitive eye and ear, and a most sympathetic heart." At a time when Grace was shy and perhaps unaware of her intellectual gifts, he encouraged her to enter a French composition contest in which she won the prize.[3] As a student for whom French was a second language she must have found this a very satisfactory, confidence-inspiring accomplishment.

By the time of her graduation Grace King had attained fluency in French and a good reading knowledge of both Spanish and German. Socially she had made friends with daughters of some of the city's major families, several of whom she would keep in touch with for years to come. If we compare her education with that of George W. Cable, whom she would oppose as an interpreter of the Creole character, she probably had closer friendships with Creole families than he.[4] Education and friendship would generate in her a loyalty toward the Creoles that Cable lacked.

Grace King graduated from the Institut St. Louis in 1868 at the age of sixteen. She then improved her German at the Sylvester-Larned Institut and still later studied at the Institut Cénas, a school founded by Heloise Cénas in Reconstruction times, illustrating Grace King's comment in her memoirs about the respectable Creole ladies who opened schools to support themselves. This kind of school offered French, English, music, and drawing

3. Grace King, *Memories of a Southern Woman of Letters* (New York, 1932), 89.
4. Arlin Turner, *George W. Cable, A Biography* (Baton Rouge, 1966), 203.

together with instructions in refined manners.[5] At the Institut Cénas Grace King's primary concentration was in the study of English composition. She became a close friend of Heloise Cénas, to whom she would later attribute her ability to write well. Miss Cénas taught her to be critical of her own writing, to construct sentences and paragraphs logically, and to use words with power and grace. The style of her earliest stories would reflect that influence. It is self-conscious, literary, and somewhat pedantic; but it is the style of a person who has learned to write. Miss Cénas had been educated in Boston and her knowledge of English literature was particularly strong. She passed on to the young Grace King some of her appreciation of John Keats and William Wordsworth as well as Thomas Carlyle and John Ruskin, authors not read in a girls' school like the Institut St. Louis. Grace learned "The Eve of Saint Agnes" by heart under Miss Cénas' direction, and her introduction to Ruskin initiated what later became a great enthusiasm for his work.

Another phase of her education was private tutoring in French by Madame M. D. Girard, a widowed lady who taught New Orleans children from 1843 until the early years of this century. Grace King's 1922 memoir of her depicts Madame Girard going her rounds of various houses in 1870. She probably tutored Grace and her sisters then, when they were young women completing their education, but she may also have come to the house before the war. In the article she is a serious woman dressed in old-fashioned clothes. Stepping from the mulecar, a blue barege veil weighted down by large beads covering her bonnet, she would be ushered into the family dining room, used then as library and study as well. The table was prepared with notebooks, pencils, pens, and inkstand. The "little scholar" entered, made her curtsey, said, "Bonjour, Madame," and the lesson began. The child would recite what she had, through much repetition, memorized, the subjects in the reading assignment being history, grammar, and mythology. Then the tutor would examine her exercises in the several copybooks—one devoted to "analyse grammaticale," another to "analyse logique." At some time Grace King had certainly been the little scholar herself: she remembered these exercises "as incomprehensible as the creed, and accomplished only by an act of faith." There followed a "résumé" of the previous day's history lesson, corrected

5. King, *Memories*, 24.

with precise editing by Madame Girard, and finally the "dictée," in which she had selected for study a series of moral maxims filled with grammatical pitfalls.[6]

Grace King realized that the method of instruction was as old-fashioned as Madame's blue barege veil, that it went back to the lady's own childhood education in France in the early years of the century, and that it was still considered the only way to learn French. But the sketch of Madame Girard does convey the seriousness with which the education of young women was taken in Creole New Orleans and it indicates how a rather close connection was maintained with traditional Parisian education. Madame Girard was a gentle figure of the past who as she grew older became a kind of institution in the city. Grace King was a friend of hers for many years. The younger woman spoke French with reasonable fluency but even in her mature years asked her old teacher for assistance in brushing up on the mysteries of French verbs.[7]

Grace King's religious education continued after the war when the family resumed their attendance at the First Presbyterian Church. The children attended Sunday School there and immediately afterward were marched into the church to hear the ponderous oratory of Dr. Benjamin Morgan Palmer, whose theology was frequently beyond them, but whose heroic personality gave them a glimpse of divinity. Palmer was a bastion of spiritual power to New Orleans Protestants throughout the war and Reconstruction, and he was still preaching at the end of the century. He was one of those preachers who defended the Confederate cause when it was alive and acted as a force to hold together his demoralized congregation when it was dead. Like Grace King, George W. Cable was a member of Palmer's congregation and admired him. But Cable's seniority of seven years over Grace King and the large size of the Presbyterian church explain why their paths probably did not cross until much later in their lives.[8] During the Reconstruction years the Kings lived a great distance from their church, but it is quite likely that they attended when they could. Grandmother Miller would have insisted that the children attend

6. Grace King, *Madame Girard, An Old French Teacher of New Orleans* (privately printed; reprinted from *Yale Review*, January, 1922), 2.

7. Grace King to May McDowell, February 10, 1884, in the Grace King Papers, Department of Archives and Manuscripts, Louisiana State University. Unless otherwise stated, all manuscript material is from this collection.

8. King, *Memories*, 23–29.

Sunday School after teaching them their catechism at L'Embarras in preparation for church membership.

Grandmother Miller's death occurred on March 21, 1877, and since this was the first death of a relative that Grace King experienced, it left its mark. She devoted an unusually long space in her memoirs to the event, indicating that it was a particularly moving part of her emotional development and explaining why deaths in the family thereafter were never taken as a matter of course.

An event of importance took place in Grace King's sixteenth year (1867)— the beginning of her friendship with Charles Gayarré, the major Creole intellectual of his time. Gayarré was a close friend of William Woodson King and had for a time used space in his office. As historian of Louisiana he was a man of some national prestige, who had had a brilliant career in literature, politics, and law but was to experience years of futile attempts to recover that career. He owned a plantation in the pinewoods country of Tangipahoa Parish, a few miles south of the Mississippi border town of Osyka. Invited to this country home, Roncal, Grace King and her sister May met Gayarré for the first time at the station, where he would escort them by train. He was then in his early sixties, a majestic man in satin stock, long black broadcloth coat, and tall top hat, with his beard trimmed and pointed.

The country home was disappointingly small to Grace. She had expected a mansion and found a brown stucco cottage adorned with galleries, planted with ivy, and standing on a ridge in a park with fine old trees. But the inside provided the revelation: it had the foreign quality and some of the European grandeur she was expecting. Much of Gayarré's furniture, his paintings and candelabra had been brought from Paris, where he spent several years in the 1830s when he was a young man. The Catholic Gayarré and his Presbyterian wife lived somewhat in European style, reminiscent of his Franco-Spanish ancestry and his Parisian years. Indeed, few Americans of that time were more European than this man who had been born in Louisiana in 1805, only two years after the Louisiana Purchase. His influence was to become a most important force in Grace King's education. At home her patrician but somewhat prosaic family enjoyed lively talk at the dinner table and in the parlor, but with Gayarré talk was elevated to conversation. And his conversation was pure enchantment to the two brown-eyed girls who listened to him with the closest attention.[9]

Roncal became a frequent retreat for Grace King during the years that followed. It was through the influence of Gayarré that the young girl developed her love for the history of the Louisiana Territory, which she would turn to practical use in the 1890s. The childless Gayarré cultivated the King sisters with paternal affection. In 1875, when Grace volunteered to come to Roncal to nurse Mrs. Gayarré through a dangerous illness, the Judge wrote her mother that "Grace's generous offer has moved me to tears. My heart overflows with gratitude and never shall I be able to repay the debt. Had I retained my fortune, it would have been my daily wish to have such a daughter, and to make her as happy as it is possible to be in this miserable world."[10]

The world of Reconstruction and after was indeed miserable for Gayarré because of the loss of his $400,000 fortune and the failure of his intellectual and political projects. His friendship with the Kings, and especially with Grace, was one of the joys of his later years. If there was a tendency for him to resort to melancholy, the "merry Kings," as Mrs. Gayarré described them, gave him some happiness. In Grace King's letters home from Roncal, there are many references to laughter, to pleasant outings in the country, to music and conversation, in all of which the Judge participated with dignity. Throughout the 1870s, until Roncal was finally sold because the Gayarrés were destitute, Grace enjoyed many a visit there, usually in the summer months when she took pleasure in such activities as swimming in the sandy-bottomed creek on the Judge's land.[11]

During the year 1871 the Kings had moved from the outlying district of the city, which they had endured for five years. The move to Erato Street was, however, only a slight improvement, and the house thereafter was referred to with contempt. Grace King later wrote of the wretched poverty and the misery of life, the poor food, and the unending family quarrels.[12] The reference to quarrels indicates that some unhappiness had grown up between

9. *Ibid.*, 31, 36.
10. Charles Gayarré to Sarah Ann King, November 3, 1875, in possession of John M. Coxe, New Orleans.
11. Grace King to May King, September 7, 1875.
12. Grace King Journal 1886–1901, January 3, 1900.

individual family members, possibly aggravated by their economic woes. But the King family tended to quarrel over relatively slight domestic problems even in times of prosperity. They were proud as a group, but they were also proud as individuals who gave way to emotional self-expression.

Grace King was twenty in 1871. She was then a small, pert-looking young woman with curly reddish brown hair and brown eyes. She enjoyed clothes and knew how to make herself look stylish, even if she was not strikingly beautiful. Her intelligence, manners, and appearance made her reasonably attractive to men. There is no record of every young man who visited her during the decade of the seventies; however, she did save a series of letters from Garrett Walker, a young man who professed a deep love for her and wanted to marry her at a time when his career with a railroad company was only beginning. Walker was not afraid to tell Grace he loved her in his letters, and it is also significant that she kept these letters, though because we have none of her replies, it is difficult to determine what her feeling for him was.

Walker lived at Pass Christian, Mississippi, on the Gulf Coast, which may explain the existence of any correspondence at all; other courtships may have been as serious without producing any letters. Grace King may have met Walker at Pass Christian, since that had been a favorite vacationing place for the King family in their more prosperous years.

The three characters in the little courtship drama were Walker and Grace and her mother. Grace had tentatively accepted Walker, but he met with her mother's objections on the grounds that she was too young and he was not sufficiently established financially to support a wife. Mrs. King imposed a two-year waiting period before the marriage, and her daughter acquiesced, probably without much objection since she was only nineteen. In September of 1871 the courtship reached a point of crisis when Grace, despite her tentative acceptance of Walker, began to follow her mother's line of thinking—expressing her own doubts about Walker's future. In time he was to become a successful railroad man, but since there were not enough signs of that future in 1871, he was finally rejected. One of his letters at this time suggests his extreme disappointment and also reveals by implication the pronounced financial aims of both mother and daughter in the poverty-stricken times of Reconstruction:

You do me a terrible and awful injustice and one undeserved. I am as ambitious as you could be but not more of fame than happiness. You accuse me of wasting my time in idleness. Some truth may be in this accusation but at the same time you have not known the whole—The Railroad on which I was engaged paid me well, guaranteed me a good position and more chance of advancement than I could have hoped for in any other position. When I asked you to wait those two years the RR was paying $150 a month with the promise of advancing my salary.[13]

Another of Walker's notes indicates that Mrs. King took some form of drastic action at this time to end the courtship she didn't favor. "I am truly pained and surprised that your mother should act thus to me," he wrote. "How much so I can hardly say—You of course must obey her. I would not counsel disobedience in any one but do not suppose that if you see less of me it proceed from any doubt of you—I am willing to wait the two years and my promise binds me as surely as an oath." When Grace was absent on a trip, probably in 1875, her mother wrote her that Mr. Walker had "taken the hint" and no longer visited the family, indicating her pleasure that they were rid of him.[14]

He had been a sincere suitor; in one of his letters he showed as keen an insight into Grace King's character as anyone would:

I intend justifying what I said last night although you know perfectly well that it was all true. There are two (pity I cant say three) Graces in you as distinctly different as day and night. One is ever ready to court public inspection: a brave easy unembarrassed young lady of the day, who has all the little peculiarities of her sex and claims to differ from them in nothing. Religious to the extent required by the rules of society and who pretends to wage guerilla warfare against everyone pretending to authority over her. And with the usual mild contempt for any thing romantic or to use the common expression highflown. Sentiment strictly eschewed. This is the Grace one sees in company, and who bravely sustains the character when upheld by her sister's presence. But under all this is hidden the other

13. Garrett Walker to Grace King, September 1, 1871.
14. Walker to King, undated; Sarah Ann King to Grace King, undated, c. 1875.

and *real* person. This last is a timid shrinking frightened little Grace who differs in almost everything from her young lady friends. True and faithful in her friendships. Deep, earnest and constant, in her love, I *believe*. With a mind which necessarily draws a romantic idea of its fellow creatures from its own goodness and purity. This Grace is a loving and obedient daughter and sister and I believe deeply and sincerely religious. The one Grace is to me a true and faithful friend brave to defend me when unjustly attacked and eager to find an excuse for my shortcomings. The other loves me well (I have never doubted it) and believes in my faith and constancy. And yet this last Grace is so afraid of me that I must seek to call her to me but seldom if I would wish, not to inflict pain on the one I love best in the world. But this fear she must overcome. Would you wish to distinguish the difference between these two Graces. The voice is enough. The one is unembarrassed in conversation ready and quick. The other timid and shy with an almost painful effort to control herself. The first Grace I admire but it is the hidden, the real Grace that I love and wish to *see more* of. Have I explained myself?

Yours

Garry[15]

The double character Walker perceived in the young Grace King fore-shadowed that of the mature woman. Even at nineteen she put forth a public front that reflected an assured personality, whereas underneath she was less secure and deeply emotional. When she became a woman of some renown, she acted a public role that shielded the more sensitive inner person. But the public Grace King was not a false mask; rather it was a genuine persona created to protect the more vulnerable self within.

Social and intellectual activities were her main interests during her twenties, which the decade of the seventies consumed. During this period she hardly followed the established pattern for the southern patrician female. Following the educational standards of her parents, she became an apprentice intellectual with a drive to educate herself after the formalities of schooling were over. Also, she never set for herself the goal of marriage, although she would make some uncomfortable attempts to meet young men outside her

15. Garrett Walker to Grace King, undated, c. 1871.

New Orleans circle. The conventional reason for a strong social position was to provide the opportunity for the best possible marriage, but social life to her was for the joy of intellectual exchange rather than for the pursuit of a mate. These attitudes prepared her for a serious creative career, one that might not have bloomed at all if she had married.

Grace King made trips to spa towns occasionally and reported to her mother her lack of success in finding eligible young men. Since she made this report more than once, it is possible to conclude that she really found the average young man at such places a bore. And since she was not the stereotyped southern belle whom the average young man sought, it is quite possible that he found this learned lady too bright for her own good.

The quality of social life improved as the Kings moved closer to the center of the city. In 1877 they moved from Erato Street to 219 Terpsichore Street, where they would live for four years. In this neighborhood they became acquainted with the John A. Morris family, who were not only New Orleans rich but Gilded Age rich. Much of Morris's wealth had come from his connection with the Louisiana Lottery, an enterprise of which the Kings would eventually show strong disapproval. But the source of the Morris wealth hardly kept the families from becoming friends. Mrs. Cora Morris took great interest in the King sisters, especially in Grace. She pretended to adopt them as her favorites and encouraged them to call her "the Foster," which meant that she was their rich foster mother, who could provide for them more lavish entertainment and social opportunities than their own parents. Cora Morris was a middle-aged woman who dressed gorgeously and entertained with ostentation. When she was not in residence at the town house in New Orleans, she might be at the Morris country estate at Throg's Neck, Westchester, New York, or she might be cruising on the Morris yacht in the Gulf of Mexico, or traveling in Europe, toadying to minor nobility in hopes of marrying her daughter to a title.

This friendship opened to Grace King the social world of the very rich and enabled her to travel outside the limited world of Louisiana. She was invited by the Morris family to make what would be her first trip north in June, 1876. By train she traveled via Montgomery, Louisville, Columbus, and Cincinnati to New York. She visited Cape May, then Philadelphia for the Centennial Exposition, after which she paid the Morrises a visit on their luxurious

Throg's Neck estate near Fort Schuyler. She had not known such excitements before and in a letter home commented, "There is one thing certain—all the down will be off this peach by the time I return." [16]

She was impressed with the large scale of the buildings of Philadelphia and had to admit that the way of life was better than that of New Orleans, yet she added, "I must say that the people, tho' they are ever so much more stylish and dress ever so much better, do not strike me as being genteel as with us, and the men and women on the sidewalks do not look like gentlemen and ladies." [17]

She visited Saratoga, where the atmosphere was "like going from a circus to a Presbyterian church. . . . Every body is polite and kind but so stiffly proper and respectable." [18] Again writing from Saratoga she assured her mother that she wanted male companionship, but it wasn't easy to come by: "There seem to be some very nice gentlemen parading themselves around and how I do long for someone to introduce me, but all the longing in the world can't accomplish the impossible, and the tantalizing things cross my path at every turn. . . . that is the only drawback to my complete happiness . . . the total absence of young men, one young man would go a great way in reconciling me to everything." [19] The comment, flippant in tone, was appropriately directed to the mother, the one person who conditions a daughter to look forward to marriage and to act with a modest aggressiveness in achieving it. The daughter seems to be saying, "Don't blame me for not attracting men; there is no one here to introduce me to any of them." In her later career Grace King made a policy of cultivating men of literary importance, but her aim in such friendships was the advancement of her professional career.

As the decade wore on she made fewer comments in her letters about the search for a husband. Perhaps she saw herself as a failure in the marriage market; but what is more evident is her judgment of men—particularly her resentment of male dominance in marriage. Some years later as she considered "Subjects for a Southern Novel," in her journal, she made her strongest statement against the southern male:

16. Grace King to May King, June 23, 1876.
17. Grace King to Annie Ragan King, June 25, 1876.
18. *Ibid.*, August 1, 1876.
19. Grace King to Sarah Ann King, August 3, 1876.

The public chivalrous talk and bearing of the men; their utter contempt of the claims of women in private. Their reckless extravagance in regard to themselves; their parsimony towards women—their egotism—their dissipations—their terrible, wild depravity. I have known husbands; of the best families—claiming on the political platform and elsewhere superiority over all other men—particularly the "Yankees"—come home after the midnight hours, and ill-treat their wives—as to absolutely beating them—beating would have been preferable. Brothers—who let their sisters toil at home in wearisome unremitted drudgery; sewing even for negroes in order to gain a few cents. These brothers drinking themselves drunk on champagne—then riding until morning through the streets in open carriages to get sobered. Is slavery accountable for the degraded position of women in the South? for degraded they are, beyond belief, beyond imagination—[20]

By 1880 Grace King had begun to think seriously about some kind of career and had discussed the still vague possibility with her sisters. She had applied for a teaching post through a New York agency, but nothing came of the application. Her youngest sister Nina had similar aspirations about working and agreed with Grace wholeheartedly. When Grace was about to return from one of her frequent trips, Nina wrote her,

> I think you are perfectly right to go on & get a position if you can; it is what I am going to do as soon as I am able. I do not believe in living in this poor half starving way. Poverty & dependence crushes every noble feeling out of the heart. I do not think it lowers a woman to work for her living, on the contrary it shows courage & perseverance. I agree with you that teaching is the hardest & the less lucrative of all works & if you have a chance of getting a government office you are lucky, for they pay better & you are more independent. . . . We are poorer now than we have ever been & from all prospect are to be still poorer, but of course you will see this the first month you are home. . . . Sis, we are destined for something—there is no use to think otherwise, either good or bad. As for me I would not be surprised to find myself in 20 years from now either in the penitentiary

20. Grace King Journal 1886–1901.

or upon the throne of England. . . . I must do something. I must be something.[21]

In the summer of 1880 Grace was again visiting the Morrises at Throg's Neck and through correspondence was making her influence felt on Nina, to whom she recommended a very heavy reading project. The oldest and the youngest King sisters at this period had much in common, and the affection between them is quite evident. In October, 1880, Grace addresses Nina as "My dear little Pet" and picks up the subject then popular among American intellectuals—Herbert Spencer. Both sisters have been reading him, and Grace points out:

> By the time you next hear from me I will have assimilated from him as much as my intellectual organs can digest. I am very much afraid you will not be able to keep up the strain all winter; of course you *can* do it easily if you sleep & eat enough—that you must attend to yourself. You know by this time the importance of health, and if you have any ambition mentally, you will never be able to gratify it unless your body is strong & mind cheerful. . . . And do try to sieze as much pleasure as possible; it will keep you from getting ascetic and soured, besides making your family feel so much more comfortable.

Grace continues in her intellectual-didactic vein to discuss beautifying devices that she has seen in New York, such as "silky flat Récamier curls— most artistically mounted from $2 up to $7." Such matters are important if one follows the behests of Ruskin "to cultivate the beautiful as well as the true, for one cannot exist without the other. I for my part cannot tolerate a shabby body any more than a shabby dress. . . . Good-night dear baby Blue-Stocking."

In another letter of the same time she urges Nina to read Longfellow's *Hyperion* and some of his translations from the German. She had started reading Carlyle's *Heroes and Hero Worship*, which has increased her admiration for the Scot. The Morrises' large and well selected library—one of the accoutrements of a Gilded Age millionaire—contains many books in English, yet she feels the compulsion to read in French, German, and Spanish as well.

21. Nina King to Grace King, January 14, 1880.

It was most unusual for a southern young woman of her era to read with as much seriousness and discipline as she did. Looking forward to her return home, she wrote Nina, "I have such nice little treats of Tyndall, Darwin, and Huxley in store for you all. How people can read novels when so much good hard common sense can be procured for fifteen cents." [22]

Other activities that summer were the usual ones: attendance at the local Episcopal church, carriage rides or solitary pony cart rides through the Westchester countryside, excursions to New York to attend the opera, writing letters home, and betting on the races at Coney Island with Henner Morris, the Morrises' sixteen-year-old son. Henner was an intelligent young man who had been educated partly in Germany, where his family spent much of their time. The family had acquired the idea that culture and education were qualities expected of the very rich. Grace King, not ungrateful to be patronized by a family of wealth, was nevertheless aware of a difference in values between her own family and the Morrises. The Kings of course wished to hold their heads up in good society wherever they were, and they held on to their sound, old-fashioned pride, stemming from their antebellum experience. But they were without wealth and also without the pretentiousness of their friends the Morrises.

It is difficult to understand Grace King's continuing drive for learning and especially her wish to master the ideas of her era. She was neither a professional scholar, nor did she need much learning as a mark of social status in the New Orleans of her time. The extraordinary fact remains that her grandmother and her parents had established among the King children, especially the daughters, a genuine love of learning. This had taken place as far back as the war years at L'Embarras Plantation, when the elders were the affectionate teachers and when they were isolated from the normal sources of culture and education. All members of the family learned to read to each other out of the sheer joy of reading, and they discussed their reading experiences together as a part of the pleasure of everyday country life. The habit of reading aloud persisted throughout the sisters' lives. When Grace began formal schooling in New Orleans she had an excellent beginning so that school work was more pleasure than work. And the school experiences were followed by the friend-

22. Grace King to Nina King, October 28, 1880.

ship with Charles Gayarré, whose intellectual influence was of course a profound one. It is not difficult to see that the young Henner Morris would see Grace King as an unusually learned woman.

When he left for school in September, Grace wrote her sister May, "Henner was so unaffectedly fond of me that I was very much touched by it. I drove with him to the station, said good-bye there. He clasped me in his arms and kissed me until his father warned him that the train was going. I felt as if it were a farewell to the last romance of his boyhood."[23]

*

The most important event to dominate the year 1881 was the death of Grace King's father, William Woodson King, at the age of sixty-eight. His health had been in decline for several years, and he had sought cures to alleviate his chronic bronchitis by traveling to a variety of places with dry climates. Grace had returned from her northern trip in February of that year to find the usual commanding presence of her father "dreadfully changed. Now he looked small, thin, bent," his voice "sterile & weak." The period from February to April, she wrote in a later journal, "was one of such acute misery to me that I cannot look back upon it without pain & suffering. The world was never the same to me after the death. . . . The house seemed to me dead when I came back—all were depressed in spirit & discouraged. The life of all had been too hard and we all knew our father was dying of hard work, disappointment, want of rest, & proper comforts necessary to an invalid."

Sometime in March he suffered a paralysis of some sort. During his last days for hours at a time Grace sat on a small stool by his bedside, holding his hand. He could not speak but would waken and look at her lovingly. Her pity for him and her realization of his importance as a force in the entire past of the family increased her love for him. She believed that up to that time she had never known what love was or how profound filial love could be. Then all other forms of love paled before the strength of her devotion to her father. One night as she sat by his pillow she fell into a kind of trance and the room itself expanded; although other family members were near by, she seemed to

---

23. Grace King to May King, September 16, 1880.

be alone with her father in a vast room. She did not move from the place throughout the night until, near dawn, her brother Branch brought her a cup of coffee and made her drink it. This aroused her, and she realized that she had not moved from her vigil in twenty-four hours.

Her father died on a quiet spring Sunday, April 10, 1881, when they were living in a cottage on Terpsichore Street. Part of his face was paralyzed, but he attempted to give his children admonitions even in his last moments. He turned to Grace and said, "Sis—take care of your sisters," and then he repeated the words for emphasis. She was nearly thirty then and she never forgot that moment. Years later she would look back on the event and comment that the light of the world had gone out for her when he died.

After her father's funeral the women of the family journeyed across the lake for a brief period of recuperation. It was strange now not to have the dying man's coughing awaken them during the night. But Grace missed his agony and suffering, and his death marked a crisis of suffering in the lives of the entire family. They would be almost dead themselves for a while until their energies revived and they could start out again without their father's dominant presence. In later years Grace King pondered that dominance endlessly. She was convinced that all his children owed him "all the intellectual worth" of their lives: "He set before us a high ideal & held us strictly to it. No matter how hard the times were . . . no matter what disappointments we had . . . no matter how black the future looked before us, that radiant ideal presided over our household—its patron saint. We were not allowed for one instant to doubt the efficacy of its power."

Had William Woodson King remained prosperous and successful from 1862 to the end of his life, his daughter probably would not have reacted so strongly to his death and to his memory. To her he had become a tragic symbol, the family's head who had kept the faith during the hard times and brought his children to maturity when they could fend for themselves. His sons were now earning salaries to help defray the family expenses, his daughter May would soon marry, and in a few years Grace would commence her independent career as a writer. They were all out of the woods at the time of his death, and Grace looked to him as a martyr who had worn himself out in his endeavors for his family. She took great pride in remembering that he was an honest man who chose privation over luxury when there was any question of compromising his integrity:

> Toward the end of his life, when he saw that despite all his high endeavor he would not be able to provide for the future of his children as he hoped, he used to tell us that all he could leave us was an honest name. And such was our trust & confidence in him that he never murmured when the want of money pressed us in any way that would seem to reflect upon him. On the contrary, the sadder our hearts became, so much the greater pride we had in him. And although he saw the children of other men all around us in luxury, enjoying the privileges of education, travel, dress, of the rich, we never for a moment would have changed places with them. . . . For it was undoubtedly the fact then & now . . . that a high ideal of honour & sensitive delicacy in regard to business standards were an infallible way of not making money, & those that succeeded then as those that succeed now did so by virtue of a hardened skin of honour & a deadened sense of the odour of fine transactions.[24]

After her father's death the old aspiration that had lain in her mind since she was a girl of ten on Bayou L'Embarras came again to the fore. That desire, or obligation, to write again appeared as she saw her brothers go off to their careers—Fred to study in a law office, Branch to work in his Uncle Tom Miller's firm of cotton and sugar factors. Was she a laggard, she asked herself? What about her reading and preparation for a career; were they to come to nothing? But the time was not then quite ripe. The opportunity to write with a genuine purpose had not presented itself.[25]

*

The first marriage among the King children took place in 1884 when May King married F. Brevard McDowell, the son of an old family of Charlotte, North Carolina. Married in New Orleans, the newlyweds went to Charlotte to live permanently. Because May had been Grace's bedfellow and confidant for years, the separation was a difficult one for Grace. But the sisters would

24. Grace King Journal 1904–1906.
25. King, *Memories*, 48.

continue to confide in each other by means of letters. Shortly after the separation May complained to Grace about Brevard's indelicacy in the marriage bed. Grace, the protective older sister, responded with outrage, an emotion she frequently gave way to:

> I am sorry that Brevard was not more considerate—more delicate—or that you were not more obtuse—more of a level with him—but you have only to recollect what armies of women have gone to martyrdom before you & never be surprised & shocked at women who do for money what a hollow sham called matrimony consecrates. If I had known what all this was going to cost me—I would never never have consented to it—but it seemed to me that when girls have mother & aunts & women friends who all encourage that my own individual forebodings must be wrong. It however is only one drop more of gall that has been poured into my cup of life & now it seems to me we had all become at least reconciled to the degradation of being dependent & that perhaps the marriage might have been spared you.[26]

In a second letter written the same day some of her pessimism and outrage had abated in favor of a confessional reply to her favorite sister, with whom she could commiserate on the role of women in marriage:

> Never mind my pet—you will always be a girl sister to me or I a married one to you—for have I not been married—in imagination—or in my dreams at night & have I not trembled & blushed & felt degraded for days afterwards—ashamed to look you in the face? I do not know if all women are this way. I know I would feel as you do now—& you would feel as I do—could we change places. I am afraid we are both only quarreling with the inevitable murmuring at what we consider a peculiarity of our lot—which is no doubt the lot of all women. . . . you can't imagine how precious is to me the knowledge that you *will* write everything even things that women never wrote before to each other. I feel to you the intensity of a mother's devotion & the wild affection of a sister—

26. Grace King to May McDowell, January 16, 1884. May McDowell wrote to Grace during or shortly after the honeymoon, but the letter was not saved.

nay more——of a man who sees that necessity separates those whom love should always unite. . . . Do not regret the May King—she has entered into a higher development—painful, yes—degrading, humiliating—yet a necessary one. Remember the Saviour was stripped naked before he was crucified. Remember that mothers cease to be girls. The ornament of shame is torn away because it is no longer needed. After your letter today such a wild tumult took possession of me—but you see—it has passed away. I am submissive because, May dear, *it must have been*. What God has done must be best. He sent Death into the world. You know how hard that is to bear—& He sent women for men—not men for women. . . . I hated Brevard today—but now I feel an infinite tenderness for him. He could have been better—but also how much worse. . . . I think you will always have to look out for your own comfort. Do it boldly. Don't risk any more annoyance or discomfort thro' a sense of delicacy. You see he has always been used to country people & they are coarse." [27]

It was a somewhat cynical, Genesis-inspired view of marriage, that woman was victimized from the beginning. And it tends to confirm the possibility that Grace King remained single at least in part through her own preference. Her use of the phrase "the degradation of being dependent" on the male illustrates what she found to be the most objectionable disadvantage of being female. In her letter she was of course thinking of physical submission, but she would also have included economic dependence, which she found galling within her family. And it was the onerousness of this dependence that played a forceful role in her eventual decision to work for a living. She had such a move in mind in 1880 when she made an application to a teacher's agency in New York to be considered for a teaching post. She did not take such a post, but the thought and desire for financial independence was early in her mind. The death of her father strengthened her will to attain it. Although her father had not regained his former wealth, he had brought his family through their worst economic crisis and reestablished them in a respectable environment. Once he was removed from the family scene, however, Grace and her sisters became dependent on the three working brothers with whom they lived. There

27. *Ibid.*, January 16, 1884.

were occasional family quarrels on this score that created an atmosphere of tension and bitterness.

Later in 1884 she became more accustomed to May's absence and quizzed her about the mysteries of marriage:

How is it now with you & Brevard? Do you begin to feel at home with him? Isn't he becoming the least in the world a necessity tò you? As I now constantly lay awake half the night I wonder myself almost wild & if souls were marketable, would give a long lease of mine just to catch a glimpse of you two. Nature is a puzzle to me & if you don't unravel some of the mysterious doings of life for me, I am afraid I shall go down into the grave uninformed. To know what is beyond marriage I would gladly get married for a brief period myself.[28]

A few weeks later she wrote May, "I wish you could find a Brevard for Nan, Nina or me. We are getting pretty hard up & the future is threatening us again with all sorts of wants & no sort of means to gratify them with."[29]

In September, 1884, Grace and her sister Nan vacationed at the Gulf Coast town of Pass Christian as the guests of their Uncle Tom and Aunt Sallie. Grace was charmed by the architecture of her uncle's luxurious cottage, which even Ruskin would have approved of. It was painted dark green and red and furnished with wicker. The gallery was curtained and contained a mosquito house and hammock. Grace enjoyed invigorating swims in the Gulf waters, but she complained that during the week there were no beaux, "so we are not belles. I rather dread Sunday, when the beaux do arrive, for the girls appear so silly now, I know they will be abject fools then."[30]

Such was her state of mind at the age of thirty-two in the fall of 1884, on the eve of her first notable accomplishment. She was remarkably well educated for a southern woman of her time. In her childhood she had determined to be a writer, and that desire, vague and wavering through long periods of time, was still alive, awaiting the series of influences and encouragements that would launch her career. She had rejected the influence of the wealthy,

28. *Ibid.*, February 1, 1884.
29. *Ibid.*, February 23, 1884.
30. *Ibid.*, September 10, 1884.

pretentious Cora Morris. She had found no beaux serious enough to interest her; she questioned the value for herself of a marriage experience like that of her sister May. Marriage now being in no way an imminent possibility, she was waiting for bigger game. The idea of a writing career was ready to emerge whenever the proper opportunity arrived.

Three

The Emergence of an Intellectual Southern
Woman, 1885

The literary career of Grace King began in 1885, when she was already thirty-three years old. Two motives account for her readiness to begin to write, one almost heroic, the other practical. Since the days of the war, occupation, and Reconstruction, she had possessed so deep a sympathy for the people of the South that she felt the need to depict their lives as she had observed them and her own life as representative of the regional experience.

The practical motive was her wish for financial independence from her brothers. Fred, Branch, and Will as young men starting out in their various careers were obligated to provide some of the support for the three unmarried sisters, who in traditional patrician families were not expected to work for a living. This situation occasionally caused abrasiveness within the family. The eldest daughter, who was also the most gifted and responsible member of the family, found herself in a position where because of her sex she was expected to spend her life in activities limited to the domestic and the social.

The Kings were a cohesive and affectionate family within their circle, but they were also a particularly irascible and irritable lot. Mrs. King was a devoted mother, but an emotional one who found it difficult to hold her family together in harmony. As she grew older she began to feel a dominance assert itself on Grace's part. Quarrels, usually petty ones, arose between family members and led to hurt feelings. In April, 1885, Grace, having quarreled with her brother Branch over "some trivial affair," drew a strong rebuke from her mother (Mimi) and took such offense that she vowed she would "never get over it as long as I live." In response she left the house for a long ride in the cars to calm herself and think the problem through. She believed that her mother resented "my usurping her place in the house, & the moment any little thing offends her, out it comes, that I do not treat her right." She next made overtures to her Uncle Tom Miller, asking him for permission to live in his country place, but the effect of this was only to bring her mother to tears. Grace confided to May that her own emotional response to the incident was a state of intense shivering followed by "burning fever."[1]

There was no question that Grace would leave the household or break with her mother, whom she cared deeply for; she needed an absorbing activity that would keep her mind from the pettiness of household quarrels and open up some kind of new world for her, a world that would give her a degree of financial independence and personal freedom. Shortly after the quarrel with Mimi she met Charles Dudley Warner, whose friendship she promoted with as much aggressiveness as a southern lady was capable of. Warner was to become a family friend and enjoy the King hospitality. He would witness the joy and good fellowship this remarkable family was capable of at its harmonious best, and he also would be the instrument to rescue Grace from her constant domestic concerns and expose her to an important intellectual milieu in Hartford and New York.

Grace King's own local milieu had been many years maturing, in preparation for such a writer as she would become. In 1873, over ten years before she began to write, Edward King, a literary emissary of *Scribner's Magazine*, came to New Orleans to gather material for a series of articles called "The Great

1. Grace King to May McDowell, April 11, 1885, in the Grace King Papers, Department of Archives and Manuscripts, Louisiana State University, Baton Rouge. Unless otherwise stated, all manuscript material is in this collection.

South." The articles became a book of considerable national influence in 1875. King, who was no relation to Grace King, wrote of the state: "Louisiana today is Paradise Lost. In twenty years it may be Paradise Regained. It has unlimited, magnificent possibilities. Upon its bayou-penetrated soil, on its rich uplands and its vast prairies, a gigantic struggle is in progress. It is the battle of race with race, of the *picturesque* and unjust civilization of the past with the prosaic and leveling civilization of the present."[2]

Grace King would not see Louisiana's potentials in quite that light, but she was very much aware of the great material that her own experience and her knowledge of the state had provided her. She knew of Edward King's accomplishment in making the nation conscious of the future of the South. For this she would give credit to him in her *Memories* and also to George W. Cable, who had been "discovered" by Edward King and whose stories had subsequently been published in *Scribner's*. Cable's *Old Creole Days* (1879), the collected tales, and his novel *The Grandissimes* (1880) had conveyed to the reading public some of the excitement of Creole life of the past; they had whetted the national appetite for more fiction about the charms of the Crescent City. Indeed, Cable had done for New Orleans what a team of modern public relations specialists might have done, publicizing a city that previously had been only vaguely known and little visited by outsiders.

In 1884 New Orleans showed its own wish to publicize itself for commercial reasons by producing a successful Cotton Centennial Exposition. This fair, the idea of "Major" Edward Burke, continued until 1886, bringing the city its first modern wave of tourists and stimulating its economic growth in the years to follow. Grace King was vitally interested in the exposition and its value to the city, and she herself benefited from the outside visitors, who provided a series of intellectual friendships as important to her as her friendship for Charles Gayarré had been. There were five of these—Joaquin Miller, Julia Ward Howe, Charles Dudley Warner, Lafcadio Hearn, and Richard Watson Gilder.

Earliest of these to arrive in New Orleans was the colorful and celebrated Joaquin Miller, who came in the fall of 1884 as a correspondent for several eastern newspapers to report on preparations for the Cotton Centennial

---

2. Edward King, *The Great South* (Hartford, 1875), 1.

Exposition. Grace King's brother Fred met him on a river boat and, with his family's typical hospitality, invited him to the King home on South Rampart Street. Miller made a great impression with his long hair, scarlet scarf, and patent-leather boots. And for all his ostentatiousness the King family took kindly to him because he was sympathetic to the city and to the South. They found his manner unaffected and cordial; they enjoyed his beautiful voice as he read his own verse, and his good humor and satire enlivened the various parties he later attended once he began to be lionized.[3]

Grace King had much admiration for this literary oddity on his first extended visit to the city. Throughout the winter of 1884–1885 she occasionally took dictation from him as he wrote a poem about the Mississippi called "The Song of the Great River." His impact was quite sensational during the months of his stay in New Orleans, and Grace later wrote that "to the young who heard him, he ever lives as a poet radiant in the light of the great sun of our generation, Byron." The presence of such an attractive man who had won international fame through his untutored and humorous verse was a kind of tonic to Grace King, as he was to other literary amateurs of New Orleans. And becoming a friend of this celebrity may have made the profession of writing seem even more attractive to her. But this pioneer Byron certainly had no influence on her future writing, and when he returned to New Orleans in 1896 her attitude toward him had changed completely. She wrote May McDowell in that year: "Joaquin Miller has not monopolised us—of all disappointments, he is the greatest. . . . He was rather an amusing & interesting fraud before— now he is a stupid & boring fraud. He affects the patriarch poet . . . he wears a long beard, and his nose is redder & his bold head pimply. I suppose he expected some sort of veneration from us, but we really couldn't. We can all stand being shocked better than being bored."[4]

New Orleans and Grace King were announcing themselves in 1885, and then a costumed poet out of the West was an exciting novelty that matched the new energies of both the city and the young woman. When ten years had passed, however, the two had achieved a degree of sophistication that turned them away from the celebrated poseur.

---

3. Arlin Turner, "Joaquin Miller in New Orleans," *Louisiana Historical Quarterly,* XXII (January, 1939), 216; Grace King, *Memories of a Southern Woman of Letters* (New York, 1932), 52–53.
4. Grace King to May McDowell, undated, c. late 1896.

Grace King needed the model of an aggressive woman with a career behind her to overcome whatever doubts she might have had about the propriety of a southern lady's earning a living. Southern women of the previous generation like Augusta Jane Evans Wilson and Caroline Lee Hentz had written novels for commercial success, but such books were beneath the literary aim forming within Grace King. She believed that to work for a living by writing was not necessarily to debase one's literary ideals. In the South few women before her time had pursued intellectual careers. The one woman southern writer she admired among those already writing in 1885 was Mary Noailles Murfree (Charles Egbert Craddock). She had been publishing stories in the 1870s, and her collection *In the Tennessee Mountains* had appeared in 1884. The fathers of both Miss Murfree and Miss King were lawyers, both intellectual men who believed in sound education for their daughters—as opposed to many planters who tended to believe that a genteel polish was all a southern lady needed. Neither lawyer Murfree nor lawyer King seems to have felt any repugnance about the possibility that his daughter might work with her head for a living.

The aggressive career woman who appeared on the New Orleans scene to influence Miss King's destiny was Julia Ward Howe. She arrived in the city with her daughter Maud on December 16, 1884, on the invitation of the Centennial Exposition to direct its Women's Division. There was resentment in some quarters that a northern woman should have been selected for the post, but Mrs. Howe, who at age sixty-five was energetic and efficient, made herself welcome in many New Orleans households. Looking back to that time, Maud Howe could "remember best of all Mrs. William W. King and her four interesting daughters, in their large comfortable house on South Rampart Street. Here I felt the flavor and charm of Southern family life, which had a character all its own. Mrs. King was large of heart and friendly of manner, with such a glow of hospitality about her that I still have a warm feeling when I think of her and her kindness." In a journal Maud Howe also wrote that once at dinner at the Kings, she and her mother had "Bouillabaisse better than we had in Marseilles."[5]

In her memoirs Grace King gives great credit to Mrs. Howe's accomplish-

5. Maud Howe Elliott, *Three Generations* (Boston, 1923), 205, 207.

ment as head of the Women's Division. To show the importance of New Orleans history she collected furniture, jewels, laces, documents, and miniatures that had been hidden from the public eye in old Creole houses. The collection was a pleasant surprise to the citizens of New Orleans and made them more conscious of their past. To Grace King Mrs. Howe was "the embodiment of the Victorian ideal of womanhood. She was small of stature, with a poise of exquisite dignity. Her head wore simple bandeaux of white hair, under a real-lace cap. Her voice once heard could never be forgotten, richly musical and modulated to the tone of high society. In manner she was cordial as well as reserved; she had a smile that can be described as sweet politeness."[6]

In her public pronouncements Grace King was careful to make polite comments about people she had known, but these might not always be her final word. In calling Mrs. Howe "the embodiment of the Victorian ideal of womanhood," she of course did not mean the ideal of the self-effacing mother confined to the duties that kept her at home. Mrs. Howe was well known as an aggressive public figure, a career woman devoted to feminism among other causes. She was the Victorian woman zealous with humanitarian spirit, much of which she had poured into the writing of the famous "Battle Hymn of the Republic." Although she was well received and admired in New Orleans, there were occasional abrasions. Mrs. King, it was said, left a gathering in some offense at a time when Mrs. Howe was urged to sing the Battle Hymn. And Grace King took some satisfaction in scorning "these Bostonians" (though Mrs. Howe was born in New York) when she wrote privately to her sister May McDowell. At lunch, she wrote, "They literally 'grabbed' for food—& eat & drank like cormorants." She later described an excursion through the countryside: "The bridge over a bayou having been swept away, we were obliged to ford & make a long detour in the lake—the waters of which came up to the floor of the carriage. Mrs. Howe screamed & yelled, & implored us to save her—not to let her be killed etc etc—which made me feel like ducking her in the water. . . . One's character can never be so well studied as on these excursions. . . . The old lady, perches herself up and looks like a ridiculous old owl." In the same letter Grace King asked for Henry

6. Grace King, *Memories*, 54.

James's novel *The Bostonians*: "I would like to read any thing that ridicules these Bostonians."[7]

Grace King, however, demonstrated that she was also highly stimulated by the presence of this celebrated woman. Not only did the Kings and the Howes exchange visits with some frequency, but Grace eagerly participated in a small literary club that Mrs. Howe revived for the exchange of ideas. The Pan Gnostics held weekly meetings to discuss literary subjects or to hear an original paper by a member. Grace King's paper, prepared for the club, became her earliest published article. One can also conjecture that Grace admired Mrs. Howe's feminist attitudes, since she herself was on the threshold of a career in which she would achieve a large measure of independence through her own individual expression.

Maud Howe, in contradiction to the stereotype of the prim young Bostonian, was extraordinarily beautiful and sought after by men as distinguished as General Pierre Beauregard. Her popularity tended to vex Grace King, who as the soul of southern propriety, was in sharp contrast to the Yankee belle fully enjoying the stir she made among the men. The sociable Maud gave frequent parties at her mother's house. Grace King met Charles Dudley Warner at one of these, but she was ill at the time and made no attempt to cultivate him. At a second such evening party at the Howe home early in April, 1885, she met Warner again and was more determined to gain his friendship. He was safely married and more than twenty years her senior. She wrote her sister May that the party "was stupid in all but the opportunity it gave me of prosecuting my acquaintance with Charles Dudley Warner. I had dragged through a long evening talking 'scraps.' . . . But I watched my opportunity & snatched it when it came. Mr. Warner made an engagement with me to call on the Gayarrés. This morning at 11 oc he came for me & we had a very nice time of it. He is about fifty—grey haired & bearded & married— but so clever, refined & original. Of course we are affinities & of course the fashionables are racing after him & he doesn't meet me anywhere & notice it—tant pis."[8]

Warner was fifty-five—five years older than Grace King supposed—and was at that time at the peak of his career. Editor of the Hartford *Courant* and literary critic of *Harper's Magazine*, he was in demand as a lecturer on literary

7. Grace King to May McDowell, March 4, 1885.
8. *Ibid.*, April 11, 1885.

subjects. His books, especially his essays and travel works, were enjoyed by a wide audience. He found Grace the most enthusiastic of guides to New Orleans and obviously enjoyed her company. Two weeks later she wrote that "he came & spent nearly the whole day here (It rained so he couldn't leave) & then he proposed that I should go with him & visit the 'Straight University.' We had a very funny time. As he said, I was there under false pretenses—for they took me for a Yankee & talked accordingly. He asked them all sorts of leading questions & I was delighted when their report tallied so well with my version of the darky question. He is a very nice man—so refined & quiet, & yet so full of humor." [9] On another occasion she took considerable pride in taking Warner the celebrity to a meeting of the Pan Gnostics.

During his first stay in New Orleans, Warner eagerly met all the writers he could, keeping his editor's eye open for talent. He spent a memorable evening with Lafcadio Hearn in his quarters at the corner of Gasquet and Robertson streets, beginning the acquaintance that would in time encourage Hearn to write for *Harper's Magazine*. No two intellectual people could have been more different in character or background than the respectable Miss King and the melancholy, eccentric Hearn.

The diminutive Hearn, no more than two years her senior, had been born on a Greek island, the son of a British army surgeon and a Greek mother with a strain of Arabic and Moorish ancestry. His strange pilgrimage as a youth from Greece to Cincinnati was like that of no other American author. He had none of Grace King's love of appearance, her sense of respectability, or her pride in ancestry. She would have been appalled, for example, had she known of his liaison with a mulatto woman in Cincinnati before he was commissioned to come to New Orleans to do a series of political articles. Later in New Orleans he began to write regularly for the respectable *Times-Democrat*, but then he had turned his interests to French literature, which he both translated and analyzed. Grace King read the *Times-Democrat* regularly and began to feel his influence probably even before she had read any of his fiction. She had long since been exposed to classic French literature, and Hearn's contribution to her development was likely that of making her aware of contemporary French writers, since his great admirations were for Gautier, Flaubert, Baudelaire, and Maupassant.

9. *Ibid.*, April 26, 1885. Straight College became Dillard University in 1930.

Warner brought these two together. Without telling the shy Hearn where he was taking him to lunch one day, he brought him to the North Rampart Street home of the Kings. When the door was opened, Warner had to urge Hearn to come in. To Grace King "he seemed small, slovenly and gauche, and he acknowledged Warner's introductions in a thoroughly scared way, half swallowing inaudible monosyllables. All through luncheon he sat looking as if he were suffering acutely and nobody was able to pry a word out of him. In fact he gave the impression of being on the point of making a break for freedom at any moment." Hearn felt uneasy among the trappings of grandeur or what was indeed no more than old-fashioned nineteenth-century southern class. Grace King later heard from Henry Mills Alden of *Harper's Magazine* that Hearn had told him her parlor was "as big as a cathedral and all hung with pictures."[10]

Hearn's visit was important to her, although there may have been no other meeting between them. How much of his own fiction was to influence her is unclear, but surely she learned much from his articles in the *Times-Democrat.* That reading helped her to use French writers as models for her own fiction. In a 1915 letter to Professor Fred Lewis Pattee of Pennsylvania State College, she wrote, "Charles Gayarré influenced me in my writing & so did Lafcadio Hearn, but no one else. I am not a romanticist. I am a realist à la mode de Nlle Orléans. I have never written a line that was not realistic—but our life, our circumstances, the heroism of the men & women that surrounded my early horizon—all that was romantic—I had a mind very sensitive to romantic impressions, but critical as to their expression."[11] By this statement she meant that Gayarré influenced her writing of history, Hearn her writing of fiction. This is probably the only comment she made on the influence of Hearn, and we can assume she meant that she was influenced by Hearn's analysis of the fiction of such authors as Maupassant. She might also have been thinking of Hearn's fiction, which like her own was an expression of the romance of real life. Both authors depicted commonplace reality, but the backgrounds and characters they chose were unusual and unstandardized.

Warner's first noticeable influence on Grace King was his support of her paper "Heroines of Novels," which she prepared for the Pan Gnostics. He

10. Edward Larocque Tinker, *Lafcadio Hearn's American Days* (New York, 1924), 257.
11. Grace King to Fred Lewis Pattee, January 19, 1915, in Robert Bush (ed.), *Grace King of New Orleans* (Baton Rouge, 1973), 398.

showed her his own "Modern Fiction," in which he defends idealism in the American novel as opposed to commonplace realism. "One of the worst characteristics of modern fiction," he wrote, "is its so-called truth to nature." Art, to him, is "selection and idealization, with a view to impressing the mind with human or even higher ideas."[12] Although Grace King does not champion such a position in her article, part of her contrast between the heroines of German and French fiction is that the former are idealized and the latter are not.

She was self-conscious and nervous about her own ability even to read with assurance before a small critical audience, but Warner's encouragement probably forced her to do something she might not have done or might not have done so well. She described her feelings about the paper to her sister May: "Next week, I am going to devote myself to it & if I can only manage to steady my voice enough to read it—am determined to make a tremendous effort. After all Warner's encouragement, I am as bold as a lion—& if I make a failure it will be an audacious one."[13] Years later she described the paper as "a rather caustic review . . . and an arrogant one. I read it at the club meeting in a trembling voice and could hardly believe my ears when I heard expressions of compliment and applause."[14] The paper was published on the *Times-Democrat* literary page for Sunday, May 31, 1885, and signed "P.G.," which probably stands for "Pan Gnostic." That Grace King did not use her own name was entirely proper for a young woman of New Orleans, where the achievement of newspaper publicity was frowned upon.

"Heroines of Novels" is neither a landmark of literary criticism nor did it presage a particular talent for criticism on the part of the author. It does tell us that a southern woman is engaged in thinking and writing seriously about literature, which for its time was unusual. In the essay Grace King compared the character of fictional heroines in the literature of the recent past of Germany, France, England, and the United States. She was writing in effect an essay in what is now called comparative literature. Even more extraordinary, she exhibited a wide learning in the four literatures she was considering, indicating that she had prepared herself in her subject as well as if she had been expecting to pursue a professorship. Her interest was women in litera-

12. Charles Dudley Warner, "Modern Fiction," *Altantic Monthly*, LI (April, 1883), 464.
13. Grace King to May McDowell, May 9, 1885.
14. King, *Memories*, 58.

ture, and this was to become her major theme in fiction. At the very beginning of her career she was establishing herself as a kind of advocate, interpreter, and apologist for womankind.

She first compared the idealism of the woman of German fiction as opposed to the greater realism of the French concept of woman. Curiously, this illustrates a dilemma in Grace King's own mind, for she quite clearly admired the superlative spiritual values represented in the German heroine, whereas she admitted that "the heroines of French novels have never been considered very proper acquaintance for ladies." They were a "brilliant fascinating set of creatures . . . possessing in perfection the two supreme arts for women—*l'art de se faire jolies et l'art de se faire aimer*. They are a consommé of all that the French sensorium and a century has discovered to be the most alluring physically, the most charming mentally." For an Anglo-Saxon Victorian this was what made the French heroine shocking and often repellent. But, unusual for her time, Grace King was aware that "artistically the novel has reached perfection in France alone. No painter has been so devoted to his art, no physician to his profession, as the novelist to the novel. He goes through the most painful apprenticeship, frequents morgue, hospital, jails, hangs over dissecting tables, follows the criminal from trial to judgment and execution, to achieve outward exactitude, and then diseases himself morally for the inner sensations." She was here showing herself to be among the few Americans who could champion the French advances in fiction technique, but she was still Victorian enough to shy away from the sordidness that accompanied naturalism. In discussing the English novel, as far as the depiction of women was concerned, she put Charlotte Brontë and George Eliot ahead of Dickens and Thackeray for their greater fairness and closeness to the observed truth. In *Jane Eyre*, Charlotte Brontë had proven that a plain woman could be made thoroughly interesting in fiction—a great exception to the prevailing idea among the English male novelists. George Eliot also "felt the injustice of necessarily beautiful heroines. She makes selfishness the corollary of beauty and contrasts it with unselfishness and plainness." She added that George Eliot "did not idealize women. She did not feel the need of it for herself and her friends. She tried to write of them as she knew them, and has left much information about them, valuable chiefly from a psychological point of view."

Grace King's interpretation of the American heroine was less fully defined because relatively few important novels had been produced by 1885. Referring no doubt to the popular novel, she found little closeness to reality in the women in most novels, with the sole exception of those in the fiction of Henry James and William Dean Howells. She very much admired James as novelist but was astute enough to see something lacking in his heroines, something that a woman alone could divine:

> James once caught an American girl, and he has been keeping her by him, under a microscope, ever since. Day by day he jots down in a diary every perceptible variation in her demeanor. It makes no difference where she is . . . his eye is on her, and he is going to tell. . . . He has done every possible thing to the poor specimen except to let her die and make her speak. Women know, because they feel that it is *he*, not *she*, talking all the time. He may observe and study, and watch and examine, but never a word will he obtain from her. . . . Could James only stop enumerating, one after another, discoveries which are new only to him; would he, once only, talk to his heroine, love her, make her love him—for women have wide doors to their hearts, but no windows—you can walk in, but you can't look in; could he only know what the plowboy knows by intuition, his works would no longer be a deluge of words (brilliant, it is true) on a desert of ideas.

She concluded that "the American heroine is not romantic enough for the American novelist, nor does the American life offer those delightful contrasts of position which so effectually disturb the course of true love in the old world. . . . If you take away the pandemonium caused by the social results of an irregular civilization you might just as well take away from the novelist his pen and ink."[15] Her statement was a good one, and it reflected what many a greater author had said before (James himself, for example, in his *Hawthorne*). America was hardly an "irregular civilization" to the social historian, and in 1885 the novelist might find American life too level, too undramatic, too smiling, as the earlier novels of Howells proved it was. Grace King's insights from her wide reading of fiction provide a kind of prediction of the quality of the fiction she herself would write: it would be technically based on principles

---

15. P. G., "Heroines of Novels," New Orleans *Times-Democrat*, May 31, 1885.

derived from the French fiction writers, and as for the quality of life, she would find drama and color and interest in writing realistically about the ready-made setting for the regional writer, the city that had less of American life's regularity or sameness than any other—New Orleans.

When Richard Watson Gilder made a spring trip south in April, 1885, he was a well-known editor and author. In New Orleans he was caught up in the relatively small group of intellectual and social men and women who wrote or taught or read good books. In his pocket diary of the trip he recorded the various pleasures of his brief stay in the city. On two occasions he mentioned meeting "the Misses King," which would mean Grace King and her sisters Nan and Nina. He met them first at a party following a dinner at Mrs. Howe's home on April 14. On the night before he left the city he saw them again at a performance at the French Opera House. Gilder's particular connection with New Orleans was that in both *Scribner's Magazine* and its successor *Century* he had published the series of stories by George W. Cable that became *Old Creole Days*. He visited Cable's former home in New Orleans and met his mother and sister. It may have been a shock to him to discover the extent to which respectable New Orleanians disapproved of Cable for what they considered his disparagement of the Creole character and his sympathetic treatment of quadroons in his fiction. Entertained at the Boston Club, Gilder "met George Dupré. . . . Mr. D gave acct. of Cable's inaccuracies (alleged)."[16] He was undoubtedly put on the defensive on this issue wherever he went in the city.

The hostility to Cable had developed gradually over the previous five years, the years of Cable's most significant publications. His novelette "Madame Delphine" (1881) dealt with miscegenation in a way that suggested he approved of it. Although he did not, he was deeply sympathetic to the dilemma of the quadroon Olive and the white banker who loves her. During the period when Reconstruction was still freshly remembered, Cable went beyond the New South writers who advocated full cooperation with the Federal Union to the radical extreme of championing the rights of the freed slaves. In his novel *Dr. Sevier* (1883), this once wounded Confederate soldier speaks authorially to the Union soldiers, admitting the justice of their cause:

16. Richard Watson Gilder Pocket Diary, 1885; excerpt for April 14, 1885 in Robert Bush, "Grace King: The Emergence of a Southern Intellectual Woman," *Southern Review*, XIII (Spring, 1977), 280, 81.

"saviors of the Union; your cause is just. Lo, now, since nigh twenty-five years have passed, we of 'the South can say it! 'And yet—and yet, we cannot forget'—and we would not."[17] Certainly his "we of the South" represented a very small minority in 1883.

Cable saw his Creoles as picturesque and exotic rather than ideal and heroic. The central impression of the Creole in the novel *The Grandissimes* is that of a proud planter who punishes a recalcitrant slave with unspeakable cruelty. Cable had put his scholarly facts together in *The Creoles of Louisiana*, published in 1884, the year before Grace King met Richard Watson Gilder. That book outraged Creoles like Charles Gayarré because it implied that they were descended from women of French houses of correction and Indian and African women whom the French and Spanish soldiers had married in Louisiana. Grace King would wait many years to write her own account of the *Creole Families of New Orleans* (1921), a work that traces the origins of many of the important families to distinguished European bloodlines.

The hostility of New Orleans to Cable had much to do with his permanent move to Northampton, Massachusetts in 1884. Grace King felt that hostility as much as anyone. Several references to him in letters indicate a probability that she was at least acquainted with Cable, although she was seven years his junior and her social realm was rather different from his. It was the subject of Cable the apostate that spurred her in 1885 to begin writing fiction. She and several friends including her brother Branch were at the Pickwick Club, making plans to go to supper. Always interested in cultivating the intelligentsia, she suggested that Gilder be invited to accompany them. After supper she found herself paired off with him, and he brought up two highly sensitive subjects. He told her that his brother-in-law, a Union officer, had died during the occupation of New Orleans, and his funeral had been jeered or laughed at by a lady from her gallery. Grace King knew of the incident and attempted to explain that the lady had indeed not laughed at the funeral, but at the antics of a child. Through this misunderstanding she had been arrested and sent without trial to Ship Island, where she was guarded solely by Negro troops. The incident was an outrage to New Orleanians.

Miss King and Gilder continued in this controversial tone when he asked

17. George W. Cable, *Dr. Sevier* (New York: 1896), 377.

her why intellectual New Orleans so undervalued Cable. In her memoirs she recalled that she "hastened to enlighten him to the effect that Cable proclaimed his preference for colored people over white and assumed the inevitable superiority—according to his theories—of the quadroons over the Creoles. He was a native of New Orleans and had been well treated by its people, and yet he stabbed the city in the back, as we felt, in a dastardly way to please the Northern press."

"While I was speaking in all earnestness and desire to inform him," she recollected, "I could feel a cold atmosphere emanating from him and chilling me to the bone. He listened to me with icy indifference, and the rest of our walk was accomplished in silence, except for one remark. 'Why,' he said, 'if Cable is so false to you, why do not some of you write better?'" The one remark was to her a "rankling taunt," a challenge made to a whole society that had produced an internationally famous author and then rejected him for his analysis of the complicated problems of their society. The incident was what Grace King needed. After shaking hands with Gilder and bidding him what must have been a less-than-cordial good night, she lay awake in bed, tormented with the challenge. "The next morning," she recalled, "I was resolved to do at least my share in our defense, a mighty small share I felt it to be, possibly a hopeless effort. Brave with the courage of desperation, I got paper and pencil, and on the writing-table in my bedroom wrote my first story, with not an idea in my brain except that I must write it or forfeit all my allegiance to self-respect."[18] This was the moment at which all the pressures of her life came together—the Confederate heroism, the need for money to restore the family position and to give her independence, and her wish for recognition through the fulfillment of her talent.

The words "allegiance" and "self-respect" are important indications of Grace King's characteristic *pietas*, her strong loyalty to the principles in which she had been reared, her feeling for family, for her native city, and for the South. She and her friend Charles Gayarré really meant it when they said that Cable wrote for his own monetary success, and to please the northern press, because neither Grace King nor Gayarré could understand any degree of heroism when it violated the old Roman virtue of *pietas*. But no scholar today

18. King, *Memories*, 60, 61.

would look upon Cable as less than the most genuine and unselfish of writers when, in his early career, he championed the rights of the freed Negroes as no other southerner had done before him. He might have explained his behavior toward New Orleans by saying that he exercised self-reliance: if your conscience dictates principles at variance with those championed by your native city or your region, it is of course your conscience that prevails, not dogged loyalty to principles you no longer hold as valid. Even Grace King or Gayarré would have abandoned the *pietas* principle if they had felt strongly enough about change in their society. But they did not: the champion of *pietas* is usually the conservative; the person of self-reliance is the liberal or revolutionary.

Grace King knew that in writing about life in New Orleans she was ironically a follower of her arch-enemy Cable himself. But her approach was quite different from his. Cable, with his unusual talent for creating the picturesque in character and setting, had written stories about antebellum times. And little of the subject matter of his early stories is closely connected with his own life, though his own views were of course embodied in such characters as Joseph Frowenfeld, the liberal Philadelphian of *The Grandissimes*. Grace King's use of background for her first story, "Monsieur Motte," was determined by her own experience as a student in the later 1860s at the Institut St. Louis, a private school for girls; she took from life the school's headmistress and the quadroon hairdresser Marcélite. At the very beginning of her career she was establishing herself as realist rather than romantic. Here there was no glance back to the past for its own sake. She would point out one of the principles central to her fiction—that because in New Orleans the real and the contemporary were both likely to be picturesque and interesting, there was no need to go back to a romanticized past. She was never to ally herself to the school of Washington Irving; her closest models were probably Daudet and Maupassant, and later she followed a concept of the short story that suggests Chekhov.

In her memoirs Grace King gives the impression that "Monsieur Motte" was written in some haste. The first draft may well have been, but it was not until late August, 1885, that she considered it ready to submit to an editor. A good deal of polish went into the story in the meantime—polish that her friend George C. Préot was partly responsible for. When it was ready she thought it appropriate to submit it to Gilder: it would stand as her answer to his challenge. But she submitted it anonymously through a bookdealer. *Century* rejected the story without comment, but it is not clear whether Gilder himself read it and returned it.[19]

George C. Préot was the one friend within the city whose assistance was important to Grace King during the crucial year of 1885. A notary and a writer for the *Times-Democrat*, he became genuinely interested in her ability to write, although he had nothing personal to gain by befriending her. He encouraged her to publish "Heroines of Novels" in the *Times-Democrat* and paid many visits to South Rampart Street, meticulously helping her polish her earliest stories, "Monsieur Motte" and "Bonne Maman." After *Century* rejected the first of these, Préot strongly urged the reluctant Grace King to send the story to Warner in the hope that he could place it for her in a northern periodical. During this period she refers to Préot as her "mentor," and in 1892 she would dedicate *Tales of a Time and Place* to him as her "critical friend and friendly critic." It is true that returning from Paris in 1893 she would denigrate Préot as one of the minor intellectual brotherhood in her city; nevertheless, when he was dying in 1901, she was deeply moved and called him "the truest and the most unselfish friend I ever had. I can never have another like him."[20]

After Charles Dudley Warner returned home to Hartford in the spring of 1885, he wrote Grace King that he had heard that she had published "Heroines of Novels" in the *Times-Democrat*. He would have been pleased to help her find a publisher for it, he said, and offered himself as a friendly agent, willing to serve her "in any literary way."[21] Encouraged by Préot, her immediate answer was to send the manuscript of "Monsieur Motte" to Warner. The brief period during which she awaited his answer was a crucial one in her career. She was unsure of her abilities and decided to let Warner's pronouncement of the success or failure of her story determine her entire future. He was to be the "supreme court" that would ultimately judge her competence.

While she waited for his answer, another quarrel developed within the family that made her all the more determined to achieve financial indepen-

19. *Ibid.*, 62.
20. Grace King Journal, September 22, 1901, in Bush (ed.), *Grace King of New Orleans*, 385–86.
21. King, *Memories*, 64.

dence. She wrote May, "you can imagine what anxiety I am in to hear from him, particularly since my flare-up with Will. This young gentleman is adding the very last impulse I needed to my desire to be independent." Will, her youngest brother, had been employed as a cotton weigher at respectable wages, a part of which were contributed to the household expenses. But to Grace, Will lacked energy and ambition; he missed opportunities for advancement that would fit him appropriately into her plan for the success of the King family. She hoped he would be accepted in her Uncle Tom's company. Outspoken like other members of the family, Grace offended Will by her comments on his failings, and when even her apology failed to smooth his ruffled feelings she was placed "in a horribly embarrassing position, from which Warner's letter can only extricate me." Even a minor success with her story would enable her to contribute to the household expenses and save her from the humiliation of having to accept support from Will. Grace confessed to May what a painful lesson she had learned by making other people's interests her own. "My only quarrels in life," she wrote, "have been for the advancement of others. I have centered all my interests in the family. Consequently, all that I have suffered in life has come to me from the home circle. If I can throw myself into some all-absorbing employment, this will cease." [22]

In the meantime, Warner was playing his role in her life by turning her manuscript over to Henry Mills Alden, editor of *Harper's Magazine*. Some time later, however, he met Professor William M. Sloane, who was putting together his first issue of the *New Princeton Review*. Because Sloane needed a good story for his magazine, Warner retrieved "Monsieur Motte" from Alden's desk. Sloane read the story and accepted it without hesitation, but Warner was later rebuked by Alden, who would have published it in *Harper's*.

Grace King had been spurred to write by an emotion felt by a great number of intelligent New Orleanians. She was writing almost as a representative of those people, who may have wished to set the record straight in their opposition to Cable. One might expect that the story would itself be a kind of answer to Cable's opinions on the Creoles and Negroes or quadroons. But Grace King's fiction could never be a direct "answer" to Cable because she was always to reject any direct use of propaganda. "Monsieur Motte" does

22. Grace King to May McDowell, September 15, 1885.

imply a strong position on race relations, as it records many instances of loyalty and even sacrifice to their former masters on the part of black or quadroon women in the period of Reconstruction. In September she wrote Warner of "my own endeavor to call attention at least to some of those relations brought on by slavery, honorable to all concerned. It seems to me, white as well as black women have a sad showing in what some people call romance. I am very tired, but as I recollect these things, I think I shall try to write them—if no one else does it better. One of these days they may prove a pleasant record and serve to bring us all nearer together blacks and whites."[23] In November she reinforced her motive, saying that "the only vocation I feel, is the desire to show you that a Southerner and a white person is not ashamed to acknowledge a dependence on negroes, nor to proclaim the love that exists between the two races, a love which in the end will destroy all differences in color; or rather I had better say—that that love is the only thing which can do it."[24]

The central figure of "Monsieur Motte" is Marcélite, quadroon hairdresser for the girls' school, the Institut St. Denis. Deeply attached to Marie Modeste, the white child of her former master, Marcélite supports her throughout her school years. But since she fears the Creole girl might be disgraced if it were known she was supported by a former slave, she creates an imaginary uncle, Monsieur Motte, whom the girl never sees but believes is her sole provider. When the secret is dramatically revealed and Marcélite seems to be exposed, she is in fact elevated to the status of heroine. Marie Modeste has nothing but the highest devotion for her. Grace King wrote three sequential stories during the year that followed to complete a kind of episodic novel published as *Monsieur Motte* in 1888 by A. C. Armstrong and Son. In the final episode, "The Marriage of Marie Modeste," the bride will have only Marcélite attend her, acknowledging fully her love for the hairdresser and her debt to her.

Cable had emphasized the cruelties of the masters toward their African slaves in *The Grandissimes*. His "Bras Coupé" is a symbol of slavery itself and the resistance to slavery by the unconquerable human spirit. Even Cable's female slaves in that novel show little but hatred for their masters. Grace King,

23. Grace King to Charles Dudley Warner, September 17, 1885.
24. *Ibid.*, November 22, 1885.

writing about another era and confining herself to the relations between females, quadroon and white, wanted to show that her sacrificing hairdresser was representative of an entire group of trained servants. She wished to imply that house servants were generally so well treated in antebellum times that hatred for the slaveowner was the exception and loyalty and love the rule. She based this belief on her recollections that her parents and relatives had treated their slaves with decency and humanity.

Early in December, 1885, a check for $150 arrived for "Monsieur Motte." Grace King had made her experiment to achieve a measure of financial independence and she had succeeded. She wrote her sister May that "a great calm seemed to fall on us all—Nan & I of course got weak, Nina maintained her equilibrium and commenced immediately to advise me how to spend it. . . . I went out to get some white toweling to make Branch and Will some toilet mats of; and as I walked on the street I felt very proud I can tell you, the first really well satisfied moment of my life." [25] The comment was not so much an exaggeration as it seems. The moment she knew that she had arrived was the moment when the check came for her first significant publication, not the moment of acceptance or publication. With her $150 for the first time in her life she could enjoy the fact of financial independence. Her first gesture, the purchase of material to make gifts for her brothers, was more than a gesture of kindness or gratitude for their financial help in the past; it was also an announcement that she now had financial power of her own and that she would make it her business to maintain that power in the future.

Early in the new year she saw the story in print and had the satisfaction of hearing that it had received good notices. Since it was appearing in the first issue of a new review, it achieved considerable attention. Published anonymously, it also took on a certain mystery in the eyes of the reviewers. Warner summarized the reception in a letter:

> One paper said it was a "selection" from foreign contemporary fiction. The N. Y. Tribune had ten lines of hearty praise. The N. Y. Post attributes it to Cable, the Springfield Republican to Mr. Janvier. The Boston Herald . . . said it was the sort of fiction found in the "Revue des deux Mondes," and that we ought to have more of it. All of my friends, who have read it,

25. Grace King to May McDowell, December 22, 1885.

are thoroughly entranced with it, think it very strong, vigorous, pathetic, and wonderful in giving pictures with a few strokes of the pen.[26]

The friendship with Warner continued for many years. Grace King was to be his guest several times at Hartford, and he would return to New Orleans with regularity for spring visits. Their friendship never threatened Warner's marriage or Miss King's respectability, but their early correspondence is that of a couple who love each other. She rather proudly circulated his letters among her sisters, only one of whom, Nina, seems to have objected to the use of the word "love" and other endearments in the letters of a married man. Warner was a man of tact, who was able to maintain friendships with women other than his wife without disturbing the marital waters. There are passages in his letters that suggest that, had he been free, he would have enjoyed having a wife like "dear Grace." In October, 1885, he wrote her, "How I should like to lay down the pen, and go off to Florence, or Mexico—or New Orleans, and have you tell me stories about the darkey, and give me your good comradeship and let me receive the loving-kindness of your gentle heart." In the same letter he carried on with her the typical romance of the southern belle with the sympathetic Yankee: "Didn't you know that I was an abolitionist and prayed seven times a week for the destruction of slavery, and hated rebellious people as much as you did Yankees? . . . You could not have been born in the North, no, but it was inconsiderate to be born so far away from / Your affectionate friend / C. D. W."[27] She played the sectional game with him, accepting him in her affections but never letting down the cause she stood for:

> You needn't fling your being a Yankee and Abolitionist at me; if you can stand it, I can. That's one of the things that makes you so fascinating—the contradiction of the least Yankee of persons coming from the most Yankee of places.— Indeed, my kind friend, when I think of the trials, humiliation, and suffering—the, in short, anguish of body and mind involved in the honorable bearing of the title of Southerner I thank God that you can honorably be on the successful side. When I contrast your position now, with what it would be as a Southerner, I don't believe I would mind (if it

26. Warner to Grace King, December 22, 1885. Thomas Allibone Janvier (1849–1913) was an American author known for his sketches of life in New York and southern France.
27. *Ibid.*, October 9, 1885.

were out of my sight and soon extinguished under a torrent of daily activities, duties etc.) You will never know what a blessing your friendship has been to me—but it's no use going over it all again. I have not seen any of the Tulane people yet. They are dreadfully busy getting the University in working order. I hope they will drag you out here; in fact my heart is set upon it. I am ambitious that your name should be the one remembered by the scholars as that of the first Northern man of letters who personally helped the cause of (white) education along down here. If you do not come out, I do not know when I shall see you again, which is not a threat, only a very melancholy reflection from

Your Affectionate   G E K [28]

She could not have admired Warner had he not been sympathetic to the recovering South. She congratulated him on an article, "Society in the New South," pointing out, "You have no abolition flings to make and little revengeful memories to air. It is presumptuous for me to give you my opinion of your work, but you must remember that you were only born, for me, last year and I can't help ignoring your long brilliant reputation made before I knew you. I admire so many writers, but so few men—and it's to the man in you that my heart goes out when I read such articles." [29]

He was frank in his admiration of the mind that produced the stories he widely advertised. They jested with each other about making love, as he made it clear that he preferred her for herself even over her writings: "You perfectly understand, my child, that making love to the likes of you at a watering place would be one thing, and it is quite another thing with any one you can chance to pick up. . . . I confess, I am so weak minded, that I would rather see you in your new white silk, cut as the Presbyterian fashion demands, than to read all that your genius can put on paper. But also it is true that I expect to get a good deal of reputation as your friend, the friend of the writer of those charming stories of New Orleans life." [30] Here he was jesting and he was not; a first rate local-color writer in the middle 1880s was an editorial property of high value, and presumably he hoped that she would become in the future more important than she in fact did become.

28. King to Warner, October 18, 1885.
29. *Ibid.*, January 19, 1885.
30. Warner to King, October 9, 1885.

Grace King genuinely admired and loved Warner and found in him the cosmopolitan friend she needed, the man who surpassed the local beaux, none of whom seems to have been adequate for her during her youth. She was always grateful to him for his kind offices in seeing her into print and praising her work in public as he frequently did. He was the friend who really led her into the cosmopolitan intellectual world, which was to change her life exceedingly in the years after 1885. Through him she would establish her friendship with Mark Twain and his family, one of the most important associations of her career.

As for the other three outsiders who had come to New Orleans, almost, it seemed, to be a part of her developing life, their influence thereafter was less strong than Warner's and less personal. She did succeed in getting to know Richard Watson Gilder better, and he, who had probably refused "Monsieur Motte" for *Century*, welcomed the briefer "balcony stories" that she wrote during the 1890s. As for Lafcadio Hearn, she never became more than an acquaintance of that strange man, whose wandering career in 1887 took him to Martinique and in 1890 to Japan, where he was to spend the remainder of his life.

The city paid an official farewell to Julia Ward Howe at the end of May, 1885, when that lady was honored by the Cotton Centennial Exposition for her strenuous labors for the Women's Division. Grace King indulged her acerb pen in describing the convocation to her sister May:

> Mrs. Howe presided, as a matter of course. She presided at everything & has done it so long that her air, manner, smile & language are actually threadbare, from constant use. It is a pleasure to know that if she presides in the next world—which she will do, if she has a chance, that she will be regenerated and renewed. . . . Maj Burke presented her with a basket of flowers & a ton of "taffy." This was highly appreciated by the audience who knew perfectly well the warfare that has been going on between them for months. In her thanks for the flowers, Mrs H informed us of very much that she thought & knew, & gave us a peep at Boston & the position the women occupied there.[31]

31. Grace King to May McDowell, May 31, 1885, in Bush (ed.), *Grace King of New Orleans*, 379–80. "Major" Edward A. Burke was director-general of the New Orleans Cotton Centennial Exposition, which owed its inspiration to him. Accused later of embezzlement and fraud, he spent his last years in exile.

It would be interesting to know what Mrs. Howe said about the position of women in Boston. Among other comments, she probably said that women were relatively independent there and free to follow such careers as they chose. To southern women the elderly Mrs. Howe herself was the admirable example of this independence. The side of Grace King rooted in the Old South recoiled at such a woman historically famous as an abolitionist; it was this side that took pleasure in ridiculing the Bostonians. But her other side had eagerly joined Mrs. Howe's Pan Gnostics, accepting the club's intellectual discipline with its fellowship. She herself was embarking on a long career as a writer of fiction and history and as cultural leader of her city. Her own independence began in 1885, when this old woman from Boston brought new ideas to a New Orleans that had opened its doors to them with the Cotton Centennial Exposition.

Four

The New Confidence, 1886–1888

By the beginning of 1886 Grace King had achieved as much as she had hoped for. With no more than a single rejection she had seen her first story published in a distinguished new journal in the North, and that story had won her relatively widespread praise. She was a magazine writer, which according to the standards of the era was the promising status that led to book publishing. It was a higher form of literary activity to write for the national magazines than for the newspapers, and from this time forth she would take pride in this, almost as if it were a social ranking. This was the road by which a southern lady could become a "southern woman of letters," as she would eventually think of herself.

Her hitherto purposeless career had assumed a purpose. She felt a new excitement in making her contribution to the South, and she enjoyed the financial independence that she had sought. Her former activities had been social and domestic in addition to the heavy amount of reading she had always indulged in. Now the reading was done with a greater view to the search for models for her fiction. Warner urged her to remain at her home base in New

Orleans because he knew that the city was the fountain of her inspiration.[1] He may have realized that when Cable left New Orleans he lost touch with the source of his stories.

Within her circle of family and friends her image changed. In a city that was not a publishing center she had become an anomalous genius—someone to be regarded with some awe and someone who had been recognized in the Yankee world. Garrett Walker, the suitor of her early youth, now past forty, wrote admiringly of her work: "I knew years ago what others have found out to-day."[2] She thought a great deal about the effect of her success on the family circle. May McDowell and their mother were both proud of her accomplishment. But her sisters Nan and Nina and her brothers Branch and Will showed less enthusiasm—a fact that worried her and somewhat marred the joy of her sudden recognition as a writer. Because they were a close family and the three unmarried sisters would live together throughout their lives, feelings of envy sometimes made the home life difficult. Rumblings within the family about money continued as well; the brothers were struggling with their careers at the time, and there were pressures for the successful sister to contribute to the group's general support.[3]

Throughout the year, however, for all her joy in success, indications of her shyness persisted, as her personality became more exposed to the public view. She had published her first story anonymously, which seemed almost a device to excite the curiosity of the critics. Now, after the story "Bonne Maman" was accepted by *Harper's Magazine*, the question arose as to what name she should use in the future. Warner was to help her select a pseudonym since, as she had insisted, "I decidedly will not allow 'Grace King' which Warner persists is an ideal name for a writer."[4] In the fall of the year she was alarmed about the prospect of being publicized in a proposed article on the new southern writers by Charles W. Coleman, Jr., for *Harper's*. She wrote Warner, "Of course I don't believe in advertising, & I consider this advertising but I

1. Grace King to May McDowell, February 10, 1886, in the Grace King Papers, Department of Archives and Manuscripts, Louisiana State University, Baton Rouge. Unless otherwise noted, all manuscript material is in this collection.
2. Garrett Walker to Grace King, January 3, 1887.
3. Grace King to May McDowell, November 14, 1886.
4. *Ibid.*, February 10, 1886.

Grace King, about 1886

couldn't afford to be left out of such a list, so I will only go in after they have got permission of the others." She was willing to have her photograph taken to send to Warner for the article, a portrait that would be engraved for publication in *Harper's*. When she sent the photograph to him she wrote of Coleman as if he were an advertising man rather than a critic: "I have a chill whenever I think of that man. If you were out here I wouldn't mind it but it is dreadful to face publicity all alone in a community so much opposed to publicity. All my friends will I am sure see it only the craving for notoriety." She asked Warner to urge restraint on Coleman: "Do not let him put in too much. *No word of personal accomplishments*, no over praise of my writing, and above all no venturesome prophecies."[5] This of course hardly meant that Grace King did not seek a good reputation in the literary world. She was ambitious to become a name, but that name should be achieved as a natural result of her writing and not through any artificial or commercial attempt to create it. The attitude was thoroughly appropriate to her status as southern lady.

Throughout the year 1886 she corresponded regularly with Warner, who was her chief advisor at *Harper's*, although at home she accepted occasional advice on style from her friend George C. Préot. Warner revisited New Orleans in April, 1886, and again Grace King accompanied him in his explorations of the city. She attended his lectures as his chief Louisiana friend, and together they went over the proofs of her first story for *Harper's Magazine*, "Bonne Maman." He advised her to put the sewing away and confine herself to reading and writing, but she assured May McDowell that "I shall never be able to concentrate my mind on literary business, when there are so many divergent calls in the house. My surroundings are not intellectual."[6] Warner also advised her in the writing of the second story in the Monsieur Motte series, which would first be published as "Madame Lareveillère" and in the future book as "On the Plantation." She found the process very trying: "He was so determined to root out any and all faults or danger of faults." She rewrote much of the early draft under his direction.

She and Warner were invited to be guests for several days of the wealthy

5. Grace King to Charles Dudley Warner, December 26, 1886.
6. Grace King to May McDowell, April 6, 1886.

Avery family, who lived on what is now called Avery Island in the southern part of the state, remote from New Orleans. She regarded this as a social coup of the first order, and she dressed well for the occasion. "It nearly kills me," she wrote her mother, "to spend my money—but the Avery crowd dress so fine here that I had to make a good appearance. I have had a black straw trimmed with all my old black feathers to wear." [7] This was her first trip to the Salt Island owned by the Avery family. The extraordinary beauty of the island that rises out of the forested swamp enthralled her. She felt sure that "a more favored spot does not exist on the face of the earth." The Avery family planned activities for their guests for each of several days—a trip to Jefferson's Island with picnic lunch in the woods, then a daylong excursion on the Bayou Teche, on the banks of which they chatted with many Acadian families. They inspected the salt mines and drove over the extensive Avery sugar plantation. When Good Friday intervened the party began the day with devotions in the parlor. Quantities of fish provided the food for the day, then a ride through the forest and a literary conversation in the evening. In order to visit St. Martinsville, seventeen miles away, Warner had to spend the night at a hotel in New Iberia and engage a hack to drive him there in the morning. Grace King was most anxious to accompany him, but there was no third person to go along. Because her own notions of propriety forbade her being alone with him for such a long period of time, she stayed in New Iberia and went to church instead.

While Warner was in New Orleans he gave a series of lectures, which she of course attended. Popular as Warner was socially, he was not memorable as an orator and failed to inspire his New Orleans audience. But when his readings from his own essays failed to do them justice, Grace King defended them as "capital in conception and style—full of suggestions, and a perfect treasure to a beginner like myself." After the evening lectures he customarily came home with her and her sisters, they all drank mint juleps and he smoked a cigar. [8]

While Grace King continued to build her reputation and her income and

7. Grace King to Sarah Ann King, April 17, 1886.
8. Grace King to May McDowell, April 27, 1886.

reinforced her friendships in the North, her old friend Charles Gayarré continued to suffer the misery of old age and poverty.[9] In 1881 he had been forced to sell his charming country home Roncal, where she had spent numerous summer vacations in her youth. By 1885 most of his possessions had disappeared, and the Gayarrés had settled in a humble cottage on Prieur Street in New Orleans. They were in almost constant communication with their friends the Kings. There were frequent evening visits, and Mrs. Gayarré and Mrs. King were the closest of friends. Gayarré tried again and again throughout the decade of the 1880s to reestablish himself either by publishing a novel, giving lectures, or obtaining a political appointment. Most of these attempts came to nothing but disappointment, probably because his plans were ill conceived. In the summer of 1882, for example, he and his wife had traveled to Montreal and Boston with the hope of arranging a lecture series, without taking into consideration the fact that lectures would draw almost no one until fall. Occasionally Gayarré lectured successfully in New Orleans, where he was well known, but this brought him very little income.

Until the summer of 1886, when a quarrel estranged them, the relationship between Gayarré and Grace King had been an affectionate one, rather like that of father and daughter.[10] Intellectually she had been partially sponsored by him, although he had no influence on her career as a writer of fiction. When she would begin to write history in the early 1890s his influence was to be more heavily felt.

Gayarré had written two articles based on his own early recollections as a boy on the sugar plantation of his grandfather, Étienne de Boré.[11] Read by Grace King and her mother, these manuscripts were heatedly criticized in the presence of Mrs. Gayarré. The King ladies objected to passages in the judge's reminiscences describing the chasing of a Negro runaway with bloodhounds and the killing of several Negroes after they were surrounded in a "cabanage" in the swamps. Mrs. King became incensed with the details, and as Grace

9. See Earl Noland Saucier, "Charles Gayarré, The Creole Historian" (Ph.D. dissertation, George Peabody College for Teachers, 1933), 219–64.
10. See Robert Bush, "Charles Gayarré and Grace King: Letters of a Louisiana Friendship," *Southern Literary Journal*, VII (Fall, 1974), 100–31.
11. See Charles Gayarré, "A Louisiana Sugar Plantation of the Old Regime," *Harper's Magazine*, LXXIV (March, 1887), 606–21.

King admitted, "a great many imprudent things" were said.[12] The objections may be assumed to have been on the ground that reports of whites' brutality to blacks should be suppressed lest they provide ammunition for the champions of racial equality.

Both the Kings and the Gayarrés were conservative on matters of race, but Gayarré saw no reason for suppressing the truth, especially if the incidents gave color and meaning to his own personal history. Mrs. Gayarré, deeply offended by the heated attack on the judge's articles, had gone home in distress. Gayarré himself took up the quarrel, apparently not at all over the issue of publishing details about brutality against Negroes, but on the more refined question of the offense to his wife who had been a guest of the Kings. A small volcano erupted between the families and especially between Gayarré and Grace. The old Creole's sensitivity was sharpened by Grace King's new confidence in her success and by his own poverty. She cared deeply for the "dear judge" even though she often found him and his projects tedious. But her pride was offended by an exchange of letters in which both parties insulted each other. In one of his letters Gayarré summarized his complaint in this manner:

An old friend of your father and yourself, bowed down by age and adversity, informs you that a certain occurrence at *your house* has deeply wounded his wife and himself. He writes to you that you sent her home sick and miserable. The question whether her impressions were more or less well founded is not *debatable* according to established usage in polite society. It was enough that you had been informed that she had been made sick and miserable by what had happened *under your roof*, where she was a friend and a guest. The wildest barbarian would tell you what you should have done under such circumstances on the slightest complaint.

Instead of expressing regret and mortification at what had happened, you find it in your heart to reply with a sneer which it would be hard to qualify. You say: "I am exceedingly sorry that your wife felt ill after the visit of the other day. Nannie left her about five o'clock of the same

12. Grace King to May McDowell, July 1, 1886.

evening and reported her in her usual state of health." What does this mean, if not that I told a lie, or that my wife affected to be ill and miserable in my presence, when she was not really so? This is so pointedly impertinent and so deliberately insulting that it would be doing you a favor to suppose that you wrote this in a fit of spite or anger bordering on insanity, because in that case you would appear in a better light. An insulting letter is always returned, and therefore I send yours back.

· ·

This controversy closes here. Remembering the degree of esteem and attachment which I once had for you, it is consoling to me that if old and cherished ties are to be dissolved, it will be at the moment the least painful to you, as our separation will be effected at the point of our earthly travels where you are on the high road to a prosperity which I hope to be without vicissitudes, and we in the opposite direction on our way to the grave in affliction and poverty.

Still with lingering affection
Your old friend
Charles Gayarré[13]

The significance of the letter was clear. The famous hospitality of the King family was for the first time being questioned and by their closest friend. Grace King saw no reasons for apologies to the judge. She wrote her sister May:

Monday, through the Post, I received the most outrageous letter from the Judge imaginable. Accusing us of insulting his wife under our roof—and then proceeding to insult me and the whole family. . . . At first I was tempted to write a very curt answer—and tell him in polite language to go to the devil with his wife—but I wrote a few words saying, that there was nothing in my note to him, warranting such an answer. . . . Yesterday there came another letter—talking to me as if I were a dishonest servant: attacking us in the most violent language for not apologising instantly to Mrs. Gayarré for our "outrageous assault" upon her.[14]

13. Charles Gayarré to Grace King, June 30, 1886, in Bush, "Charles Gayarré and Grace King," 123–25.
14. Grace King to May McDowell, July 1, 1886 in Bush, "Charles Gayarré and Grace King," 126.

The quarrel was an unfortunate one since it ended a significant friendship, the close relationship between the eighty-one-year old Creole and his "Américaine" protégé. After ninety years it would be difficult to pass judgment on which party was more to blame. Was it the fault of the judge in his melancholy old age, intensely proud and conscious of the punctilio with which he had been reared in the early part of the century, or was it the fault of Grace King at a point of high confidence in her burgeoning career, not willing to unbend even to a testy and aged friend? Out of his exasperation for the injustices of fate that plagued his later years, was the judge focusing his indignation on the one person who came closest to being the daughter he never had? And could not that one person have afforded to smooth over his ruffled feelings if only because he was an unhappy old man and an old friend? Because neither was willing to apologize, the quarrel estranged them until 1888, and their meetings thereafter were undoubtedly less cordial than in the old days.

Grace King never mentioned her quarrel with Gayarré in any of her frequent writings about him. This was quite true to her essential nature and code: such a revelation would imply a criticism of him and it was her duty to maintain a loyalty to her family's most eminent friend. Because he was a symbol of Creole intellectual accomplishment and a representative of the best of the Old South, nothing should be said to disparage him. This setting forth of a correct public image accounts also for Grace King's objection to the publication of stories about the cruelty of whites to Negroes in the distant past. Her generation, children of war and Reconstruction, had been conditioned to think defensively on questions of race. One should not publish material that might tarnish the old image or harm the old cause. Gayarré, whose attitudes were those of the 1830s and 1840s, felt no need to suppress the truth. His generation had assumed the legitimacy of slavery, felt no guilt for it, and made few excuses for it.

*

During the year 1886 Charles Dudley Warner had the strongest influence on Grace King's choice of reading material. Before she began to think of herself as a writer she read with almost scholarly concentration the French, German, English, and American books—chiefly fiction, biography, and history—that enabled her to master the literature of the past for such an article as her

"Heroines of Novels." Now, however, she spent more time reading fiction that would guide her own efforts as she struggled for a style and an attitude about the writing of stories. By September she had begun reading Russian fiction, an experience that numerous American writers were discovering in the 1880s. Leo Tolstoy affected her profoundly as she read him in French. She preferred *War and Peace* to *Anna Karenina*. "I have never been so much affected by a novel," she wrote May McDowell. "It is grand and comes to me like an inspirer. If I had only had it last month! Things get so prosaic and flat at times, that I get in despair, and fear that I shall lose my way of looking at things, but a novel like this, revives me and gives me the note I want. It is so suggestive. It is not so beautiful or exciting, but Tolstoi's perfect knowledge of human nature and his perfect art in representing it—the real and ideal sides of it." Introduced to the major Tolstoy novels, she was "determined to go through the whole Russian repertoire and train my eyes as much as possible after their manner of looking at things."[15] In October she had bought Dostoievski's *Crime and Punishment* and in September of the following year (1887), in Farmington, Connecticut, she was excited about Gogol's *Dead Souls*: "Some passages in it are as fine as Cervantes. Such broad rich humor."[16]

*

In May, 1887, *Harper's Magazine* published as lead article "The Recent Movement in Southern Literature," by Charles W. Coleman, Jr. The article is made up of a series of sketches of the lives and accomplishments of twelve contemporary authors with their portraits. Coleman's introduction indicates that he had a good knowledge of the major contributions of southern authors before the Civil War—Edgar Allan Poe, John Pendleton Kennedy, Augustus Baldwin Longstreet, William Gilmore Simms, and Nathaniel Beverley Tucker. He was fully aware of the difficulty the southern authors of the past had had even gaining an audience in their own section—especially such important ones as Simms and Poe. By 1887 it was clear that largely as a result of the breaking down of the old barriers between North and South and the growth of an admiration for realism, a number of writers now constituted a kind of early

15. Grace King to May McDowell, September 23, 1886.
16. *Ibid.*, September 1, 1887.

southern renaissance, even though they developed independently in various parts of the section. The fiction writers whose reputations by 1887 could be called established were George W. Cable, Thomas Nelson Page, Joel Chandler Harris, Richard Malcolm Johnston, and Charles Egbert Craddock (Mary Noailles Murfree). Lafcadio Hearn was also included in Coleman's list as well as a series of names that have faded—Amélie Rives, Julia Magruder, Frances Courtenay Baylor, Robert Burns Wilson, and M. G. McClelland. Second to be discussed after Cable was Grace King, her sketch illustrated with the engraving made from the photograph she had had made for the article. The portrait shows her at the time—a pleasant but not beautiful face characterized by a slight plumpness and a rather sharp nose. Her hair (reddish brown then) is arranged in a natural, almost wind-blown coiffure.

Her inclusion in the article was of course a triumph in spite of the excessive abhorrence she had shown at having her name advertised. It was especially remarkable because she was being ranked with established authors like Cable on the basis of the publication of four stories and, as yet, no book at all. In addition to her "Monsieur Motte," the second episode of the series, "Madame Lareveillère," had appeared in the *New Princeton Review* (April, 1886). *Harper's Magazine* had already published two stories that would later be included in *Tales of a Time and Place*—"Bonne Maman" and "Madrilène" (July and November, 1886).

It would be easy to say that Charles Dudley Warner had had much to do with this generous prominence in *Harper's*, but it is also true that the few stories she had published had been quite widely read and admired. Coleman was justified in giving prominence to Grace King. Although he was certainly unaware that she had begun to write in opposition to Cable, he discussed her work directly after Cable's because both wrote of the same places. It is curious how widely divergent these twelve southern authors were, writing in and about many different locales. The "movement" was, in fact, simply a vogue of regionalism that the reading public found fascinating, and it reflected a nationwide interest in the quality and character of American life. The Coleman article, recognizing Grace King as an authentic interpreter of southern life whose stories might well be remembered as a part of the permanent literature of her section, paved the way for her visit to Hartford the following year.

During the early months of 1887 she was "busily and happily writing my stories," when she was invited to visit Warner and his wife in Hartford.[17] The gregarious Warner had been host and would continue to be host to many literary people, and Grace King was one of his favorites. For her the invitation provided an entrée into the literary East almost unparalleled for a novice. She was aware that the visit was "an undreamed-of opportunity," for although she had previously spent a great deal of time associating with the millionaire class at Throg's Neck as guest of the Morris family, the new invitation would take her for the first time to New England. Even more important for her future, the world of Hartford's intellectual Nook Farm community would broaden her outlook in a way that social Westchester could never have done. "No place in the world could be more different from New Orleans," she would recollect, "no place more grateful to me at that time, than Hartford."

The visit of several weeks in June with the Warners was filled with new experiences and pleasures, meetings with an intellectual world on an almost purely social level. The very look of Hartford was exciting to Grace King, the neatness, the lack of poverty, the sense of affluence. Even the Connecticut architecture of the 1880s opened her eyes since the poverty-stricken South had not yet produced a contemporary architecture. The Warners' spacious Anglo-Victorian brick house on Forest Street, surrounded by large trees, was a kind of residence rarely found in the South at that time.

The Warners shared their southern guest with their neighbors, and Grace thus soon met the Clemenses, who were to be close friends for years. Mark Twain was not to become so intimate a friend as Warner had become; she would always be "Dear Miss Grace" to him in the relatively few letters he wrote her. But she felt comfortable with him as an uprooted southerner, and he respected her as a southern lady with whom he could exchange stories about old times on the Mississippi. She knew the river as a steamboat passenger; he knew it as pilot. The well-known Captain Horace Bixby who had taught Mark Twain navigation was a friend of the King family who visited them occasionally in New Orleans. Olivia Clemens would find a close confidant in Grace King. The self-effacing "Livy," who was refined and domestic rather than intellectual, found her the most sympathetic of women.

17. Grace King, *Memories of a Southern Woman of Letters* (New York, 1932), 73.

Grace King in 1887

Grace King described to her sister Nan her first meeting with Mark Twain after Warner took her to the Asylum Hill Church one Sunday. He joined them as they walked home and kept her giggling with his condemnation of Sunday, calling it " 'The most horrible, detestable day' that ever was invented. All his life he had been trying to get rid of Sundays. He was so glad to get to Chicago that time on Sunday. Cable went round Psalm singing in three churches & he played billiards till midnight in a saloon winning his agent's money from him."[18] She not only welcomed the humor, but as on other occasions she enjoyed any joke at the expense of George W. Cable; Mark Twain did also, but for rather different reasons. She soon observed the more serious side of her new friend, realizing that "He is a powerful intellect without a doubt—a genius in disguise of a humorist." Certain characteristics of the famous man, however, repelled her. On one occasion an English clergyman "was busy showing off before 'Mark Twain,' & Mark Twain, who is not nearly so nice as Mr Clemens, was showing off for him. It was a cross firing of anecdotes, some of which I had heard too often to enjoy much."[19]

She wrote two "impressions" of him in her notebook for the year 1887, both of which indicate that she saw the complications of his character. In the first of these she sees him as the product of the Gilded Age; he is an American prophet who uses the appeal for money as the standard by which American greatness is to be measured:

> He said that in a hundred years from now America would be leading the world—in art, letters, science, and politics. Our population would be so great that we would be the market—the customers of the world's intellectual commerce. We therefore would set the fashions, regulate the taste —would have an opinion to express, an opinion that would have a cash value, as we would have the money with which to back it. Opinion is the authoritative expression of the supreme court of art, morals, science. His reasoning followed naturally from the premise and sounded irrefutable— but across it all—there was felt the want of spiritual provision in his argument. Money, or pay in his opinion would call out the best work

18. Grace King to Annie Ragan King, June 5, 1887, in Robert Bush, "Grace King and Mark Twain," *American Literature*, XLIV (March, 1972), 32.
19. Grace King, ms fragment probably to May McDowell, October 14, 1887, in Bush, "Grace King and Mark Twain," 38.

Mark Twain in 1888, a photograph presented to Grace King

everywhere—and money would be the highest reward. He did not consider those who, working for a higher aim, would disdain the prompt-paying American market. He seems to have made a slave of his soul—& condemned it to trudge along with him as he shakes his cap & bells—clipped the wings—and put out the eyes—making it a physical impossibility to see the world above.

At the beginning of the "Second Impression" Grace King records Mark Twain's kindness in meeting her at the railway station in Hartford, probably in October, 1888, when she made a special visit to the Clemenses. The train reached Hartford after dark, and after she got off she saw his gray head under a slouch hat as he rapidly went from car to car searching for her. When she finally caught up with him in the station, his welcome was "warm and sincere."

There is a good fellowship in his manner that is most pleasant. He is an easy man to get along with socially, in his own house, and with his own family. He is quick to catch your idea—and nice to it, after he catches it. He does not impose his opinions, at least on me he did not—and he listens—at least to me—with attention. His spirits rise easily—his fun is never asleep—at a wink it is alert. When he talks—there is something delightfully unpremeditated in the way he brings in his stories; good or bad, appropriate or inappropriate, egotistical or otherwise. He is not an egotist—but he is always, at any party, the entertainer, I may say, the entertainment.

She pointed out that he was not one to draw his conversational material from books but rather from his own life experience. She thought that "the pleasantest trait in his intercourse" was the absence of an "uneasiness about the opinion of others." Her next comments were about his stature as an artist and thinker:

He has the great mind of a great humorist—not the great mind of a great philosopher or moralist. He is not critical—nor picturesque. If he were he would be a great novelist. He ought to be a great realistic novelist—but he is not. I cannot suspect such a mind as he has of limitations. I would rather

accuse it of underdevelopment. On the side of reverence there is lacking—and in the region of poetry—there are chords missing. History
does not enter willingly into it.[20]

The impressions are penetrating and valuable. Today, almost a hundred
years later, we are startled by the one particular weakness of Grace King's
analysis—that Mark Twain, according to her, *should be* a great realistic novelist but that he is not and that he is not a great moralist. Such a comment was
appropriate at the time it was written. Modern critics, of course, would say
that he was both a great moralist and a great realistic novelist, a judgment
largely based on a knowledge of *Adventures of Huckleberry Finn*, which Grace
King probably had not read at the time she was writing her "impression."
Even many years later she was reading *Tom Sawyer* for the first time and
regarded it as Mark Twain's best work.

On a rainy Sunday evening, June 19, 1887, she wore her sister's borrowed
blue silk gown to attend a sumptuous dinner given in her honor by the
Clemenses. Protected by waterproofs and umbrellas, she was escorted across
the lawn by Charles Dudley Warner. Mark Twain took her in to dinner; Mrs.
Clemens was on the arm of the other guest of honor—General Lucius
Fairchild, Union war hero, one-time governor of Wisconsin, and long-time
commander-in-chief of the G.A.R. His memories of Gettysburg, where he
had lost an arm, were as bitter as Grace King's memories of occupation and
Reconstruction. She was quite dazzled by the brilliance of the large round
table with cut glass bowl in the center filled with daisies, ferns, and grasses. A
nosegay of white roses was at each of the ladies' plates, and twisted silver
candelabra held shaded yellow candles. There were olives, salted almonds,
and bonbons in curious dishes, and decanters of wine. The sherry-flavored
soup was followed by fresh salmon with white wine sauce and sweetbreads in
cream.

The dinner would have been a joy to remember for her, had it not been for
the fact that the conversation turned to General Fairchild's recent, controversial "palsy speech." Passionate Republican and Unionist that he was, he had

20. Grace King, "Mark Twain, Second Impression," undated, in Bush, "Grace King and
Mark Twain," 40.

recently spoken intemperately in condemning President Cleveland for his gesture of reconciliation with the South in ordering the return of Confederate battle flags captured during the war. In his much publicized speech Fairchild had implored: "May God palsy the hand that wrote that order. May God palsy the brain that conceived it, and may God palsy the tongue that dictated it." At the dinner Fairchild reiterated his extreme contempt for the president's action and said he had no regrets about the speech. Mark Twain was later mortified that he had not been able to think of something to change the unfortunate subject. Grace King, of course, hardly expressed her offense that Fairchild commented with some passion on so sensitive a subject at an entirely social gathering, but she later described the general as " a very good looking, sleek-faced one arm rascal. Hypocrite is written all over his face and drops from his tongue whenever he opens his mouth." [21]

She was on the one hand highly honored by the Nook Farm community; on the other hand she was all too sensitive about her sectional origin and felt she must uphold the sacred vessel of the South's honor in the midst of those who might not recognize its purity as she did. Even Mark Twain, who had had a southern background, admired the Yankee General Fairchild immensely; on occasions she must have felt that he, like Cable, had been an apostate to his own country. She was all too southern in her feeling for Harriet Beecher Stowe, of whom she has given us a vivid picture in those years when the aging celebrity was in blissful decline: "One morning as I was dressing and looking out the window, at the pretty pond, I saw a slight figure gliding rather than walking, so fast and light fell the footsteps—a woman in a light dress, whose folds vibrated in the morning breeze. She wore her hair in a single short curl tied with a black ribbon which passed like a snood around her head. Her face was indistinct, but I could see that it was full of life and animation. As she walked, she talked to herself."

When she asked the Warners about this woman, they told her that it was Mrs. Stowe, who was frequently to be seen about the neighborhood in the morning, that no one paid any attention to her. The name of Mrs. Stowe struck Grace King with considerable shock because of the popular belief that

21. Grace King to Nina Ansley King, June 19, 1887, in Bush, "Grace King and Mark Twain," 36–37.

Uncle Tom's Cabin had brought about the war and all the misfortunes that followed it. It was then that she realized fully where she was. Asked if she had read *Uncle Tom's Cabin*, she said she had not, that it was not allowed to be mentioned in the King household. But she was nevertheless fascinated by the "pretty apparition . . . in spite of her hideous, black, dragon-like book that hovered on the horizon of every Southern child." The tone of the comment, written in the last year of her life, suggests that she had never touched *Uncle Tom's Cabin* and that contempt for it, nurtured in childhood, remained with her throughout life. Intellectually curious as she was, especially about great fiction, to read an abolitionist work would have been an act of disloyalty.

The conservative Grace King had an opposite side that showed itself in Hartford: she was open and sympathetic to feminism. Introduced to the eminent Isabella Beecher Hooker, she found her "a tall, handsome woman, who talked to me about 'Woman's Rights' and converted me to her point of view."[22] This is the only comment in the memoirs about the half-sister of Mrs. Stowe, and because Grace King was never a public polemicist, her precise views on feminism remain obscure. Her acceptance of Mrs. Hooker's views is stated with too great a brevity to indicate that she became at that time any more than sympathetic to rights for women, though she seems to have followed in her early career a feminist's ideal for personal independence. Mrs. Hooker probably stressed woman suffrage—so much in the air of the times—in her conversation with Grace, and we may assume that the southerner learned a good deal more about the complicated issue of woman's rights from this Hartford expert.

The Warners organized several excursions from Hartford that increased Grace King's knowledge of the North. The most memorable one was for a weekend at Olana, the home of Frederick E. Church the landscape painter. The Warners and the Clemenses traveled with her by train to Hudson, New York, and by carriage to the hilltop on which the Moorish-Victorian house overlooks the Hudson. The romanic beauty of the house and its decor enthralled Grace King. Again it was a lavish and exotic architectural style to which she had not been accustomed. The little group enjoyed leisurely drives

22. King, *Memories*, 76–77.

about the countryside, Bible readings in the sitting room, storytelling in the evening, Mrs. Warner's expert piano playing, and Mark Twain's frequent readings from Browning. They dressed formally for dinner, though Grace King noticed that on one such occasion Mark Twain "started in very correctly in full evening dress—but soon after dinner was over he shuffled in amongst us in slippers with a big pipe in his mouth." After writing with admiration of his "very profound vigorous intellect," she added, "He is not at all refined,— wore slippers all the time at the Church's and smokes a pipe, and ate like a corn-field darkey."[23]

Warner and Mark Twain took Grace King to New Haven, where she met Professor Thomas R. Lounsbury and toured the Yale campus. Its grandeur impressed her: it was the largest and wealthiest college she had seen; but Lounsbury himself made an even greater impression. He was handsome and well mannered, which according to her knowledge was unusual for a Federal officer in the late war. Furthermore he spoke sympathetically of things southern—education and architecture. He had been stationed during the war in Charlottesville and had had something to do with helping to save the university from Federal attack. He believed the grounds were the handsomest of all American universities, handsomer than Yale's. Lounsbury was sincere, but he was also a superb diplomat. On his work table was a curious device called a typewriter, which she had never before seen. He showed her how the machine worked by inserting a sheet of paper and typing out James Ryder Randall's famous words: "The Despot's heel is on the shore, / Maryland! My Maryland!"

The little gesture touched her deeply and she felt a love for this man, wishing that other Federal officers might have possessed his heart and his understanding. In her New England visit this was a moment of high compensation for the contempt she had felt for her fellow guest of honor at the Clemenses—General Lucius Fairchild. She had met in Professor Lounsbury one of the most distinguished interpreters of Chaucer in his day. Men who knew the poets also knew the human heart better than the politicians did. She thereafter began to read Chaucer with some energy and enthusiasm, finding a fascination in medieval verse that she never had before. She would also

23. Grace King to Nina Ansley King, June 10, 1887, in Bush, "Grace King and Mark Twain," 35.

maintain a sporadic correspondence with Lounsbury in the years to come.

A visit to Northampton produced a different response. Cable the apostate lived there, and she was shown the house built by this successful man, who, as she believed, had written in a manner to please the northern press. She was told of "Cable's oft-repeated assurance that he never felt at home until he came to New England, and had never before felt that he was surrounded by his own people."[24] In expressing her contempt for such statements, Grace King was probably not taking into consideration the fact that Cable's mother was of New England origin and that both his parents had lived in Indiana before he was born. In Northampton she also saw the Smith College campus and several representative students. The physical setting was handsome enough, but she questioned the naturalness of the isolated life for young women. "Three hundred girls off from home," she wrote her mother, "given over to a college life this way. It seemed unnatural. They didn't look pretty and girlish a bit." The nurturing of femininity was to her important in women's education—an element of southern conservatism she would never abandon.

When her visit to the Warners was over Grace King took a room for six weeks at the Elm Tree Inn in the village of Farmington, near Hartford, where she could work in partial isolation for the remainder of the summer and into the fall. In October she was invited to be the guest of the Clemenses in their odd Victorian house where she had been entertained before. She exulted in the luxuries of the establishment and the flattery in being accepted as an intimate of the family. She was particularly close to Mrs. Clemens, and Susy and Clara looked upon her as a glamorous elder sister whom they called "Tetty." Mark Twain was touched to hear that *Innocents Abroad* was the one book her father could afford during a period of Reconstruction poverty. And now she could jest with him easily. "Mr Clemens is of course at his best at table," she wrote her mother, "and he just talked along as if he were writing another 'Innocents Abroad'—I've got over any timidity with him, and so can 'talk back' & have lots of fun. The country here is all wild about the 'American board of Missions,' which recently had a meeting to determine whether to preach to the savages probation or not. . . . Well after a long contest, they

<hr>

24. King, *Memories*, 79–81.

decided by a vote of 80 against 53 that there should be no probation after death, & that the ancestors of the savages had to burn, nolens volens. So Clemens came in with the paper this morning with 'News! News! Hell's elected by thirty majority.'"[25] When she prepared to return to New Orleans that month, she was invited by the Clemenses to spend a longer visit with them the following summer.

The months that followed were happy ones in New Orleans, months in which she could congratulate herself for her literary as well as her social conquests. Her correspondence with Warner continued. On March 15, 1888 he wrote, describing to her "the greatest snow of the century," and adding, "I would have given much money if you had been with us through all this—it would have given you some idea of a real storm."[26] She did not retort, but she might have, that Louisiana had *real* storms also, known as hurricanes.

Her second visit to the Clemenses was arranged to begin in the middle of October, 1888, and to last a full month. The most memorable excursion during this visit was a trip to New York, during which Grace King went to the theater, met Augustin Daly, and later made the important acquaintance of William Dean Howells. Accompanied by Mark Twain, his wife, Clara and Jean, and a German maid, the group traveled by chair car from Hartford. They stayed at the Murray Hill Hotel in New York, which the Clemenses patronized because of its location, but which Grace King found somewhat shabby. She shared a $10.00 double room with Clara. After lunch she and Mrs. Clemens went to Madame Fogarty's dressmaking shop, where the cheapest dress was about $250.

Back at the hotel Mark Twain had arranged a meeting between Grace King and Augustin Daly, primarily for the purpose of submitting a dramatization of "Monsieur Motte" to him in the hope that he would see fit to produce it. She was surprised at Daly's appearance; he seemed "a slouchily dressed, thin— most *un*theatrical looking person" with "a literary look and a very artistic face." Their interview was private except for Mark Twain, who sat in as chaperone. Daly was cordial, telling her that he welcomed dramatic manu-

25. Grace King to Sarah Ann King, October 8, 1887, in Bush, "Grace King and Mark Twain," 38.
26. Charles Dudley Warner to Grace King, March 15, 1888.

scripts for production, that such productions were the most lucrative of all literary endeavor, but that she should not be discouraged if the dramatization she had written was rejected. She presented the manuscript to him and would await his decision.

Grace King and the Clemenses next set out to pay a visit to the Howellses, who then lived in a third floor flat on Stuyvesant Square. They climbed two flights of stairs to find that only Howells's daughter Mildred was at home, much to their disappointment. They sat down for a rest in a room that "seemed to be parlor, dining room and sitting room—furnished with the inevitable Turkish rugs on the floor, and striped portieres dangling from the door ways—with some bric-a-brac, and otherwise, artistic attempts scattered around on tables, and pinned to the walls."

Later while they were having dinner in the Murray Hill and talking about the episode, Grace King recognized Howells as he approached. As he sat with them during their dinner, she found that he was everything the Warners and Clemenses had described:

> Unaffected, modest, but perfectly charming in conversation and manners. He and Mr Clemens laugh and talk together like two schoolboys. He was exceedingly pleasant and cordial to me. We went into our rooms after dinner—sent for the children, and until theatre time, were just as sociable and family-like as possible. How the man can write his stories is a puzzle to me—there is nothing cold and critical about him—but he has a sad face—and a hopeless look about his eyes—which shows that he is a pessimist at heart. His language in talking is as exquisite as his writing— his division of sentences exactly the same as in his books.

Augustin Daly invited the Clemenses and Grace King to a performance at his theater, where they occupied his stage box. She found the production of *Divorce* with Ada Rehan and Mrs. John Drew so professional that she began to realize the inadequacies of her own dramatization of "Monsieur Motte." A few days later Daly did indeed send the manuscript back to her with a note saying that he did not find a producible play in it. He did not explain why, but in addition to the fact that she had made no attempt to study dramatic writing and could not have been expected to produce much of a play, her story was perhaps too heavily feminine in its point of view and in its number of characters.[27]

Before she departed for home she spent a short time as a guest of the Warners in Hartford. During this visit a few flaws developed in her friendship with them. She had spent an especially long time with the Clemenses, which had given the Warners some offense. Also, a rivalry had developed between her and one of their frequent guests, Isa Cabell. She had met Mrs. Cabell during the summer of 1887, and although she believed her clever, she thought of her as her opposite in personality. Isa Cabell earned the superior salary of $130 a month writing for *Appleton's Encyclopaedia* and for a series of newspapers; but Grace King prided herself in being a magazine writer, which she thought the more prestigious career. When she mentioned Mrs. Cabell in her letters to her sister May, she automatically revealed something of her own personality. In the previous summer she had written, "Mrs Cabell talked incessantly. I amuse myself by watching her and every now and then the thought strikes me how you would dislike her. . . . She is not at all pretty but lots of go in her—and . . . is hail fellow well met with everybody, just of course the opposite of me in every respect. She has told me lots about herself; among other things that Mr Warner had written her regularly every other day for five years, and that he has given her every nice thing she possesses; that she loves him better than the whole world."[28] And to another sister she wrote:

> She is tremendously clever, and much better equipped for making her way in this world than I with my offish, severe manner. She insists upon being very intimate with me & that as you know is a style I abhor. I am very much relieved to find that Mr Warner is really more intimate with her than with me. She goes off with him for hours, and sits up in his study alone, a thing I have been very careful about, and Mrs Warner doesn't seem to mind it at all. It is so hard here to find out what etiquette really is—people are so puritanical about some things and utterly lax about others. It seems necessary for Mr Warner's happiness that he should be

27. Bush, "Grace King and Mark Twain," 42–45.
28. Grace King to May McDowell, June 28, 1887.

helping some person along and having intellectual people about him and I really do not think he cares who or what it is—so it is a she.[29]

Grace King believed that Mrs. Cabell was Warner's mistress. This might have been true, although it is difficult to conceive of a Victorian husband inviting his mistress to visit him in his home in the presence of his wife. Two unexplained references to Susan Warner's "humiliation," however, in letters to Grace King from Olivia Clemens, might substantiate this assumption. Grace King continued to be distressed by the Warner-Cabell relationship until the end of her visit of 1888. At that time an unrecorded event took place in which she said something offensive to Mrs. Cabell, who was reduced to tears. The Warners heard of the incident and were less than cordial to Grace when she departed for New Orleans. But the rift seems to have been repaired during the year that followed.

Olivia Clemens' references to the incident suggest that she was sympathetic both to the Warners and to Grace King. She refers to her friend's behavior at the time as "When you are on your Matterhorn,"[30] meaning that at times Grace's pride did carry her to a peak where she towered above everyone else. The phrase was a kind of jibe, meant to chide Grace gently without wounding her. Livy was not the sort who ever showed a cold, high Matterhorn pride herself. She was a kindly, wise, and discreet lady whose perfect manners and her genuine affection attracted her to Grace King. Both Grace and Livy were symbolic types of their respective regions, and both were representative of the American late nineteenth century. Mrs. Cabell was a less-than-patrician Virginian who fell into a lucrative writing career available to women in the New York of the 1880s. The fact that she was southern galled Grace King, who liked to think of her region as incapable of producing an aggressive and indiscreet woman who would represent the South in the North.

*

While Grace King was visiting the Clemenses in October, 1888, her Uncle Tom Miller died in New Orleans. The event was an important one since her

29. Grace King to Annie Ragan King, June 26, 1887.
30. Olivia Clemens to Grace King, 1888.

uncle was the one man of wealth in the family and had maintained a lavish way of life and prospered in business during the period when the Kings struggled in poverty. He had been reasonably generous to his sister's family during his lifetime; now he had left Mrs. King with something that approached wealth. She wrote Grace in Hartford that the bulk of the estate was left to herself and her brother Henry, that they expected as much as $40,000 each.[31] But in spite of these hopes for adequate wealth to live on, Grace King and her sisters never acquired very much from the estate, and, although they managed to live well in New Orleans, they never achieved affluence.

31. Sarah Ann King to Grace King, October 20, 1888.

Five

Early Fiction: *Monsieur Motte*, *Tales of a Time and Place* and Two Novellas, 1888–1892

I n her letters to Charles Dudley Warner, Grace King had revealed the major motive in writing "Monsieur Motte"—her wish to celebrate in fiction the loyalty she had observed on the part of former slaves toward former masters. Not only is this the theme of the story, but it continues to be present in each of the three episodes or stories that follows in the complete novel. What she has little to say about is how the novel developed and just what she thought she had produced when it was published in 1888.[1]

The loyalty theme was an expected answer to George W. Cable, but other qualities of her book were more original than this and in a literary way more worthy of praise. *Monsieur Motte* was published at the very height of the vogue of local color, when the national magazines were stuffed with things American and especially with dialect fiction. During her apprenticeship Grace King had great admiration for Charles Egbert Craddock (Mary Noailles Murfree), and

1. Grace King to Charles Dudley Warner, September 27, 1885, in the Grace King Papers, Department of Archives and Manuscripts, Louisiana State University, Baton Rouge. Unless otherwise noted, all manuscript material is in this collection.

even though she deplored the attitudes she found in Cable, she recognized his genius as a writer.[2] She was to outdo them both in her treatment of dialect. For however enthusiastically Miss Murfree was read in the 1880s, her Tennessee dialect is almost unreadable today. And Cable chose to present his Creoles as frequently speaking in broken English, that being one of the elements of charm the American Cable found in the Creole. But it is only a charm as heard through the ears of an American or an Englishman, and it is thus appropriate for Joseph Frowenfeld of *The Grandissimes* to enjoy the substandard English of the Creoles because he is American. Grace King, however, realized that Creoles were a French-speaking people whose use of English was exceptional and often nonexistent. Almost invariably she presents her Creoles as speaking French to each other and avoiding the second language which they have improperly mastered. She does this by imitating in English the tone, the lilt, the expression of French and by occasionally using a French phrase or a literally translated phrase. In her first version of "Monsieur Motte" she overused the French phrases to a point of affectation, but she became aware of the fault before she finished the book. Then having mastered her balance between French and English, she conveys the illusion that her characters are speaking French. Miss Murfree had little choice but to reproduce the difficult mountaineer dialect of Tennessee, but she ought to have simplified it and made it intelligible. Grace King avoided using dialect at all, and today she is more readable than some of her contemporaries.[3]

A reviewer for *The Nation* recognized her accomplishment in *Monsieur Motte*, pointing out,

[She] totally discards the dialects, verbal corruptions, jargon, which have been reproduced or invented by her confreres with such astonishing facility. She sketches phases of creole life in Louisiana in easily intelligible English, relying for local color on careful description, and on thoughtful and sympathetic interpretation of the spirit of a race which she thoroughly understands. Her people speak an English which is French in idiom and incisive brevity, but which, instead of tormenting the reader, enables

2. *Ibid.*, January 20, 1886.
3. See Charles Egbert Craddock, *In the Tennessee Mountains* (Boston, 1884).

him to realize their passion, their piquancy, their folly, and simplicity, as formal English never could.[4]

The second quality that marks *Monsieur Motte* as a work of distinct originality is its form. Is it a novel, or is it a series of four stories held together by a similar background and similar characters? It can be interpreted as either, but it stands best as a novel that happens to have grown out of a series of stories. There is no indication that Grace King had a book in mind when she wrote the first story—her answer to the memorable challenge of Richard Watson Gilder. It is a long story, and it achieved a remarkable critical success. Professor W. M. Sloane of the *New Princeton Review* and Charles Dudley Warner then encouraged her to write the succeeding stories. It was Sloane who requested a second story with a rural background, and this accounts for "On the Plantation." Warner urged her to write the two final sections and suggested that each be contained within a time limit of forty-eight hours. He seems to have seen the work as a balanced unit of four parts.[5] Grace King accepted the idea of a unified series and made much of it. She was especially aware of the necessity of having the various parts stand in contrast to one another. When she was proceeding with the third part, her comment to May McDowell was that she feared the first episode, "Madame Lareveillère" and the second, "On the Plantation," "lacked dramatic force too much, but Sloane wanted the same characters, and a plantation scene and truthfully I could not depict it otherwise. The next installment I shall venture on something more dramatic."[6]

Her final work is a series of four contrasting parts, related to one another as the four parts of a sonata are related. Each of the stories has a separate identity and can stand by itself, but each contributes to the unity of the whole. Part One, the original story "Monsieur Motte," is vibrant, emotional, full of contrast and suspense. It leads to a somewhat sentimental conclusion, but a satisfactory one for this particular story. The theme is sacrifice and loyalty, interracial maternal love, and the entire movement serves as an exciting

4. Review of Grace King's *Monsieur Motte*, in the *Nation*, August 2, 1888, p. 95.

5. William M. Sloane to Grace King, February 6, 1886; Grace King to May McDowell, February 10, 1886.

6. Grace King to May McDowell, November 14, 1886.

beginning for what is to become the full novel. Part Two, "On the Plantation," contrasts with the setting of the girls' school of Part One as the slow movement of a musical work contrasts with its predecessor. The setting of the sugar plantation at harvest time is pastoral, the tempo slow. The almost plotless revelation of the engagement of two old friends, the notary and the headmistress, intentionally lacks the excitement of the first story. Part Three, "The Drama of an Evening," returns to New Orleans, where the girls of Part One are now debutantes being introduced to society at a ball. In musical composition it is comparable to a scherzo, and dance music is stressed as part of the background. The episode concludes with another revelation from the past—the young Creole recognizing his old nurse who is now poor and degraded. Part Four of the series, "The Marriage of Marie Modeste," is an appropriate finale in which Marie Modeste spurns the conventions of the marriage contract and affirms her dowry as one of love alone. The conclusion provides the most important revelation of the novel—the excitement of the restitution of the wealth of her parents to the impoverished and dowerless Marie. Even though the plot is obvious and old-fashioned, Grace King manipulates these simple elements with delicacy and taste.

To continue the comparison with musical forms, there are passages where the chitchat of the school girls is charmingly presented as vapid conversation to be appreciated merely as chitchat. This is well conveyed in the first part when the girls are preparing for commencement. It is echoed in the second part when the middle-aged women, Aurore and Eugénie, recall their school-girl intimacies of the past. In the third part we return to the girls' chitchat as they discuss their appearance before the ball; and in the final part the same girls have become bridesmaids whose chitchat is wedding talk around Marie Modeste, the bride.

Piano was a part of Grace King's education; she frequently played for pleasure, and her general knowledge and taste for music were considerable. She also greatly admired Sidney Lanier, who more than any other poet created a marriage between music and literature. It is thus possible that in developing *Monsieur Motte* she thought in terms of musical form.

When Fred Lewis Pattee discussed Grace King's fiction in *The Development of the American Short Story* (1923), he gave her a position of distinction and originality, but one of her weaknesses, he wrote, "lay in her technique; she conceived of her material in terms of the novel. Her stories are chapters. The first section of *Monsieur Motte* contains all the elements of a perfect *conte*, but in section two the story sprawls like a marsh."[7] Pattee wanted a standard novelistic development, movement without rest to the climax or conclusion; when he came to the slow movement of the "sonata-novel," he read weakness for what was in fact an extraordinary originality. If the book is to be considered a novel at all, it must be read as a series of four interrelated but independent parts.

Grace King was preeminent as a social historian, and *Monsieur Motte* as much as any work of fiction reflects the social history of Reconstruction New Orleans. That history is presented from a woman's point of view through the brief development of a young girl from her school days to her entrance into society and finally to her marriage. Almost all of the reviews and critiques of the novel grant its accuracy and importance in reflecting the quality and temper of the city when, as a result of war, a fluid society had made it possible and even desirable for an aristocrat like Eugénie to marry a plain notary like Goubilleau. And Morris Frank, the son of the plantation overseer, has become the rich planter through the shenanigans of his dishonest father.

The treatment of Negroes in *Monsieur Motte* is noteworthy. The portrait of Marcélite is as high a compliment to Negro women as that of Jim in *Huckleberry Finn* is to Negro men. Grace King professed no wish for racial equality as Cable did, but she respected Negro women and believed that under the difficult circumstances of war and Reconstruction most of them had responded well and even heroically to the situations in which they found themselves. It should be pointed out, however, that her judgment of these former slaves was determined almost solely according to the extent of their loyalty to their former masters.

Marcélite provides the ironic center of *Monsieur Motte* as Jim provides it in *Huckleberry Finn*. She is so conditioned to the principle of racial inequality that she is ashamed to have her immense sacrifice for the white child Marie Modeste known. Were it not for her social inferiority as a quadroon she would of course be proud of her sacrifice to the child she reared with greater care and devotion than most white mothers would have done. The ancient division

---

7. Fred Lewis Pattee, *The Development of the American Short Story* (New York, 1966), 324.

between master and slave was the cause of this profound irony. It was possible for black and white to love each other as intensely as mother and child. It was possible for domestic slaves, especially women, to maintain their old fidelity to their masters' families even into the era of freedom. Love transcended the barriers of class, of the enslaved and the free, and of color itself, but in doing so it created a powerful irony that implied a great fact about the human spirit in spite of the shameful fact of debasement because of race. Grace King did not imply that racial differences were to be eliminated in the social world. She was hardly a believer in the concept of integration. She was speaking for females rather than males, and she was capable of seeing the mother principle as being the single spirit that could transcend racial barriers.

The most conservative part of her implied thesis is that in order to inspire the devotion of certain female slaves of the old order, the master families must have treated them with consideration and kindness—no whips, no harshness of manner, no cruelty. She seemed to want to set forth such a view of the benevolent and paternalistic class of slaveowners like her own father. She certainly knew that the master-slave relationship had not always been a perfect one, but she did not wish to give ammunition to those who thought the antebellum relationships had been marked only by cruelty and exploitation. Her thesis of white benevolence was that most of the female domestic slaves had been treated with humaneness, and that during Reconstruction they more than often returned this treatment in the form of loyalty. She wrote that *Uncle Tom's Cabin* was a forbidden book in her family when she was a child, and it may be that she never read it at all. Although Mrs. Stowe's aim is hardly comparable to Miss King's, the character of Uncle Tom in the Kentucky setting of the early chapters reflects the same closeness between the domestic slave and his master as appears between former slave and master in *Monsieur Motte*.

Grace King mentions only briefly in her *Memories of a Southern Woman of Letters* the novella "Earthlings," which appeared in *Lippincott's Magazine* in November, 1888. It is a fiction that attracted little attention except for a polite note from Mark Twain, and it may be that she gave it little importance because it is inferior to the series of stories she was writing for *Harper's Magazine*. The work has never been reprinted, but it is worthy of comment for its revelation of Grace King's creative mind during the years when she was writing relatively rapidly, full of the energy that followed her first realization that she possessed talent.

The story has the usual New Orleans setting, but the emphasis is on plot, character, and meaning rather than on local color. The themes are hackneyed and the plot involves old-fashioned coincidence and sentiment. Aglae is the sophisticated young woman who has inherited a fortune that in truth belongs to Misette Omer, the daughter of an impoverished Creole aristocrat. The attempted restitution of the fortune comes too late for Misette, who pathetically dies before she can enjoy either it or the love of the young lawyer Feltus. "Earthlings" has elements of plot that derive from earlier nineteenth-century fiction—Misette may be an echo of Dickens' Little Nell. The theme of the poverty of worthy New Orleanians after the Civil War had already been exploited by Grace King in *Monsieur Motte* and "Bonne Maman," and it would remain the chief theme of her fiction because her own family was essentially the model for such suffering. If she treated the subject unconvincingly in "Earthlings," she would treat it with more convincing irony in *The Pleasant Ways of St. Médard* (1916). The persistence of this theme in her work indicates some lack of variety in her creative mind, and although at her best she succeeds admirably with the theme, in "Earthlings" it entrapped her in sentimentality.

The more interesting character of "Earthlings" is Aglae, who, after spending several years in Europe as a southern heiress, returns home with a stricken conscience because she has been living in luxury on money which she has done nothing to deserve. The Aglae story reflects a possible influence of Henry James, whom Grace King read with enthusiasm in the 1880s. James's Isabel Archer of *The Portrait of a Lady* also inherited a fortune, which she was challenged to use under the guidance of her conscience. Had Grace King placed her emphasis on the money theme rather than the poverty theme she might have produced a better fiction. She had already written in her "Heroines of Novels" her belief that James did not fully understand women. In "Earthlings" she touches on this interesting idea through the man (Feltus) to whom woman is an unfathomable mystery:

The mystery of woman nature!—what can man understand of it, what make of it? A few external caresses given and taken,—that is the end of man's knowledge about women! and yet what is life but just man and woman? His own mother who brought him into the world! His existence had passed through her, but he had not come any nearer the arcana of her sex. If she were here she might enlighten him! If he could but know one with certainty! but—— Madame Dominique, obese and vulgar,—the woman in her under all her obesity and vulgarity was as impenetrable to him as the woman in little Misette, the woman in Aglae, the woman in the degraded specimen who ogled men for a living.[8]

When Grace King pondered this mystery she had a fresh subject of which she possessed insight, but unfortunately she grazed without penetrating the tantalizing possibilities.

Mark Twain read "Earthlings" with an enthusiasm that one tends to bring to the work of personal friends and family guests. His letter reflects a kindness and a politeness that is not insincere:

Hartford, Nov 16/ 88

Dear Miss King:

    I do suppose you struck twelve on Earthlings. It does not seem possible that you or any one else can overmatch that masterpiece. I cannot find a flaw in the art of it—I mean the art which the intellect put there—nor in the nobler & richer art which the heart put in it. I *felt* the story, just as if I were living it; whereas with me a story is usually a procession & I am an outsider watching it go by—& always with a dubious, & generally with a perishing interest. If I could have stories like this one to read, my prejudice against stories would die a swift death & I should be grateful

Sincerely your friend
S L Clemens[9]

Mark Twain's praise of "Earthlings" is quite credible. Like the editor who accepted the novella for *Lippincott's*, he had his sentimental Victorian side and was moved by the depiction of such genteel, pure-minded women as Misette and Aglae.

---

8. Grace King, "Earthlings," *Lippincott's Magazine*, XLII (November, 1888), 653.

9. Mark Twain to Grace King, November 16, 1888, in Robert Bush, "Grace King and Mark Twain," *American Literature*, XLIV (March, 1972), 41–42.

Around 1890, after Grace King had accepted the commission of Dodd, Mead and Company to write a biography of Jean Baptiste le Moyne, sieur de Bienville, she seized the opportunity to write a work of historical fiction. Immersed as she was in the facts and lore of eighteenth-century Louisiana, it was almost inevitable that she would try her hand at fiction set in a past far beyond the experience of her own or her parents' lifetimes. The work she produced, which she called a "novelette," was written for the *Chautauquan* and published in July, 1891, as "The Chevalier Alain de Triton." An example of a short historical romance, the work should have been published in a less obscure magazine; it added little to Grace King's reputation, and few critics of her work seem to have read it. Madame Blanc, the French friend whom she would not meet for several years, admired the work and thought about translating it into French for the *Revue des Deux Mondes*, but no translation was ever made and the story was quite forgotten.

Grace King wrote "The Chevalier Alain de Triton" at a time when the tradition of Sir Walter Scott and James Fenimore Cooper had developed the sophistication of such contemporary work as William Morris' "The Haystack in the Flood." That is, the author immerses herself in the lore and feeling of her historical period to create credible characters and real settings; the New Orleans of "The Chevalier" has mud in the streets and snakes that breed among the weeds in the gutters. Grace King recognized Cooper's importance to the tradition of American literature, writing, as late as 1902, that "Cooper was our first and, as it seems, our last great American romanticist. The day was, if it is so no longer, when American children (not Eastern, Western, Northern, or Southern children) read their Cooper with their Walter Scott and learned to companion Coeur de Lion and Uncas, Long Tom, Leatherstocking, Ivanhoe, in their hearts as in one heroic heaven."[10] This was the very tradition of Grace King's childhood and youth, but her comment that Cooper was "our last great American romanticist" can be interpreted as meaning that romanticism in the Cooper fashion was dead. Perhaps the only element her work has in common with Cooper's romances is the love of the past in a particularly fascinating locale. She was as inspired by her city's history and the excitement of the wilderness of the upper reaches of the Mississippi as

10. Grace King, "A Southern View," *Outlook*, LXXII (December 6, 1902), 787.

Cooper was with the New York State frontier. Alain de Triton has much of that love of the unexplored and the strange in nature that Leatherstocking has, but Grace King had no wish to embroil her characters in endless adventures that would involve them in Indian captivity and hair-breadth escapes from mortal dangers. Rather she looked for archetypal characters she believed to be representative of eighteenth-century New Orleans and set them in motion in such a way as to present imaginative social history.

The chevalier himself is not very well defined as a person, but as a youth who is pleasure loving and full of the zest for adventure possessed by the *coureurs de bois*, he stands for what must have been the universal romantic urge to conquer the unknown, such as was possessed on a grander scale by the great early Canadians whom Grace King so much admired—La Salle, Iberville, and Bienville. Her creation of Louis Belisaire is an even better example of this old spirit. The chevalier represents that worldly side of the old-time adventurers as his sister represents the other extreme—piety carried to the extreme of bigotry. The sister, Odalise, is religious for the wrong reasons. She carries her piety almost to a point of vanity as a kind of domestic nun. She grows old in her pious obsession, a dried character, intransigent in her beliefs and contemptuous of the worldly life and sinners like her brother the chevalier. The two main characters embody Grace King's attempt to represent the polarization of the age of discovery from the point of view of the Europeans in Louisiana.

There are two love affairs in the novella, about as much of the amorous as we are to find in the whole of Grace King's fiction. The Chevalier's love affair is with an Indian maid, Tinta, who has a daughter by him and later dies. The love has that element of the romantic in it that Grace King may have found in Chateaubriand, but the fact that the bride of the wilderness bears a daughter who is to be the chevalier's responsibility after her death, suggests that we have progressed from idyllic romance to realism. The baby is brought home to the chevalier's sister, who reluctantly assumes responsibility for her, while her brother sets out on the next episode of his vagrant life. The infant will become a beautiful convent schoolgirl, who will fall in love with a handsome cousin at the conclusion of the story.

The trouble with Grace King's first attempt at historical romance is that she seems to have had little feeling for the structure of the short novel. She develops themes that are not dramatized sufficiently, when the fiction demands that they should be. The reader wonders why she named the work for the chevalier only to destroy him in a shipwreck midpoint in the fiction. "The Chevalier Alain de Triton" has an untidy plot that progresses through two generations with a series of loose ends. Perhaps the author would defend her fiction with the point that in reality there are no such things as neat plots; life in actuality is full of characters we meet for a while and then see no more. The career of the chevalier, however, seems to have no point whatever except the love he shows for the wilderness and the camp fire; and nothing in the plot explains his death by shipwreck. If Grace King defended this conclusion by saying that such omissions are true to life, we should answer her that standard fiction even up to our own times must convey meaning of some value if it is to be worth remembering.

If Grace King failed in structure and plot with this relatively short work, she succeeded in writing with an elegant style that resembles the lady herself. It is somewhat intricate and frequently poetic, invariably the style of the educated narrator who sees through the complications of her characters and has a full knowledge of their background. As we read the work the style carries it along gracefully and gives us the impression that it is more carefully conceived as fiction than it really is. Grace King failed here to present a unity of impression and purpose—something she had succeeded in doing so admirably in her first fiction, *Monsieur Motte*. If she had reached a point in the development of the historical romance well beyond the abstract and verbose style of James Fenimore Cooper, she had not supplanted his famous action with enough drama to sustain the interest of her reader. And although she admired the poetry of Poe, she had not learned the essence of his contribution to short fiction—his emphasis on the unity of effect.

Nevertheless, "The Chevalier Alain de Triton" has undeniable virtues. It conveys the excitement of pioneer days in Louisiana very well indeed. With her expert knowledge of the period, Grace King gives us the full panorama of the emotions of the Canadians and the Creoles, set before a background of the beginnings of New Orleans and the marvelous presence of the Mississippi as it flows through the wilderness. Her chapters that deal with the eighty-year-old Louis Belisaire are particularly appealing. Belisaire is the ideal *coureur de bois*, a man of romantic heart who lacks the avarice of the average man, a brave and tender person who has grown old as he has become a legend. That legend began with his story of his mother being scalped when he was a babe at her breast and the later story of his love for the slender woman who chose him from the soldiers who waited for their wives to arrive from France. Belisaire is more interesting than the chevalier, and his own story might better have been the central one for the novella.

The prose that deals so often with the mysterious landscape of the Mississippi of a hundred and fifty years earlier, as Grace King imagined it, has a sustained lyric beauty about it. It is a literary prose with studied, balanced sentences and admirable imagery:

> In the early dawn when the paddlers felt through the mist for the water they could not see, the rising veil never rose but on the unexpected; and each successive hour held its sensation, as they pushed their way along the sinuosities of the great hieroglyph of the river. It was a course that baffled astronomical knowledge, rendered useless the willing guidance of the stars, and confused all but the sure piloting instinct of the Canadians and Louis Belisaire.
>
> The sun seemed to rise at will on the one hand or on the other, and appointed its setting place capriciously, behind, before, or on either side of the ascending pirogues, which paddling round and round the compass in a day's journey, paddled, as evening neared, and the journey closed into ever widening, deepening, increasingly glorious revelations of color,—or into the reflections of it, into undreamed-of violet landscapes or golden yellow landscapes or into rose or emerald lighted vistas through which the river ran glistening and glimmering like a melted rainbow; the trees all around darkening into chimerical monstrosities, and the evening star flashing into brilliancy at any point it chose; while the distant voice of the Canadian leader musically signalled the night's camping ground.[11]

While she was writing the sequence of four parts that were to make up *Monsieur Motte*, Grace King was also proceeding with other stories not related to that series. The original "Monsieur Motte" story, published in January, 1886, was followed in July of that year by "Bonne Maman," her first of

11. Grace King, "The Chevalier Alain de Triton," *Chautauquan*, XIII (July, 1891), 426.

many short works to be published in *Harper's Magazine*. "Bayou L'Ombre" appeared in *Harper's* a year later (July, 1887), "The Christmas Story of a Little Church" in *Harper's* in December, 1888, "Madrilène; or, the Festival of the Dead," also in *Harper's* in November, 1890. The final story that was to make up *Tales of a Time and Place* was first called "The Surrender of Paris" when it appeared in *Arts and Letters* in June, 1887; in the volume it is called "In the French Quarter, 1870."

The collection of five Louisiana stories, published by Harper in 1892, lacks the structural unity of *Monsieur Motte*. It begins with the best three stories and ends with the two that are least interesting. First to be published serially and second in the volume is "Bonne Maman," a major story among Grace King's works and one that has much of the meaning and feeling of "Monsieur Motte." It is another indirect answer to Cable. Bonne Maman is an elderly Creole aristocrat living in a poor quarter of New Orleans, where the black population predominates. Her son has been killed in the war; his wife also is dead. The old lady lives with her granddaughter and supports herself by sewing for black women, who put demands on her as she has put demands on slave women in former times. Also typical of this period of Grace King's fiction, the story involves several revelations. Aza, who was once the pet slave of the young Bonne Maman, is now the madam of a brothel that flourishes nearby. When Bonne Maman dies, the affluent Aza by chance enters the house and at first is shocked to find it occupied by white people, then overcome to find her beloved mistress prepared for her funeral. As in "Monsieur Motte," the slave was so well treated by her mistress that nothing but devotion and loyalty well in her heart. Bonne Maman's heroism lies in her allowing her old associates to think she has gone to France to live at ease, when in fact she has chosen to suffer in anonymity and poverty for the rest of her life in her own country. Aza's function is to summon the various relations and friends of early days to Bonne Maman's funeral. They swell the old-fashioned procession, honoring the past, and they also make provision for the future of the granddaughter.

The extremes of poverty and pride keep this story from being as effective a piece of social history as it might have been. The characters tend to become types. The most telling incident is the conclusion, and the most interesting character is Aza. Having debased herself at the funeral by wearing an old slave dress and leading the blacks at the end of the cortege, she returns secretly at night to the brothel, going in the back way lest she be seen in such shameful garb, for "the piano had already commenced its dances."[12] Grace King avoids comment on her conclusion, but her dramatization of the ironic values of black women like Aza is clear: there was no shame in being gaudily dressed as the madam of a brothel. That was the true freedom to Aza.

"Bayou L'Ombre, An Incident of the War" is the first story of *Tales of a Time and Place*, indicating that the editors considered it the best of the series. It was written in the summer of 1887, while Grace King was staying at the Elm Tree Inn in Farmington, Connecticut. At that time when she was full of ideas for stories and produced them with some rapidity, her mind went back to the memorable period of her childhood, when the city-bred Kings were living in a kind of exile at L'Embarras Plantation for the duration of the Civil War. The background of the story is the plantation itself, and the plot derives from Grace King's memory of the excitement of the arrival of a Union gun boat on the bayou. Aside from their experience in escaping from occupied New Orleans, this incident was the closest the patriotic King children came to the war. The plot constructed from this incident, however, is somewhat contrived. Prisoners in Confederate uniforms are locked in the smoke house by officers in blue uniforms, but it is eventually revealed that both forces are in disguise. The officer in charge is a Confederate and a cousin of the family. The children, anxious to help the war effort, release the prisoners without realizing that they are in fact Union soldiers. An added denouement occurs when the final revelation is made that the rescue of the prisoners has been quite futile because Lee has surrendered and the war is over.

The story's value lies in its authentic details of plantation life and in one brilliantly rendered scene in which the black laundresses show their joy when the presence of "Yankees" makes them believe they have been freed. In this scene Grace King is at her best in her earthy depiction of ordinary plantation life:

> Little clouds of steam rose from the kettles standing around them over heaps of burning chips. The splay-legged battling-boards sank firmer into the earth under the blows of the bats, pounding and thumping the wet clothes, squirting the warm suds in all directions, up into the laughing

12. Grace King, "Bonne Maman," in *Tales of a Time and Place* (New York, 1892), 115.

faces, down into the panting bosoms, against the shortened, clinging skirts, over the bare legs, out in frothy runnels over the soft red clay corrugated with innumerable toe-prints. Out upon the gunnels the water swished and foamed under the vigorous movements of the rinsers, endlessly bending and raising their flexible, muscular bodies, burying their arms to the shoulders in the cool, green depths, piling higher and higher the heaps of tightly wrung clothes at their sides. The water-carriers, passing up and down the narrow, slippery plank-way, held the evenly-filled pails with the ease of coronets upon their heads.[13]

A small girl runs to the women, announcing the arrival of the "Yankees," electrifying the group and fully changing their complacent mood. When the significance of the news takes its effect, shouts of "Glo-o-ry!" are heard and the women's response is like the emotionalism of their church services:

With a wild rush, the hesitating emotions of the women sought the opportune outlet, their hungry blood bounding and leaping for the midday orgy. Obediently their bodies began the imperceptible motion right and left, and the veins of their throats to swell and stand out under their skins, while the short, fierce, intense responsive exclamations fell from their lips to relieve their own and increase the exaltation of the others.

"Sweet Christ! Sweet Christ!"

"Take me, Savior!"

"I'm a-coming! I'm a-coming!"

"Hold back, Satan! we's a-catching on!"

"De blood's a-dripping! de blood's a-dripping!"

"Let me kiss dat cross! let me kiss it!"

"Sweet master!"

"Glo-o-ry! Fre-e-dom!" It was a whisper, but it came like a crash, and transfixed them; their bodies remained bent to one side or the other, the febrile light in their eyes burning as if from their blood on fire.[14]

As the women naïvely think that freedom will mean no more labor for them, they set off on the road. There follows a bitter and bloody dispute between two of them, a mother who abandons her baby and her mother-in-

13. Grace King, "Bayou L'Ombre," in *Tales of a Time and Place*, 22.
14. *Ibid.*, 27–28.

law who forbids her to leave. The entire episode is carefully developed and exciting, resembling Émile Zola's struggle of the laundresses in *L'Assomoir* (1877).

"Bayou L'Ombre" is a nostalgic piece, a unifying of several themes of plantation life awakened by the appearance of the gun boat on the bayou. Henry Mills Alden, Miss King's editor at *Harper's Magazine*, admired her style but urged her in a letter to prune her work:

> It is not often that the robust strength shown in the washing scene on the bayou is accompanied with such elaborate skill as you have shown in every sentence. . . .
>
> You add to poetry and wit the charm of rhetoric—to such a degree that I am reminded of DeQuincy, as I read. And yet there is nothing stilted, nothing extravagant. Your mind dwells upon your subject, & not a shade of meaning escapes it; & your prodigal imagination develops subtle meanings, catching & holding evasive shadows.
>
> It seems strange that I should find fault with the results of so rare & so strong a faculty. But I think I shall only reflect your own judgment when you re-read your story (& shall, therefore help you) when I say that to the very best effect, greater economy & reserve are necessary. If your structure were not so grand—so capable of impressing the reader, & you depended mainly upon this expansive & exhaustive elaboration, I would not say a word.
>
> On the other hand I would not have you prune severely. Sometimes expansion of a thought gives a reader exquisite satisfaction. Sometimes the suggestive treatment is more impressive. You must judge where you will draw the self-delimiting line. . . .
>
> But while you are so full in elaborate detail, you sometimes leave the reader in a little doubt as to your main meaning.[15]

Alden had pointed perceptively to what may have been a major weakness—the emphasis on detail to the detriment of a unified total meaning. Did her excellence in rendering detail get in the way of the major power of her story? Was this to be a characteristic of her fiction generally? If she were

15. Henry Mills Alden to Grace King, April 21, 1887.

aiming to write like Maupassant the answer would be yes. But throughout her career as a practicing fiction writer plot would be secondary to character and social history, both of which would be the main source of the meaning she wanted to convey.

"Madrilène; or, The Festival of the Dead" provides an exception to the comment of the June 1892, Editor's Study in *Harper's* that Grace King did not use local color as a varnish for her stories. That danger of overelaboration of detail that Alden had warned her against is present in this story and tends both to date the work and to divert the reader's interest from the rather melodramatic plot. Grace King thought of All-Saints Day as one of New Orleans' most attractive and characteristic traditions; here she provides enough comment on that day's grave-decorating customs to fill a descriptive travel account of the city. The information is interesting and attractively presented, but to what extent does it detract from the action of the story? Her likely answer to such a question would be easy to determine. The story is a pathetic melodrama leading to the death of the heroine; therefore, the somewhat macabre background of the cemetery is the best preparation for such a conclusion. The implication of immortality, symbolized by the candles and flowers of the grave decorations, reinforces the story of a supposed quadroon girl who enjoys no happiness in this world because of her debased social position. Actually, Madrilène is a white girl whose father happened to die in the house where she has since been reared as a servant by the evil Madame Laïs. Taught to read by an elderly white man, the sexton of the cemetery, the young girl has developed an instinctive preference for the Caucasian over the Negro. She has a melancholy wish to be rid of the indignities of life, hoping she may be accepted as white in the next world even if she is not in this one. The opportunity is given her when a villainous quadroon, Palmyre, attacks her at night and gives her a mortal blow with a knife. The excitement of the incident brings the police and causes Madame Laïs's old voudou enemy Zizi Mouton to reveal that Madrilène is white. The story begins in low key and gradually works itself into a passionate melodrama. It has its place among the tales of unhappy quadroons, whose only means of escape from their plight is to be discovered to be white, as in Cable's "'Tite Poulette"; to pass as white, as in his "Madame Delphine"; or to commit suicide, as in Grace King's later and more effective story, "The Little Convent Girl."

At the conclusion of his letter about "Bayou L'Ombre" Henry Mills Alden had assured Grace King that he wanted her to give *Harper's Magazine* "the first offer of your stories." And he added a request for "a strong story for our Christmas No for 1888." Christmas stories in nineteenth-century magazines were more likely to be sentimental than "strong." Her answer to him was "The Christmas Story of a Little Church," the fourth of the *Tales of a Time and Place*, and a story that is indeed more sentimental than strong. It attempts to weave together the lives of several people, using a humble church as a unifying principle. Two episodes complement each other, one involving a mother's neglect of responsibility, the other a sister's willingness to sacrifice happiness for the sake of responsibility. The pastor of the little church rights the extremes in both cases, but his agency is not enough to make one story of two separate episodes.

The final story of the volume, "In the French Quarter," is woven around the impact of the news of the French defeat at Sedan on a group of poor Creoles in a rooming house. In spite of a sentimental plot, Grace King undoubtedly reflects accurately the deep Creole patriotism for France as late as the time of the Franco-Prussian War. Even after their participation in the Battle of New Orleans and the Civil War, the Creoles still felt that they were French and celebrated the Fourteenth of July rather than the Fourth.

In 1892 Grace King was publishing almost exclusively for *Harper's Magazine*, and it was the firm of Harper and Brothers that published *Tales of a Time and Place*. Not unexpectedly, a note of high praise for her work appeared in the "Editor's Study" in the June, 1892, issue of the magazine, presumably written by Warner, who had taken over that column in the spring of 1892 when Howells had abandoned it. The Editor's Study asserted that although many contemporary authors wished to saturate their works with local color, a great author like Nathaniel Hawthorne would not have known the term but would never have sought out superficial characteristics with which to embellish his fiction: "He wrote of that into which he was born, and his creations, even when they were in foreign settings, glowed with that internal personality which is never counterfeited by veneering." The Study then paid Grace King the compliment of comparison with Hawthorne.

> *Monsieur Motte* was a striking example of the unconscious expression of the life of a community, without the slightest effort on the part of the writer

to make that life visible by exaggeration of peculiarities. There was no question here of the truth of dialect or the external characterizations of race; the author wrote out of her experience; this was a life she knew so thoroughly that she was not trying to exploit it in telling her story. The result, as we know, was as perfect a representation of creole conditions and social life as Hawthorne ever made of New England. And the two results were produced exactly in the same way. Neither author used "local color" as a varnish.

The editor further noted that the new volume (*Tales of a Time and Place*) had already attracted attention and it proved that "the South here has a born interpreter. 'Bayou L'Ombre' is a picture of the reflex action of the late war that can scarcely be matched. And for the episode of the rising and bacchantic march of the negresses when first the idea of 'freedom' came to them, that has a dramatic quality and a raciness of humanity that our critics have been accustomed to find only in the French masters of fiction."[16]

When she read the column in London, Grace King wrote her thanks to Warner, realizing that "to be formally introduced in such a manner & in such a column, into the literary world, as an accredited writer, will go far to make me one." But she later pointed out that the high praise of her as a regional writer was in contrast to William Dean Howells' attitude toward her "school" of fiction when he wrote the Editor's Study:

> I have never read a "study" of Mr Howells without feeling disheartened—and his utter want of sympathy for the school to which I belong, was acting, I felt, to the detriment of the literature of the whole country, for he seemed to be trying to confuse literature to "life shown, not through many, but one personality." And if you desire to know when I joined a school & how I define myself, I answer that in Paris we all belong to schools and that mine is "realism as we see it," which seems to me to be a

16. Charles Dudley Warner, "Editor's Study," *Harper's Magazine*, LXXXV (June, 1892), 155–56. Although Warner succeeded William Dean Howells in the Editor's Study in April, 1892, Lawrence Hutton, the literary editor, certainly approved of and might have written this part of the unsigned column. In the summer of 1892 Grace King's mother wrote her in Oxford that she had met a friend of Hutton's in North Carolina, who said, "Mr. Hutton says that you are the only Southern writer whose works he ever would review, that you are in his estimation entitled to the *first* place—and that he said so, in the article he wrote in the June Harper." Sarah Ann King to Grace King, August 12, 1892.

very ancient & trustworthy school, and much broader than Howells, which is "realism as Howells sees it."[17]

She was showing her displeasure here against what she considered Howells' narrow interpretation of realism and probably against his persistent attacks on all forms of romanticism and traditionalism for its own sake. Her friend Warner was himself the more traditional critic who defended idealism and other qualities that Howells rejected. Grace King always considered herself a realist, but although her kind of realism usually dealt with commonplace life, it was intended to be the more fascinating because that life was in a city where customs were not yet standardized.

Since Reconstruction times Howells had played an important role in reconciling North and South by encouraging young writers of merit. As editor of the *Atlantic Monthly* he had "discovered" such southern writers as Mary Noailles Murfree. But in his criticism he had warned regional writers of their tendency to fall back on a sentimental imitation of authors like Dickens. In writing of Miss Murfree's work he would begin with complimentary remarks and then proceed to point out the flaws of the romantic tradition. The incredible sacrifice that ends *The Prophet of the Great Smokey Mountains* is like that of Sidney Carton in *The Tale of Two Cities* and was to Howells sentimentality which was in no sense the truthful treatment of material.[18] Although he did not, he probably would have said something similar about the grand motive of Grace King's theme of sacrifice on the part of Marcélite, the quadroon hairdresser, for the benefit of her beloved Marie Modeste in *Monsieur Motte*. He would have found romantic sentiment in the devotion of Aza to her former mistress in "Bonne Maman." But these plots of Grace King's early work were not thought to be excessively sentimental either by their author or her early sponsors—Warner, Sloane, or Alden.

Howells was of course far more advanced in his concept of realism than any of these editors, but it is not true that he disliked the regional or "local-color" school of writers. Whenever they dealt truthfully with their material he was the first to praise them, especially if their work was "without the

17. Grace King to Charles Dudley Warner, June 19, 1892.
18. William Dean Howells, "Editor's Study," *Harper's Magazine*, LXXII (January, 1886), 322.

emotional foolishness of manner or the contorted pseudo-dramaticism of method which cause the compassionate to grieve over so much fiction, especially our lady-fiction."[19] In one of his finest essays in the Editor's Study he gives first-rate advice to the southern regionalists: "Do not go to Poe, we should say to Southern writers . . . but go to Life. Do not trouble yourselves about standards or contempts or compassion; but try to be faithful and natural; and remember that there is no greatness, no beauty, which does not come from truth to your own knowledge of things."[20]

It may have been this kind of comment that disheartened Grace King, even though Howells hardly intended that effect. But human that she was, she was elated and encouraged by the praise of her work in the later Editor's Study, even though it probably went too far in its praise and made her think her early fiction better than it really was.

Consciously or not, most American fiction writers of the 1890s were probably influenced by Howells as they came around to Continental attitudes toward realism. Grace King reached that more mature period in her writing when she published *Balcony Stories* in 1893. Howells would have been more likely to approve of this volume than of her first two, which may explain the comment of Hamilton Mabie, who wrote her around that time that he "had some talk with Mr. Howells about you over our segars and he spoke most cordially. He said he was reading you with 'growing appreciation.' As you belong to the school he doesn't like this means a good deal."[21]

Between *Monsieur Motte* and *Balcony Stories* Grace King divested her fiction of what Howells might have called "literosity," as well as of sentimentality. If she had heard him speak at the dinner given him in New York to celebrate his seventy-fifth birthday in 1912, she would have agreed with his assertion that "we studied from the French masters, the continental masters, to imitate nature, and give American fiction the bent which it still keeps wherever it is vital."[22] Like Howells, she had had misgivings about using traditional English

19. *Ibid.*, 323.
20. William Dean Howells, "Editor's Study," *Harper's Magazine*, LXXV (September, 1887), 639–41.
21. Hamilton W. Mabie to Grace King, undated.
22. Edwin H. Cady, *The Road to Realism, The Early Years 1837–1885 of William Dean Howells* (Syracuse, N.Y., 1956), 175.

and American writers as models for fiction. Like him she had studied the French masters and imitated nature. In the long run there was little difference over principles of realism between Grace King and Howells except that her commonplace subjects were observations of picturesque and unstandardized American life.

Six

The First European Trip, 1891–1892

Because Grace King had had a French Creole education in her native New Orleans, she was prepared to be one of the few nineteenth-century Americans who fully understood and appreciated French civilization. Her first exposure to Europe was therefore of high importance to her intellectual development. It is meaningful that in her *Memories of a Southern Woman of Letters* (1932) she would devote four chapters to that first European trip. This was a period of great variety in her life, but it also signaled her achievement on the cosmopolitan level. Her background had prepared her to pursue friendships among the French, and she was accepted by French people with unusual affection.

In the fall of 1891 she sailed with her sister Annie (Nan) on the White Star steamer *Britannic*. There were to be three such trips in her lifetime, the first two more important than the third. The immediate motive for the first voyage, according to her memoirs, was that her mother and her brother Branch felt that if she returned from a visit at the home of the Frederick E. Churches on the Hudson, she would become embroiled as a partisan of the antilottery forces in New Orleans, so passionate was her opposition to the

Louisiana Lottery. For the good of her career they urged her to go to Europe and to take Nan with her.[1] It is not likely that she required much urging: for some time she had had the idea in her own mind, and her plans for the trip were quite definite. From Liverpool the two women went to Manchester to stay with the family of an English friend they had met in North Carolina. They next went to London, where awaiting them at Brown's Hotel was the page proof of *Tales of a Time and Place*, which Grace King began work on immediately. The European tour from the beginning was to combine social and cultural enrichment with work.

At Cambridge the New Orleanians met Anne Jemima Clough (1820–1892), sister of Arthur Hugh Clough and first principal of Newnham College. Miss Clough's accomplishment as a pioneer in university education for women greatly interested Grace King. Entertained at dinner in the college dining hall, she was asked about the state of literature in the South since the war, a question she took some pride in answering. She revealed here her extraordinary admiration for Sidney Lanier as "the greatest poet America had produced."[2] The choice was not an absurd one: we should not expect Grace King to have admired Walt Whitman or to have heard of Emily Dickinson, and she was astute enough to recognize in Lanier a poet of genuine originality. She also admired Poe and Longfellow, but they were well-known poets; Lanier, who had died in 1881, was not, and to her he was the symbol of the new southern energies of the postwar era. In transatlantic conversations of this sort Grace King was a vigorous participant and eager cultural ambassador of the South. In Europe she made it clear to her new friends that the Kings were Americans from the South and that that made a great deal of difference. Miss Clough asked her to speak about Lanier to a class at Newnham College. This made her fear she had been excessively voluble on one of her pet topics, but she accepted and gave a successful talk on the poet before Miss Clough's English class. She wrote later of being "terrified at the idea of talking to a class at Newnham," but "for the sake of the South" she had agreed to do it. She believed that her influence was a healthy one, since Lanier was subsequently put on the list of American poets in the Newnham curriculum. She recalled in

1. Grace King, *Memories of a Southern Woman of Letters* (New York, 1932), 103.
2. *Ibid.*, 117.

her memoirs that "afterwards I found him well known in Oxford," implying that she would like to believe that her influence carried even that far.[3]

But England was not to be the major attraction in Europe that it was to so many American authors of her generation. To the New Orleanian, the mother country was France and the mother of New Orleans was Paris. In Paris the sisters found themselves "in a fine big New Orleans." Having recently come from England, Grace King was bold to say, "we certainly understand the French here, better than the English there." She was to make frequent comparisons between New Orleans and Paris as she established her routine there. "Paris is a great place," she wrote her brother Branch, "but New Orleans is very much like it. By carrying New Orleans out to its highest expression of wealth and beauty . . . you have an idea of what the mother of New Orleans is. We try to feel strange here but we cannot; everything seems so natural, so what we are accustomed to."[4]

On the advice of their English friends, the sisters went to the *Institut*, a tall apartment house in the *Quartier de l'Europe*—a residence for women supervised by the Vicomtesse du Peloux. A handsome, middle-aged lady customarily dressed in black silk and a cap, the vicomtesse was "the perfect prototype of a Creole lady of New Orleans." The Americans had to climb five flights of polished stairs to a room that they delighted in. There was a great double window with a heavy gilt cornice and chintz curtains overlooking the courtyard. They had two small beds, easy chairs, and a mantelpiece that framed an open fire. When they entered the dining room, they were introduced to twelve other boarders—a laughing group of young women—French, German, English, and Russian. Everyone spoke French, and the King sisters found themselves very much at home, feeling greater social warmth than they had felt in England. The vicomtesse was paid the deference demanded by her rank: she entered the dining room first, gave the signal for her charges to leave, and no one sat while she stood. She was a woman of sharp wit who dominated the table conversation.[5]

Grace and Annie King, with some frequency, would hasten off in the

3. *Ibid.*, 111–12.
4. Grace King to Branch King, November 29, 1891, in *ibid.*, 117.
5. King, *Memories*, 113–14.

morning to the Sorbonne to hear lectures. In the first week of December, 1891, they attended a matinee performance of *Andromaque* at the Odéon, followed by a *conférence* on Jean Racine by Ferdinand Brunetière. A week later they heard Ernest Renan lecture at the Sorbonne—an event that brought a kind of forbidden excitement to them when they remembered that their grandmother had thought of him as anti-Christ. But now, in the final year of his life, he struck Grace King as "a charming old man, very short and fat, with long white hair. He was ever raising his eyebrows, screwing up his mouth, shrugging his shoulders, as he talked in the most intimate, personal tone in his critical examination of the Pentateuch. He read from the Hebrew and explained what it meant in the most exquisite French. In fact, his language was the perfection of the most perfect language in the world." [6]

In the final weeks of 1891 she absorbed as much of the dramatic and intellectual life of Paris as she could, at the same time working on her two current projects—a biography of Bienville, the founder of New Orleans, and her series of "balcony stories" for *Century Magazine*. Her social and intellectual breakthrough came early in January, 1892, with a letter of introduction to Madame Marie Thérèse Blanc, who wrote under the name of Th. Bentzon. Madame Blanc was a corresponding friend of Mrs. James T. Fields and Sarah Orne Jewett. At the request of Henry Mills Alden, Mrs. Fields wrote her, introducing Grace King. [7] Madame Blanc was an aristocrat of such impeccable reputation that even an American Victorian could approve of her. In her youth she had been a protégé of George Sand and had since written much criticism and fiction for the *Revue des Deux Mondes*. No two women in France and the United States were likely to find more sympathy for the national culture of the other. Grace King was in the forefront of her times in her understanding of French civilization, and Madame Blanc was as well informed on the literature and the position of women in the United States as any of her compatriots. Although she had erred in the ludicrous task of translating Mark Twain's "Celebrated Jumping Frog" story into French, [8] she did introduce the American regional writers to readers of the *Revue des Deux Mondes*. In time she would publish an article on the work of Grace King, who in turn

6. *Ibid.*, 116.
7. *Ibid.*, 119–20.
8. See Mark Twain, "The Private History of the 'Jumping Frog' Story," *North American*

would write a series of articles on Madame Blanc and her circle for American magazines. Madame Blanc invited Grace King and her sister to attend her Monday afternoon salon in her small bright apartment, which was located on the rue de Grenelle and furnished with fine portraits and white and gold Louis Seize chairs.

Madame Blanc next recommended the American ladies to her friend the Baronne Blaze de Bury, whose salon proved to be a serious intellectual experience. Rose de Bury lived near the Invalides in quarters that, like herself, were almost shabby in appearance. She was a large Scottish woman of about sixty, the widow of a French nobleman. Seated beside an open fire, she received her guests with personal warmth. When Grace and Nan King attended the salon for the first time on Saturday afternoon, they found her a tall, uncorseted woman with large limbs, her once handsome face horribly marked with smallpox. She wore a wig and was dressed in a black skirt and gray jacket brightened by a vivid red silk belt. Her shoes were shabby. She talked constantly with a strong and determined voice, often about a political figure like Bismarck, one of her most intimate friends. She of course dominated her salon by shifting the subjects of conversation to whatever she wished to talk about. The Kings were particularly enthusiastic about Paul Desjardins, a close friend of the baronne's, but when they would try to draw her out about him she would bring the conversation back to her favorite topic of the afternoon, the latest encyclical of Leo XIII, whom she considered the greatest man of the century. On the side, Madame Blanc whispered to Grace that the baronne was very intimate with Desjardins, but she liked to keep him to herself. Madame Blanc promised to arrange to have them meet him.

Madame de Bury made it clear before they left that she expected them every Saturday while they were in Paris. Grace King came away deeply impressed with the baronne, who, being conversant on a wide range of subjects and acquainted with a great number of eminent people, was one of the most versatile intellectuals she had met. The American southerner thought of her as "the most prominent literary woman of Paris."[9]

Both Madame Blanc and Madame de Bury were greatly attracted to

---

Review, CCCCXLIX (April, 1894); Robert Bush, "Grace King and Mark Twain," *American Literature*, XLIV (March, 1972), 46–48.

9. King, *Memories*, 121.

Grace, who was flattered by their efforts to introduce her to their circle. But although she admired the eccentric baronne, her deeper affections were appealed to by Madame Blanc, who had done so much for her. She conveyed her excitement to Charles Dudley Warner:

> How kind she is! And how much I admire—I may say love her? For I have never learned to admire without loving—or vice versa. And through Madame Blanc, I am made welcome at Madame de Bury's—and so on, into the very literature of Paris. I cannot speak my pleasure in this intellectual atmosphere—it is too deep—almost too sacred. It is so mysterious—so wonderful. . . . It is almost too much for me. A book last week excited me, to painfulness—and this morning, a sermon, or rather an address—has filled my brain and heart to actual lightness. I sometimes feel that I have glimpses of Keats' ideal—*thinking* by sensation instead of by thought.[10]

Grace King was in France at the time of the transition from the reliance on scientific thought, as represented by Renan and Hippolyte Taine, to the hunger for a new idealism represented by Henri Bergson and Brunetière. Her admiration for Renan seems to have been for his charm as a learned old man who spoke perfect French rather than for his analysis of religion on historical and not theological principles. She of course had high respect for historical principles, but she was also a fairly devout Presbyterian. Her real enthusiasm would quite naturally be for the new spiritual strength she was to find in the group with which Madame Blanc and Madame de Bury were associated. They were strong supporters of "L'Union pour l'action morale," a movement being formed in 1892 that would flourish under that name until 1904, when it would become "L'Union pour la verité." The founder was Paul Desjardins (1859–1940), a writer who attacked the current attitudes of dilettantism, decadence, and immorality that he believed were sapping the national strength and spirit. The movement was also called "neo-Christian" by those who followed it: both Catholics and Protestants were involved in it, providing a healthy ecumenical atmosphere.

10. Grace King to Charles Dudley Warner, February 28, 1892, in the Grace King Papers, Department of Archives and Manuscripts, Louisiana State University, Baton Rouge. Unless otherwise noted, all manuscript material is in this collection.

Grace King found herself deeply interested in the new movement, though she was not then fully aware of the major changes going on in the French intellectual world. Later, when she was writing her memoirs, she realized how very important a dividing line the year 1892 was. Taine and Renan were in the final years of their lives, and "France was emerging from an epoch of intellectual dryness and materialism that had culminated in its literature and philosophy. Taine, Renan, and Zola were the titular exponents of life. In their hands God and man, the world and the soul, were reduced to insignificance. The heart was dispossessed of what erstwhile had been its joy and its greatness. Patient and cruel workmen, they had pulled to pieces the universe as they would a watch to explain its mechanism. No place was left for poetry, mystery, or faith."[11]

"L'Union pour l'action morale" was only a sign of the desire for a change of attitudes. To those involved it seemed more important than it really was, and Grace King thought of herself as associating with the most important literary figures in Paris. Indeed, several of them did count for much in 1892, but the impact of the movement was hardly to be as crucial in French society as its leaders hoped; rather it signaled a desire for the abandonment of the scientific spirit and the revival of basic Christian principle. Certain important figures were involved in the movement—Brunetière, Melchior de Vogué, and the future Marshall Lyautey.

The founder, Desjardins, a minor essayist and teacher, achieved great importance as a cultural organizer whose primary aim was to direct the thought of French civilization. Two essays were influential in launching the new movement: "Le Devoir Present" by Desjardins and Madame de Bury's "The Spiritualisation of Thought in France." The first of these became the movement's manifesto, an article that Grace King had read in preparation for her first visit to Madame de Bury's salon. In this brief work Desjardins' primary point was that humanity has a purpose and a destiny that all classes of society can participate in, that French education should be turned from its exclusive reliance on science and that it should be inspired by a new spiritual and moral aim. Desjardins condemned the present state of society and culture because they were based on sensation alone. Drunkenness and drug addiction

11. King, *Memories*, 131.

were rife among the lower orders, and love was too often reduced to mere sensuality; the soul no longer played the primary role it should play in the life of the intelligence. To bring spirit and soul into life was his movement's primary goal, and when this was achieved French civilization would attain a higher seriousness and a higher morality.[12] Politically the movement opposed all forms of state socialism but encouraged liberal democracy and free enterprise.

In her article "The Spiritualisation of Thought in France," Madame de Bury used the term for the movement "Desjardinism," comparing it to the pre-Raphaelite movement in England but adding that its scope was wider, "since its ultimate outcome is the spiritualisation of *all* thought, in whatever mode or region it may manifest itself." She believed that the movement had its starting point with the Paris Exposition of 1889, which was supposed to "represent the total sum and achievement of man's inventiveness in tangible things. But the revelation it really made was the revelation of his psychic power."[13] The development of the movement, she announced, was an indication of France's revulsion against the corrupt state of her own literature.

The idealistic and even transcendental quality of the philosophy behind the movement made it particularly appealing to Grace King. Although she did not become a friend of Desjardins, she later corresponded with him when she was preparing a sketch of his life and work. He was a supersensitive and even self-effacing man, a devout Roman Catholic. His friend and ally, Charles Wagner, was quite different—robust, impressive, handsome, and Protestant. Wagner was a neoromantic who loved nature as deeply as Thoreau had, who saw God in all things as much as Wordsworth or Emerson had. At the same time he was a man of the deepest compassion for humanity, a selfless minister who threw the energies of his mature career into the Union for Moral Reform. On her second visit to the salon of Madame de Bury, Grace King was impressed by the forcefulness of this man's personality before she had ever met him. Madame de Bury, who as usual did most of the talking in her own salon, discussed the need for "moral revolution" in France; her article in the

12. Paul Desjardins, "The Present Duty," trans. Madame Blaze de Bury, in Charles Dudley Warner (ed.), *The Library of the World's Best Literature*, (30 vols., 1896–97), II, 4600–4605.

13. Madame Blaze de Bury, "The Spiritualisation of Thought in France," *Contemporary Review*, LX (November, 1891), 640.

Contemporary Review had just been published. Wagner himself spoke eloquently about the ideals of the movement and was so convincing that when he left Grace King found herself wanting to know who he was. When she was told that this was a major leader of the movement and a "great Protestant minister," she determined to hear him preach. She and her sister heard him on the following Sunday at the *Salle Géographique*.[14]

Pastor Wagner was a tall, powerful man whose rugged appearance made him seem like the figure of an apostle to his congregation. Grace King was later to write an introductory sketch of him for an American translation of his book *The Simple Life* (1901), and there she described his spiritual and intellectual development in terms that suggest the principles of the American transcendentalists. Wagner was a countryman, reared in Alsace, and he early developed an almost pantheistic insight into nature. Then, as he was trained in the rigors of Lutheran orthodoxy, he discovered that his simple childhood faith had been obscured by "a black veil of sin, suffering, punishment." Almost unconsciously he began a quest for the God of his childhood. He studied at the Sorbonne, at the Universities of Strasbourg and Göttingen, constantly questioning the theology he was taught and never accepting anything that insulted his soul. He began preaching in Paris, gradually drawing a large congregation from all classes of society.[15] Grace King responded to the sermon she and her sister attended with deep emotion: "We felt a great religious experience taking possession of us; not the excitement of a revival, but a still voiceless sentiment, overpowering in its sincerity and force. No theology in his sermon, no dogmatic recriminations, only a single, direct talk on solidarity and love and helpfulness."[16]

She later met Wagner, who encouraged her to come often to hear him. After Madame Blanc and the Baronne Blaze de Bury he became the third Parisian with whom she was to maintain a long friendship. In addition to the introduction to *The Simple Life* she would publicize his work in articles in *Harper's Bazar* (September, 1896) and *Outlook* (September, 1907).

Indeed, the Paris experience was to provide subjects for a series of essays

14. King, *Memories*, 123–25.
15. King, "Introduction and Biographical Sketch," in Charles Wagner, *The Simple Life* (New York, 1901), xxv.
16. King, *Memories*, 125.

on all the individuals of importance whom she met. Grace King created her own version of the biographical sketch—the profile as personal impression rather than factual biography—which fitted the needs of *Harper's Bazar*. She combined the knowledge her acquaintance with the subject had provided with pertinent facts of the person's life to create a kind of symbol. The final impression is that of a representative man or woman of the era. In her first portrait of Madame Blanc she explains the process as the putting forth of something like a private confession: "Personal impressions are almost too private to be made public. Outside of one's religious convictions there is nothing so personally private as personal impressions. They are really confessions." In her friend she found "a woman in whom one can recognize the untrammelled, simple, full development of her type." Her "type" was that of the modern French intellectual woman, but the word "type" may be misleading since Grace King saw Madame Blanc as an ideal intellectual woman. Not only was she skilled as a novelist and critic but she was a lady of impeccable character as well.

How does the visitor feel on entering the apartment of Madame Blanc? "One feels the pleasantest sense of intellectual isolation and harborage. Indeed, in the great overwrought, intense Paris this tiny retreat reminds one of a quiet thought in a superexcited brain." Grace King next focuses on the portrait of her friend as the young woman Thérèse de Solmes; and she then delves into her early association with George Sand and the series of novels written largely as a result of that association. After some praise of the perfection of Madame Blanc's salon, where there is neither "blue-stockingism" nor "the affirmation of wealth," Grace King is about to reveal some of the talk, but she hesitates and concludes her profile, fearing that she is "verging upon indiscretion!"[17] The impressionistic biographer never gives away the confidences of private conversation. Grace King's restraint appears excessive from a modern point of view, but when one's friends are the subjects this may be understandable.

The portrait of Madame de Bury is done in a similar way. The apartment is described selectively as the background of the symbol. The Scottish lady sits by her fireside—a kind of oracle who dominates her own salon with her

17. Grace King, "Theo. Bentzon—Madame Th. Blanc," *Harper's Bazar*, XXIX (August 8, 1896), reprinted in Robert Bush (ed.), *Grace King of New Orleans* (Baton Rouge, 1973), 347–51.

opinions on current politics and her memories of major figures of the past.[18] She comes across to the reader as so deeply serious and even passionate about her beliefs that no touch of levity ever brightens her salon. Like Madame Blanc, she is an internationalist with wide knowledge of other countries. Madame de Bury, long a widow, and Madame Blanc, long separated from her husband, represent intellectual independence. One can easily see why Grace King, the independent, unmarried American woman, would appeal to them both. The three women were very different as personalities but similar in that they were independent of male support yet quite prepared to follow the spiritual guidance of men like Desjardins and Wagner.

Grace King would write other articles on the French, but for the present her major work was concerned with Louisiana. She completed her biography of Bienville, founder of New Orleans, and had sent her manuscript off to Dodd, Mead by April 7, 1892. She also proceeded with an article on Iberville that had been requested by Henry Mills Alden for *Harper's Magazine*. In her research for the article she was assisted by the Baron Michel de Pontalba, great-grandson of the famous Baroness de Pontalba, whose father was Almonaster, the rebuilder of New Orleans after the fire of 1788. The baron introduced Grace King to the *Archives de la Marine*, where she found all the official correspondence relating to the history of Louisiana. He was a French-man who had in common with her a strong interest in Louisiana history. She had begun corresponding with him long before she visited Paris, and she would maintain her friendship with him for many years to come. Also aided by Henri Vignaud, a New Orleanian who was secretary of the United States legation, she did research at the *Bibliothèque Nationale* in an attempt to discover the map that Iberville mentioned in his journal about his discovery of the mouth of the Mississippi—a map once captured from the Spaniards and obtained by Iberville from a buccaneer in Havana. Grace King knew Iberville must have returned the map with his official report; she left her request with the head of the cartographic section of the library, who promised to make a search for it.[19]

Late in May, 1892, the two sisters spent several days at a small boarding

18. Grace King, "Madame la Baronne Blaze de Bury," *Harper's Bazar*, XXVI (September 16, 1893), reprinted in Bush (ed.), *Grace King of New Orleans*, 335–42.
19. King, *Memories*, 134–36.

place in Barbizon, where they enjoyed the company of painters and the grandeur of the Forest of Fontainebleau. Three letters of importance arrived while they were there. The first was from Olivia Clemens inviting them to spend the month of October at Villa Viviani, near Florence, where the Clemenses were staying. Because this was an invitation they could not refuse, they changed their plans to spend the final part of their trip in England, intending now to sail from Genoa late in the year. A telegram from the *Bibliothèque Nationale* urged Grace King to come to the cartographic section on her return to Paris. When she arrived the department chief had for her a large display of seventeenth-century maps of French explorations. Among them she found what she believed was the map used by Iberville—a plain, undecorated map with the mouth of the Mississippi clearly drawn on it. She was elated with what was largely her own discovery. The map was photographed and sent with her article on Iberville to Henry Mills Alden.[20]

The third letter had come from Madame Blanc with the proposal of an interesting literary project. She and a friend, Madame Foulon de Vaulx, were interested in a series of letters that had been published in *La Revue Illustrée* and were presumed to have been written by George Sand to Michel de Bourge. Madame Foulon de Vaulx thought the "Lettres d'une Femme" should be translated for publication in an American magazine. When Madame Blanc suggested Grace King as translator, Madame Foulon de Vaulx invited her to dinner to discuss the idea. The evening was a memorable one: the seven guests entered an exquisite salon with gilt chairs, a grand piano, walls heavy with paintings and a rare tapestry. The guest of honor was Stéphanie, Comtesse Tascher de la Pagerie, grandniece of Napoleon through the Empress Josephine. A frail woman of seventy-eight, she was dressed in black lace cap and old-fashioned dress of brown changeable silk, with large ruby pendants over her high collar. She carried a fan tied with reddish brown ribbon that passed in loops over her wrist. Grace King took mental notes of her as a subject of a portrait out of the past. A witty, intellectual woman, the countess had been one of the ornaments of the court of Napoleon III and the Empress Eugénie.

The mental notes developed into another profile for *Harper's Bazar*,

20. *Ibid.*, 150–51; see also Grace King, "Iberville and the Mississippi," *Harper's Magazine*, LXXXIX (October, 1894), 722–32.

"Madame la Comtesse Tascher de la Pagerie." Again Grace King followed the pattern she had used before: she described the setting in which she had met her subject, assembled a limited number of biographical facts, and finally presented the lady as a representative personality. An authority on the court life of Paris before 1870, the countess spent her time writing her memoirs, which would be published in 1894. She held the other members of the dinner party in some suspense when they wanted her to discuss the royal figures of the past, saying "Wait until you read my 'Souvenirs'; it will all come out there." Much had changed for this lady since the emperor had been captured at Sedan and later deposed. He and many of his lieutenants were dead, but the Empress Eugénie would live on in England until 1920, and the comtesse herself was dedicating herself to writing her defense of the fallen court. Grace King theorized that although most of the men of that era were forgotten, the women survived after such catastrophes to serve as the chroniclers and defenders of the old cause:

> The men of the Second Empire, they seem to have sunk into a common grave with their chief. All that is not a reproach seems silence and obscurity around them and their names. Not so the women. The cup of sorrow, on the contrary, contains a drop of immortality for women, and it is not too much to say of them that there are but few who after disaster do not live for the betterment of the worldly reputation of the cause for which they suffered—even for so poor a cause as the Second Empire.[21]

In such a comment Grace King must have looked back on the defeat of the South and seen herself as one of those surviving women who live on and gain their drop of immortality by defending the old cause.

As for the letters of George Sand, Grace King did not begin their translation until after her return to New Orleans. Although she was somewhat shocked by their eroticism, she admired them for their literary value. Wishing to give Charles Dudley Warner the pleasure of reading them and undoubtedly seeking his opinion on the propriety of publishing them, she sent the letters first to him. "He jumped away from them as from a fire," she recalled, "and wrote me a severe scolding for translating them. No magazine would publish

21. Grace King, "Madame la Comtesse Tascher de la Pagerie," *Harper's Bazar*, XXVI (September 30, 1893), reprinted in Bush (ed.), *Grace King of New Orleans*, 342–47.

such things, he wrote, and he was ashamed that I should even think of submitting them to an editor." She obediently abandoned the project, never mentioning it again, at the same time realizing that "in comparison with what magazines publish at the present time [ca. 1931] they were mere icicles."[22] Warner was of course quite right. As an editor he knew what was acceptable to respectable American magazines in 1892. But he seems to have been shocked and even embarrassed *personally* by the letters. Grace King had progressed a step beyond the provincial attitude that he reflected. She had lived long enough among the Parisians to acquire a degree of cosmopolitanism that he would never know.

Early in June the sisters set out for a second stay in England. En route they paid a visit to Rouen, in which Grace King took intense delight. Typical of the American romantic is her almost ecstatic response to the picturesqueness of the Norman Gothic city as it appeared in 1892. They arrived by train one afternoon, checked their baggage at the station, and then set out to treat themselves to the medieval. Grace King wrote May McDowell,

> Could anything be imagined more delightful than the two of us turned loose, to wander, at our own sweet wills through the fascinating old Norman Gothic town—depending upon chance to furnish us with our first sight!—and what should that sight be, but St. Ouen! I cannot tell you how curiously it feels, to see something rise up before you about which you have heard & dreamed all your life, but never hoped to see. When I saw the steeples of St. Ouen, I could only say: "Look Nan, look!" It was as beautiful as a vision, too beautiful to have been created by human hands. The stone has been bleached white by time, & the steeples & facade look so threadlike & fairy that you almost fear they will blow away some day—like a beautiful piece of lace that they are—granite lace. We walked around it, went inside, walked around again, & then went on to see more, more. The new streets are of course not interesting, but they are very few of them, & we could easily avoid them—selecting the crookedest & queerest lanes, for they were merely paved lanes, that presented themselves to us. It was like walking through an old, old volume of wood cuts—the houses, projecting over the streets and every now and then some beautiful frag-

22. King, *Memories*, 151–54.

ment—an old tower, stone doorway, or facade, around & about which all sorts of human habitations had been built, or had grown, for they clustered around just like weeds & flowers cluster around a ruin. In the remnant of one old chapel is a warehouse, and what was very curious, another, beautiful old church—St. Godard—had become a perfect nest—a beehive—little shops stuck in all around & above, dwellings way up to the tower & among the little steeples could be seen tiny rooms, some with galleries before them, with vines & pot plants on them—& people. How curious to live celled on to a church! The cathedral came upon us as suddenly as St. Ouen. Architecturally not so perfect, but to me at first sight more grandiose. It is so vast, irregular and "crumbly" & bleached so much whiter & has suffered so much more from time. It reminded me of some fine old Rip Van Winkle—of a church covered with a veil of white hair grown during its centuries of sleep.[23]

During the second visit to England the Kings divided their time between Hampstead and Oxford, sightseeing, working, and enjoying such social introductions as they could arrange. Grace King's ambivalence toward England becomes evident during this period—her willingness to appreciate what she considered the ancestral home of her father's people but her misgivings about the character of the present-day English. She completed her article on Iberville, and once she had sent it off to *Harper's* she felt free to write letters with greater frequency. To May McDowell she confessed her detestation of London women in general: "the ladies in the crested carriages are the most atrociously dressed women imaginable. . . . Really, you would never believe how hideously Eng. women dress . . . until you come here. And all that I have seen are so ugly, it makes me quite melancholy. As for Hyde Park, that was the greatest disappointment of all—a lot of stupid looking old women and badly dressed plain, stupid girls drawn up & down a road in great lumbering carriages." In the same letter she described taking tea with ladies who lived at Chiswick along the Thames: "We found our hostess with her mother & sister . . . along the backyard or garden of which flows the Thames—a cozy English home with lots of books and pictures . . . over which the eldest daughter, Miss Jane, seems to preside—a veritable mission but a most tyrannical one.

23. Grace King to May McDowell, June 9, 1892.

Intelligent, handsome, about my age—talks like a newspaper editorial—with the most radical views imaginable. She would have been bad enough alone, but she was reinforced by an old wretch who had lived much in Boston—one of the shrieking sisterhood—fervid admirers of Cable—intime of Julia Ward Howe."

One of Grace King's weaknesses asserted itself here: she could not tolerate people who favored writers or ideas in opposition to her own. The tea became even more unbearable to the southern ladies when the sensitive question of race relations was brought up:

> The first thing Nan and I knew we were being demanded to justify the attitude of the South about the negroes & why we didn't marry them, etc, etc. in the style I know so well. We tried to argue a little, but I have found out that advanced women cannot argue—they can only state prejudices and call names. Whereupon I drew myself up & informed the ladies that I thought the South intended to arrange her own affairs her own way & was not disposed to take any more advice either from Yankeeland or England—and if it were their opinion that the Southern men were still living in harems of negro women they ought to produce their facts or entrust them to men who would be held responsible. The mother & other sister seemed somewhat alarmed at Miss Jane's performance & were as sweet and amiable as mothers & sisters in that position usually are, but Nan & I were very glad that at the end of our tea & cake we had to leave to catch our car. But we were mighty mad I can tell you & we dislike England more than ever. The English women would be enough to damn paradise. They are not Eng[lish]—they are really Yankees as far as we have seen.

The entire scope of female society was unacceptable to her, especially the offense of prostitution: "As for the low dissolute women of the street, it simply makes you sick to see them—dirty, half dressed, bold, profane—carrying on their vile trade in the most shameless way. I sometimes think that the whole scheme of civilization & religion here is a dead failure. A nation that can produce & maintain such street women cannot be far from the lowest rounds of degradation."[24]

24. *Ibid.*, July 8, 1892.

Charles Dudley Warner, about 1890, from a photograph made in New Orleans

Department of Archives and Manuscripts, Louisiana State University,
courtesy of John M. Coxe

Nature was the more pleasing side of the English experience. She delighted in Hampstead Heath near their lodgings; it brought her to the conclusion that the English were at their best when they allowed nature to remain unadorned. She wrote her sister Nina,

> Whatever has been left to nature in Eng[land] is lovely, whatever art has touched is hideous—that is from Wren down. That is why there are so many beautiful landscapists here and why English art has become so narrowed in its pre-raphaelism [*sic*] & mysticism. When the artists cannot go to nature, they must go into themselves for the picturesque. It is painful in the galleries to see the immense space between the immortal trio, Reynolds, Gainsborough, and Romney & their nearest followers. In those days life, dress & [illegible word] were still picturesque & the painters had picturesque eyes. Hogarth painted what he saw. He & Dickens go together—the others go with Spenser, Milton, Tennyson. I must say that the England I see is the Eng[land] of Hogarth & Dickens. Strangers passing through & stopping at a hotel can still enjoy the Eng[land] of their reading & dreams, but to go with the middle class life as we are doing is to see what one never conceived of as the way of the ugly & commonplace. The hot joint on Sundays with potatoes—then the four days of cold joint with potatoes for both meals & the inevitable "milk pudding"—a kind of thickened baked milk pudding, which we would have discharged Cécile for if she dared to send it out of her kitchen.[25]

A New Orleanian living cheaply in Europe, like Grace King, would be understandably dissatisfied with English food. Unlike the young Henry James, however, she could not enjoy the commonplace generally in English life, which may be explained by her tendency to associate England with the American North. Because she felt committed to the special qualities of life in the South and in France, even as great a name as Sir Christopher Wren was lost on her.

Warner, who enjoyed teasing her about her prejudices, wrote her with some frequency. He wrote her in England:

> One of my great regrets, Grace dear, is that I cannot be more your companion in your development in life, in the new experiences and

25. Grace King to Nina Ansley King, July 16, 1892.

thoughts. You know that in your literature I regard you as being the most original and fresh of writers, by this I mean that you have a quality that is absent from most of our work however we cultivate it in and for any personal gratification. I am sorry not to be more in contact with you. I do not think I have so many distinct prejudices as you have, or had, but that does not hinder my having sympathy with you in that which makes intercourse with one another the chief charm of life. I shall try to see you when you return to New York.[26]

At this time she had spent five weeks in Oxford, of which three were lost in illness—a fairly severe fever from which she suffered a great deal. Possibly the lack of rest was the reason for it. She admitted that she spent much of the night working: "Since I have been over here I sleep hardly at all," she wrote Warner. They had gone to Oxford armed with a sheaf of letters of introduction to friends of Madame Blanc, but it was the season when everyone was out of town. Despite this misfortune and the fever, her impressions of Oxford were bright and enthusiastic in comparison with those of London. "I saw Oxford . . . thoroughly," she wrote, "and I wanted to stay there the rest of my life." [27]

Restored in spirit and health, she returned to London with Nan, enjoying excursions to Greenwich and Windsor, both of which made a profound impression. In mid-September, 1892, she wrote her mother of the absolute rightness of the first year abroad which she was soon to conclude. She wanted Mimi to know that she had indeed worked hard to make the trip a successful development of her career rather than a period of mere pleasure seeking. And for all the early comparisons she had made of New Orleans with Paris she had come to the conclusion that her home city society was indeed provincial in contrast with the mainstream of intellectual life she believed she had touched in Europe. She assured her mother,

> I have earned every pleasure of this trip by the "sweat of my brains"—I am not quite sure that it is not selfish for us to go on to Florence instead of returning to our posts at home. And more than once I have been on the point of giving it up. Then I think of the profit in after life—& how much better I shall be qualified to write after it—& the small chance of my ever

26. Charles Dudley Warner to Grace King, September 25, 1892.
27. Grace King to Warner, September 10, 1892.

coming over here again & I gird up my loins & clench my teeth—&
resolve to go on with it. . . . I have seen the folly over here of our so-
called society in N O—the men are all too stupid—the women too vain
& frivolous for really the expense mental & financial of knowing them. The
very thought of them makes me ill. When I think of the time and effort I
have wasted on the Préots, Ficklens & Sharps, I wonder that I could ever
have been such an idiot. I have seen what real intellectual society is & I am
not going to demean myself any more for the paltry stuff in N O.[28]

The King sisters had accepted the Clemens' invitation for the month of
October, planning a leisurely trip to Florence by way of Switzerland. They
traveled first to Paris, where they spent the night at the *Institut*, then on to
Switzerland, changing trains at Basel and for the first time entering a Ger-
manic world as they approached Lucerne. Switzerland pleased them, but the
first sights of the Italian landscape as they proceeded south were almost a
revelation. Looking out the train window as Italy revealed itself, Grace King
remembered the stereoscopic views her father had brought from Europe
when she was a child, how they had given her the earliest conception of Italy
even before she knew the name. How exciting it was to feel the memory of the
child's dream in close proximity with the mature woman's fulfillment of the
dream. They stopped briefly in Milan and Bologna before going on to
Florence.[29]

Mr. Clemens was punctually waiting at the station for them, ready to take
them to Villa Viviani, the house he had leased on the road to Settignano.
Warmly welcomed by Olivia and her daughters Susy and Jean, the King sisters
settled down for a month's stay. The villa was a relatively plain, eighteenth-
century country house, its stucco painted yellow and decorated with green
shutters. The inside was more impressive. The center of the house was its
salon, rising two stories, around which all the rest of the house was built. To
Grace King it was palatial with its "long suites of bedrooms and endless
corridors connecting them." It was a bright villa and the marble floors were

28. Grace King to Sarah Ann King, September 17, 1892; George C. Préot was literary
advisor to Grace King; John R. Ficklen, professor of history at Tulane University, would
collaborate with her on two texts; Robert Sharp would become the ninth president of Tulane in
1912.
29. King, *Memories*, 167.

"shiny and full of reflections." The grounds were exquisite: "Tall and stately pines surrounded it. Pink and yellow roses overflowed the walls and battered mossy stone urns at the gate posts. From the wall, the vineyards and olive orchards fell away toward the valley." Mark Twain loved the setting and the magnificent view of Florence from the villa, the "lofty blue hills . . . white with innumerable villas." To him this was "the fairest picture on our planet, the most enchanting to look upon, the most satisfying to the eye."

The Clemenses and the Kings took their tea in the shade of olive trees, from which they viewed the warm October countryside. On one such occasion Mark Twain smoked his pipe and commented on the gold of the late sun: "It cannot be compared to the sun on the Mississippi River." For all the beauty of the view of Florence before them the remark prompted reminiscences of Captain Horace Bixby and their various trips on river steamers. On such an afternoon Mark Twain confessed to them his fear of hell. When someone discounted the possibility of hell, observing that "Nobody believes in hell any longer!" he said, "I don't believe in it, but I'm afraid of it. It makes me afraid to die." He recollected his Presbyterian mother's teachings that were still with him and said, "When I wake up at night I think of hell, and I am sure about going there." His idolizing wife then asked, "Why, Youth, who then can be saved?"[30]

While she was with them Grace King was eager to talk about her own experiences in Paris, but she thought the Clemenses showed little interest. Things French were of minor consequence to them, things German more important. To Mark Twain the French had little sense of humor, a fact that had been demonstrated by Madame Blanc's ridiculous attempt to translate into French the colloquial "Celebrated Jumping Frog of Calaveras County."

The travelers made morning excursions into Florence, visiting such Victorian shrines as the tomb of Mrs. Browning, on which they laid flowers as a kind of literary duty. Although they visited the usual museums, Grace King felt an antipathy for the city itself as Mark Twain did. The fascination that Florence held for artists in the past and for the English and American colony

---

30. *Ibid.*, 170–73; Villa Viviani remains in an excellent state of preservation today. Relatively unchanged since 1892, it is owned by a catering establishment, and the great central salon is frequently used for banquets. Mark Twain describes the villa in his *Autobiography* (New York, 1959), 314–24.

there was quite lost on her, but she responded with deep emotion to the surrounding landscape. She took great satisfaction in visiting various friends of the Clemenses whose villas were scattered about the countryside.[31]

Having no time for Venice or Rome, they left Florence for Paris before mid-November. In her brief final visit there Grace King hurried to a lecture by Desjardins and a sermon by her favorite, Charles Wagner. She visited Madame de Bury once again as well. "Why, why must I leave Paris!" she wrote Warner, "I am nearly wild with all these last excitements—travels & shopping & theaters. Won't you tell Mr. Alden when I expect to arrive. I must see him if only for a half hour. It was a wrench to leave the Clemens[es] and their ideal interpretation of life."[32]

Sailing from Liverpool, a very confident Grace King arrived in New York with her sister on the *Britannic* on December 2, 1892, and stayed at the Marlborough Hotel.[33] No one met them at the boat because of misunderstandings in communications between her and Warner and Alden. She was upset to find herself having to pay expensive hotel rates over the weekend before she could meet the people she felt obliged to talk to. In Florence she had received the first copies of her biography *Jean Baptiste Le Moyne, Sieur de Bienville*, which disappointed her because of numerous errors she had not been given the opportunity to correct in proof. She wanted to talk to Hamilton Mabie about the matter. Warner had expected to meet her but was obliged to keep an appointment in Boston. In a letter she wrote him after her return home she expressed her displeasure about the weekend arrival, but not with any blame for him. Her own success as a writer who had made friendships with European intellectuals gave her a full confidence: she was now a cosmopolitan. The Paris experience was something that Warner and Mark Twain had never had. Warner was to prove himself a New England provincial in rejecting the idea of her publishing translations of the George Sand letters; Mark Twain showed his own limitations in his easy dismissal of the French in spite of his veneration of Jeanne d'Arc. Now Grace King, the author of three volumes, had some right to assert herself. She wrote Warner, "I saw myself losing time & money, awaiting the convenience of a lot of men—which made

31. King, *Memories*, 171–72.
32. Grace King to Warner, November 14, 1892.
33. Telegram: Grace King to Sarah Ann King, December 2, 1892.

me furious. I sent Nan around to Dodd, Mead, with an insistent request that any one of the firm should come to see me before afternoon. Mr. Dodd responded & I very soon convinced him that Bienville had to be reprinted." [34]

Before the trip to Europe she was a diligent and somewhat humble aspirant; by the time of her return home she had cultivated a new self-assertion: the publisher should answer to her for mistakes in the text of her book. What was a publisher but the medium for her labors? The author was the important party, not the publisher. The pique she expressed to Warner was only one side of her disposition at the time. She was in fact exuberant with the full satisfaction of having established herself as an American of whom some Europeans of consequence had taken approving notice.

She continued to exploit the experience of Paris even after her return home. The articles on Madame de Bury and the Comtesse Tascher de la Pagerie appeared in *Harper's Bazar* in 1893, the Iberville article in *Harper's* in 1894. In 1896 she published a second article on Madame de Bury and articles on her friends Charles Wagner and Madame Blanc. During the years 1896 and 1897 Charles Dudley Warner was engaged in the editorship of the thirty-volume series called *The Library of the World's Best Literature*. A kind of precursor of the Harvard Classics, Warner's series attempted to cover all important western authors and give brief selections from them rather than complete works. He asked Grace King to make selections and write the introductions for eight of the French authors to be included. From the authors of the past she agreed to write on Alfred de Vigny, Michelet, Lamennais, Mérimée, and Baudelaire. She undoubtedly advised Warner to include the three men closely associated with "L'Union pour l'action morale"—Paul Desjardins, Édouard Rod, and Melchior de Vogué.

Her eight introductions show Grace King as a competent analytical biographer, but since each is short she hardly established herself as a critic by writing them. They show us the scope of her abilities, however, and indicate that she might have followed the career of literary historian. Probably the most interesting of her choices is her treatment of Baudelaire. Even in the seven pages of the essay she conveys a rather full knowledge of the career and the personality of the poet. She does not quote from the poetry because she

34. Grace King to Warner, December 15, 1892.

believed that the poems are untranslatable into a foreign language. Her essay centers on her selections from his prose works, which constitute a kind of defense of his often misunderstood life. She makes a good case for his revulsion for hashish, to which he was said to be addicted, and her portrait of him has none of the prejudices from which his reputation suffered in the nineteenth century. The account is typical of criticism of that time in that it concentrates on the author's life and character rather than on his work.

So also the four other biographical sketches of earlier writers. Her treatment of the lives of Alfred de Vigny and Mérimée are thoroughly competent in spite of their brevity, as is the life of the radical churchman Lamennais. Her account of Jules Michelet is particularly interesting since he is the one historian on the list. She knew his monumental *Histoire de France* and admired his theory of history. She quotes his comments on that theory: "I had but one master, Vico. His principle of vital force—humanity, which created itself—made my book and made my education." Later she quotes him as writing that "Augustin Thierry called history narrative; Guizot called it analysis: but I call it resurrection." She herself had already embarked on her career as historian, and certain qualities of her later historical writing suggest an influence of Michelet. In *New Orleans, The Place and the People* (1895), she would produce a history in which the dead past is resuscitated. Like Michelet's, her own histories tend to be romantic and often subjective narratives with an appeal to the sense of the picturesque. And it might be said that she followed Michelet, who "saw men and facts not chained to one another, and to past and future, by chains of logical sequence,—he saw them as episodes rising in each period to a culminating and dramatic point of interest." [35]

She had heard Paul Desjardins lecture and she learned much from Madame Blanc about Melchior de Vogué and Édouard Rod. She may have met these men at the salons she attended, and we know that she did correspond with Desjardins when she was preparing to write the short essay on him. All three belonged to the movement she considered essential to one of the major reversals in French civilization. She felt that she herself was touching the forefront of a new moral direction in the civilization she most admired. She deals with each writer in his role in "L'Union pour l'action morale." Édouard

---

35. Grace King, "Jules Michelet," in Warner (ed.), *Library of the World's Best Literature*, XXV, 9982–84.

Rod, the Swiss professor, was widely admired in the 1890s as a novelist, and he was particularly representative of the new spiritual forces because he had begun as a disciple of that product of nineteenth-century science, Émile Zola. But Rod had seen the light, had experienced conversion of a sort on his own road to Damascus, and thereafter he produced novels of a more strongly human character, in which man was not a mere pawn of the forces of destiny.

Following her sketch of Paul Desjardins she published a translation of his essay "The Present Duty." And in placing him in French thought she writes that "the death-bed repentance of a century, born skeptical, reared decadent, and professing practical materialism; the conversion of a literature from the pure passion of the senses to the pure passion of abstract thought; the assumption of an apostolic mission by journalists, novelists, playwrights, college professors, and scientific masters, will doubtless furnish the century to come with one of its most curious and interesting fields of study." [36] Of course today it is a curious and interesting field of study, but it is only one phase of the general discontent of French civilization in the 1890s with the strong reliance on the scientific interpretation of life that had dominated thought since 1789. The movement that interested Grace King was a phase that also included men of greater importance than those she wrote about. She heard much of Brunetière from Madame Blanc, but she never met or wrote about him. She sees the new thought as specifically neo-Christian rather than broadly philosophical. The name of Henri Bergson seems not to appear at all in her writings.

Melchior de Vogüé was in some respects the originator of the force behind "L'Union pour l'action morale." He had written a key article on the Paris Exposition of 1889 in which he proclaimed that a new moral and humane spirit would replace scientific determinism. "The laws of the outward universe are but the reflex of the moral world within," she quoted him as writing, "and the universal force once adequately distributed in its proper channel will inspire the human heart for all the purposes of human life." Grace King could embrace a principle such as this. De Vogüé also appealed to her for his role in introducing the Russian novelists to France in his *Le Roman russe* (1886), stimulating a compassionate realism in fiction as an antidote to naturalism.

36. Grace King, "Paul Desjardins," in Warner (ed.), *Library of the World's Best Literature*, XI, 4596−99.

She also approved of his theory of history, in that he conceived of it "not as a corpse to be dissected, a tomb of the past to be explored, but as humanity itself,—alive, present, vital; a drama to be seen with one's own eyes, felt in one's own veins."[37] All of her first exposure to intellectual Paris in 1892 unquestionably left a strong impact on her thinking about mankind and history. It would influence her new career as historian for the remainder of the decade.

37. Grace King, "Melchior de Vogué," in Warner (ed.), *Library of the World's Best Literature*, XXXVIII, 15439–41.

Seven

Balcony Stories and Other Short Fiction, 1888–1907

Grace King's style and concept of the short story began to change even before the 1892 publication of *Tales of a Time and Place*. Her stories tended to become shorter, their plots less contrived; an obvious sentiment gave way to a controlled emotion. Three early uncollected stories that illustrate these tendencies are "Sympathy," "The Self-Made Man," and "One Woman's Story."[1] Although all three stories miss full success, they foreshadow what would later be known as the "balcony stories." They are told by an educated narrator in literary style, but the subjects are simple, working-class country people.

The characters in "Sympathy" are rustics, but neither they nor the setting is specifically regional. Because the tale could take place anywhere in rural America, it is not a local-color story. This does not mean that Grace King was ending her career as a regionalist, but hereafter local color would diminish in importance in her fiction.

---

1. Grace King, "Sympathy," *Harper's Weekly*, XXXII (May 12, 1888), 338; Grace King, "The Self-Made Man," *Harper's Bazar*, XXIII (April 5, 1890), 258–59; Grace King, "One Woman's Story," *Harper's Bazar*, XXIV (March 21, 1891), 219.

"The Self-Made Man" is a sketch of a professor whose vanity lies in his having educated himself. He meets the lady-narrator in the dining room of their watering-place hotel and feels constrained to dominate the conversation with the simple details of his inconsequential life, presenting those details as if they were important. This compulsive talker seems to be delivering a perpetual monologue, praising himself and disparaging his wife. When the wife appears, the irony of the story becomes clear in that she is sensitive and refined, and certainly unappreciated. Grace King appears to be satirizing the American ideal of the self-made man, showing that sometimes that type develops such overconfidence that he forgets the humbleness of his origins. The background of the story is generally American rather than specifically southern.

In "One Woman's Story" Grace King suggests that the poor may have greater reserves of endurance than the rich. She probably believed that, since her own family had shown their best character when faced with war and poverty. The background of the story is only vaguely New Orleans.

The publication of the series of thirteen "balcony stories" was a major accomplishment of the years 1892 and 1893. They were first published in *Century Magazine* beginning in December, 1892, with the introductory sketch "The Balcony" and "A Drama of Three"; the final stories, "A Delicate Affair" and "Pupasse," appeared in the October, 1893, issue of *Century*. The Century Company also published the volume *Balcony Stories* late in 1893. A second printing of the relatively popular stories was done by Graham in New Orleans in 1914, and a new edition was brought out by Macmillan in 1925. Grace King wrote two additional stories, "Grandmama" and "Joe," for the 1925 edition. *Balcony Stories* is superior to the earlier volumes of short fiction, and it sustained a mild popularity over the years, especially in Louisiana.

The enthusiastic acceptance of the balcony stories by Richard Watson Gilder, editor of *Century*, was a triumph for Grace King since he had first rejected "Monsieur Motte" in 1885, the story she had written in accepting his challenge to answer Cable's interpretation of the Creoles.[2] No reasons were sent her when that story was returned, but one can put together the reasons.

2. Grace King, *Memories of a Southern Woman of Letters* (New York, 1932), 61–62.

Century Magazine tended to publish relatively short stories to be appreciated by a wide range of readers. When Grace King produced stories that were unpretentious in style and plot and that relied more on suggestiveness than on elaboration of detail, Gilder probably recognized the little revolution that she had effected in her concept of fiction. She seems to have taken quite seriously the advice of her friend Henry Mills Alden to prune.[3]

It is also true that in the years preceding the publication of the balcony stories trends in the American short story were beginning to change from the native product of detailed regionalism and sentiment to the more sophisticated European story in the manner of Flaubert and Maupassant, where economy and suggestiveness were admired over elaboration of incident. Grace King's first two volumes represent the earlier style, in which the author shows off her command of language and her ability to create plots. In the new style the author effaces herself as much as possible and relies heavily on what is left unsaid. The result is a fiction resembling that of Chekhov and Katherine Mansfield.

The idea of the balcony stories is set forth in the introduction, "The Balcony." These are to be stories of the sort told by ladies on summer evenings as they sit on the upper galleries of their traditional New Orleans homes. The gallery is the roofed walkway characteristic of the city either in the French Quarter or in the Garden District. Grace King may have hesitated to use the term "gallery," since that suggests something different to people outside the area of the Gulf Coast. Louisiana galleries are not really balconies, but the word conveys to the general reader the idea of the overhanging upper porch of the New Orleans house. The series is a group of stories told from the female point of view and even heard by the children in the sleeping rooms beyond the gallery, where the soft, comforting "mother-voices" convey the assurance that "there is no end of the world of time, or of the mother-knowledge." It was principally the voice of Grace King's own mother that inspired this idea for the narratives—the recollections of the past told her and her sisters or some neighbor like Mrs. Gayarré. There was a kind of narrative tradition

3. Henry Mills Alden to Grace King, April 21, 1887, in the Grace King Papers, Department of Archives and Manuscripts, Louisiana State University, Baton Rouge. Unless otherwise noted, all manuscript material is in this collection.

among genteel women who amused each other with "Experiences, reminiscences, episodes, picked up as only women know how to pick them up from other women's lives,—or other women's destinies . . . and told as only women know how to relate them; what God has done or is doing with some other woman whom they have known—that is what interests women once embarked on their own lives,—the embarkation takes place at marriage, or after the marriageable time,—or, rather, that is what interests the women that sit of summer nights on balconies."[4]

Grace King was raising an oral tradition to the level of literature. Her friend Mark Twain had used this method to create a major work in *Adventures of Huckleberry Finn* (1884). She could not be expected to be aware of that novel's significance in 1892, but she was surely doing something similar in her own narrative style. It is true that the balcony stories are only rarely colloquial and they are not told by a first person narrator. But the illusion of colloquial style is present throughout the series, and one feels the rhythms of women's voices telling the stories when only moonlight comes through the shutters and "while memory makes stores for the future, and germs are sown, out of which the slow, clambering vine of thought issues, one day, to decorate or hide, as it may be, the structures or ruins of life."[5]

The themes of the balcony stories are for the most part what we should expect from Grace King—the Reconstruction experience, the revelation of racial identity, family stories of the experience of ancestors, and stories of simple people in Acadia or among the "Gascons" of New Orleans. First in the series and earliest to be published in *Century* is "A Drama of Three," a sketch of old General B_____ and his wife Honorine. The general is accustomed to the best, having spent much of his youth in Paris "to cultivate *bon ton* and an education." The Paris influence and the sense of aristocratic hauteur in a time of poverty suggest the character and life of Charles Gayarré, who was living in proud poverty and old age when the story was written. If Grace King did not directly model the character on the judge, she could not have avoided the influence. General B_____, cared for by a doting wife, sneers at Pompey, the Negro servant, and distrusts his landlord Journel, grandson of the former

4. Grace King, "The Balcony," in *Balcony Stories* (new edition; New York, 1925), 1–4.
5. *Ibid.*, 6.

overseer of the family plantation. Now that times have changed, the servant continues to serve the old man loyally, and Journel secretly sends him thirty dollars every month and then collects ten from him for the rent. The anonymous letter from Journel accompanying the monthly contribution reads "From one who owes you much." The question of what the overseer's grandson could possibly owe the general is left unanswered. Grace King seems to be saying that the older generation of Creole aristocrats, who built New Orleans as a part of the region's civilization, have indeed left their mark on the city even if they have become dotards. Journel, doubtless a great exception in reality, recognizes the general as a symbol and feels a comic satisfaction in contributing to the old man's comfort. Gayarré was in a similar position in his later years, when citizens of New Orleans helped him in various ways to show their respect for his career as judge, historian, and intellectual of the Creole past. His own response to his misfortunes, however, was the opposite of Grace King's response to hers. She was driven to fresh energies to recover the family position; he was full of unsuccessful schemes whose failure generated in him self-pity. Her attitude toward him is illustrated in the story. Like Journel, she realized that modern Louisiana owed much to Gayarré and his world. She was willing to pay that debt in whatever way she could, but at the same time she smiled at the old man in his decline. The very embodiment of the region's history had become a pathetic bore.

"La Grande Demoiselle" is one of Grace King's most effective stories because it is presented as the development of a legend. By relating the information about La Grande Demoiselle through the eye and ear of rumor, the author-narrator maintains an appropriate distance. Some of the details told about the great lady seem strained and incredible—all presented as the growth of a legend told either by the Negroes of the plantation or the ladies on their galleries. The story is replete with suggestiveness, with emotional possibilities left untold, which the reader's aroused imagination may complete. What happened when the fire burned the Reine Sainte Foy plantation house when it was occupied by Negro troops during the war? The women were carried in their night dresses to the sugar house and the contents of the house were stolen. Were the women also molested? Was that part of the extreme degradation La Grande Demoiselle suffered which brought her to such a humble position as that of teacher of Negro children after the war? Why does the old bachelor Champigny marry her if he was not interested in women and if this lady is no longer beautiful and no longer an heiress? Why does she accompany him everywhere he goes? Grace King demonstrated here her ability to select and develop highly suggestive symbols. La Grande Demoiselle never speaks in the story, and her silence causes the reader to feel the unspeakable sorrow of her loss of everything that formed the substance of her pride. So also, as much as any of the King characters, Idalie Sainte Foy Mortemart des Islets is a symbol of the ironic losses suffered when fate and history impose war on human lives. That loss was more acutely felt by a woman of grace and extravagance than by someone like Champigny or like General B____ of "A Drama of Three." La Grande Demoiselle was like the Kings themselves, who felt their losses more keenly than ordinary people because they had more to lose.

In "A Delicate Affair" there are elements that echo "A Drama of Three." Both stories involve three elderly people and a servant, the servant is abused by an imperious elder, a sympathetic and nostalgic sense of the past pervades. Both center on the once respected person now living in poverty. The point of "A Delicate Affair" lies in the ironic contrast between the imperious Josephine of the early pages, especially in her irascibility with her servant, and her softness and sentimentality in reconciling with the rival who was once her bosom friend. The combination of despotism and sentimentality had been characteristic of southern women since the days of romanticism: a woman had to run her household by commands, but among her intimates she should never lose her femininity. So the elderly Josephine, a tyrant in her household, hearing that her former friend may be dying, rushes to her and greets her with the sentimental names they used together as young girls at the time of their first communion. Grace King transfers the reader credibly from the one mood to the other, and at the end the tyrant has been transformed into the schoolgirl. Psychologically, Grace King saw Josephine as the woman who "had so carefully barricaded certain issues in her memory as almost to obstruct their flow into her life; if she were a cook, one would say that it was her bad dinners which she was trying to keep out of remembrance."[6] Old rivalries and

6. Grace King, "A Delicate Affair," in *Balcony Stories*, 209–10.

resentments keep up the tyrannous sides of our personalities until the possibility of death removes the old obstruction and reveals the heart beating underneath.

"The Old Lady's Restoration" is a less subtle variation of the theme of the aristocrat of the past, now impoverished. This woman is by chance restored to her former fortune, though once her former friends visit to congratulate her and welcome her back to the fold, she is revealed to be a person who has learned to live with the common necessities of life and appreciates them more than the luxuries. And since this appreciation goes for common people as well as common things, she also rejects the society associated with equipages, laces, and opera seats for the commonplace routine that she has become accustomed to. The visitors return to their world reporting that the old lady's mind has "completely gone under stress of poverty and old age." [7] The ironic point—perhaps too obvious in the story—is that people of wealth fail to value the basic comforts when they are not accompanied by luxury. Unlike the old lady whose fortune was restored, Grace King in her own life had labored to return to the status of equipages, laces, and opera seats; but like the old lady she gained wisdom as a result of the years on Delery Street before the Kings could again hold up their heads in the Garden District.

Grace King could not exhaust the theme of the pathos and dignity of the endurance of poverty. In one group of balcony stories she is concerned with those who put up with the state as a permanent way of life—the "Gascons" or working-class Creoles and the blacks. "Anne Marie and Jeanne Marie" is her best account of the "Gascons," and in "A Crippled Hope" she again honors the character of a black woman. The first of these is another example of her ability to see the pathetic depths of irony in human character. She contrasts two poor sisters who live in poverty—one a widow who has known some of the joys of life, the other an aged spinster who has enjoyed few of them. The first, whose lottery ticket has won forty dollars, generously says that it is her bedridden sister's ticket that has won the money. The generous sister later sees the other stealthily hiding the money from her and realizes she has never known her at all. Generosity has been repaid by suspicion.

"A Crippled Hope" illustrates Grace King's ability to show the essentially

7. Grace King, "The Old Lady's Restoration," in *Balcony Stories*, 190.

compassionate psychology of womankind. It is perhaps the most moving portrayal of a black person in her fiction. We never hear the crippled slave "Little Mammy" speak, but we hear of her character from babyhood to maturity and are told through frames at the beginning and at the end that she herself is relating the story of her life. Other authors have written similar stories—Flaubert's "A Simple Heart," Chekhov's "The Darling," Sherwood Anderson's "Death in the Woods"—which treat the lives of simple women whose only drive in life is love, women who attach themselves to one person after another as their only reason for being. "A Crippled Hope" tells of a slave who is apparently worthless because she was crippled when her mother let her fall as a baby. Born in the great dusty room of the slave-trader's auction house, where shipments of slaves constantly come and go, "Little Mammy" remains there because no one wants to buy a cripple. Instinctively she loves babies as she begins to notice other human beings, and as she grows up she learns to care for babies, children, and other people who need her care. In her knowledge of how to soothe and comfort the sick, she is the perfect nurse. The author never explains how she learns what must have been learned from someone, but the possibility that a woman might become a nurse by sheer instinct is credible. In time she becomes immensely valuable to the slave-trader, who is canny enough to want to keep his stock healthy in order to obtain a good profit. And although no planter wanted her as a child, she comes to be an asset to the slave-trader and many women seek to buy her. To have served as a nurse on a plantation would have been a more attractive life than living in the slave-trader's establishment, but "Little Mammy" never gets her wish to be bought. When the war ends, however, she finds herself free. Then she faces the world of Reconstruction, as she is hired out in various places to relieve the tensions of the sick and the demoralized after the war.

"A Crippled Hope" is the sketch for a story that never comes fully into being because it is never specific enough. We may be able to accept the silence of "Little Mammy," but because the people around her are never dramatized with any degree of precision, she herself remains a vague character who performs her useful function in the melancholy days of slavery and Reconstruction. We need only contrast the memorable scenes and details of the life of Flaubert's Félicité of "A Simple Heart" with this narrative to see what it lacks. Félicité showered her love on specific people from the children of her employer, to her nephew, to the parrot. Not enough of that rendering of scene and detail occurs in "A Crippled Hope," but even so the story is eloquent and moving. Another of its virtues is the style, which suggests a speaking narrator even though colloquial language is rarely used. Also characteristic of this story as well as the volume is the epigram. As she describes her character's development, Grace King ties her ideas together with epigrammatic generalizations, such as "God, depend on it, grows stories and lives as he does herbs, each with a mission of balm to some woe," "Out of this hatred had grown her love—that is, her destiny, a woman's love being her destiny," "Nothing equaled a negro-trader's will and power for fraud, except the hereditary distrust and watchfulness which it bred and maintained," "(A negro baby, you know, is all stomach, and generally aching stomach at that)," and "—God keeps so little of the truth from us women. It is his system."[8]

If "A Crippled Hope" is an incomplete effort to create a moving female portrait, "The Little Convent Girl" succeeds quite fully in that attempt because the character is more graphically realized. Her silence, to the reader, is eloquent and as dramatically meaningful as is her suicide. And the language gives us a good example of the illusion of the spoken voice in written narrative. Also, the story is blessed with skillful construction; even though the drama is slight, the reader is held by a subtle use of preparation and suspense.

In her personal letters Grace King rarely alluded to the writing of her fiction. Thus we can only imagine by conjecture the origin of a story like "The Little Convent Girl." She knew the lower Mississippi well, having traveled at various times on the steamboats that plied the river, and the experience was such a joy to her that she would later escort Madame Blanc by boat to Arkansas, so that her friend could share the pleasure. She also knew the famous Captain Horace Bixby, a favorite subject of conversation with his pupil Mark Twain. One can see her on one of her trips to Baton Rouge, watching such a person as the little convent girl. (As she points out, passengers were not known by their real names but were referred to by this type of descriptive title.) Grace King might have watched the arrival of the shy eighteen-year-old

8. Grace King, "A Crippled Hope," in *Balcony Stories*, 106, 110, 116.

girl escorted by two nuns and accompanied by her trunk. In the story that develops, the convent girl travels alone from Cincinnati to New Orleans. She is taken care of and treated with great courtesy by the captain, who feels a fatherly responsibility for her and even refrains from his usual cursing when she is within earshot. The narrator-passenger who provides the story's point of view never hears the girl say a word. Her silence is her character. She is nun-like because of the strictness of her upbringing, and her timidity is intended to prepare us for her inability to live in a world where her father is dead and her mother is revealed to be black. The preparation for this revelation comes early in the story when we are told, "She wore her hair in two long plaits fastened around her head tight and fast. Her hair had a strong inclination to curl, but that had been taken out of it as austerely as the noise out of her footfalls. Her hair was black as her dress; her eyes, when one saw them, seemed blacker than either, on account of the bluishness of the white surrounding the pupil. Her eyelashes were almost as thick as the black veil which the sisters had fastened around her hat with an extra pin the very last thing before leaving."[9] She is in mourning for her father, and the blackness of mourning is intended to prepare us for the appearance of her mother.

The old theme of the tragedy of mixed blood had been used many times before. With Cable it was a favorite in such novellas as *Madame Delphine* (1881); Kate Chopin would soon draw on it for her story "Désirée's Baby." Grace King's variation on the old theme is one of the most successful of the long line. The poignancy of "The Little Convent Girl" lies in the contrast between the protected life of innocence in the convent and the outer world, where racial difference and prejudice are facts of life. Even the innocence of the convent could not protect the young girl from knowing that to be part black in nineteenth-century America was something of a curse. For an innocent, cloistered person to drown herself on learning such a fact is more moving than if she had been a knowing, worldly person. How does Grace King interpret such complications in the history of our social development? She assumes no moral stand at all but projects a poetic image of the river, and this becomes her second preparation for the reader. Venturing into the captain's rather philosophical mind, the narrator mentions,

9. Grace King, "The Little Convent Girl," in *Balcony Stories*, 147.

It was his opinion that there was as great a river as the Mississippi flowing directly under it—an underself of a river, as much a counterpart of the other as the second story of a house is of the first; in fact, he said they were navigating through the upper story. Whirlpools were holes in the floor of the upper river, so to speak; eddies with rifts and cracks. And deep under the earth, hurrying toward the subterranean stream, were other streams, small and great, but all deep, hurrying to and from that great mother-stream underneath, just as the small and great overground streams hurry to and from their mother Mississippi.[10]

The image is at first presented to us as a curious possibility of natural history, planted in our minds so that it will take on a meaningful poetry at the very end of the story. After the little convent girl has drowned herself and the roust-about and the mate dive in but fail to recover her body, we are told that "she had gone down in a whirlpool." And then follows the mysterious image of the river we have been introduced to before, now presented as a poetic explanation of the drowning: "Perhaps, as the pilot had told her whirlpools always did, it may have carried her through to the underground river, to that vast, hidden, dark Mississippi that flows beneath the one we see; for her body was never found."[11]

Grace King was familiar with Matthew Arnold's poetry. Quite possibly she applied to the Mississippi his image in "The Buried Life" that Fate

> Bade through the deep recesses of our breast
> The unregarded river of our life
> Pursue with indiscernible flow its way;
> And that we should not see
> The buried stream, and seem to be
> Eddying at large in blind uncertainty,
> Though driving on with it eternally.

Arnold's theme was that we are rarely our true selves except when we love. Grace King uses the image of the buried river to suggest all we conceal about

10. *Ibid.*, 154.
11. *Ibid.*, 161.

ourselves or all that fate conceals for us. Buried in the unconsciousness of the shy little convent girl is the ironic and terrible possibility of suicide, which surfaces after she learns her mother is black. Still waters run deep, the old saw tells us. The human personality is only the tip of an iceberg. The buried river image suggests the unconscious and therefore the almost impenetrable mystery about ourselves. Another curious fact about the little convent girl is that "she could not do anything by herself; she had to be initiated into everything by someone else." She is the most passive of creatures except in the final fact of drowning herself—a profounder action than perhaps any of the other characters is capable of. It is almost as if, at the end, she has for the first time ceased to be a dependent nonentity. The tragedy lies in the fact that her first assertive action should be her own destruction.

The narrative has dignity and composure; the narrator keeps herself anonymous and never allows the style to obtrude. At times there is almost a suggestion of the colloquial tone Grace King intended in creating her picture of ladies telling stories on their New Orleans galleries. When the little convent girl sits crocheting in her cabin, she is described as "never leaning back—oh, no! always straight and stiff, as if the conventual back board were there within call." The narrator brings her reader in as part of an audience: "Every one knows the fund of humor possessed by a steamboat clerk, and what a field for display the table at meal-times affords." The little convent girl's timidity is conveyed colloquially: "The first time she heard the mate—it must have been like the first time woman ever heard man—curse and swear, she turned pale, and ran quickly, quickly into the saloon, and—came out again? No, indeed! not with all the soul she had to save, and all the other sins on her conscience."[12]

"Mimi's Marriage" may be the most modern of all Grace King's stories because the narrator relates her tale of Creole marriage in colloquial style. The story proper is told by the bride Mimi, also in colloquial style. Her father wants Mimi to marry someone other than a "nobody"; Mimi wants an ideally beautiful young man. But fate or God brings her a happy marriage with the good man next door, who is certainly a nobody and certainly not ideally

12. *Ibid.*, 152.

beautiful. Not a very profound idea for a story, to be sure, but again an ironic one indicating that our choices in life are made by God, or chance, rather than by ourselves, and sometimes that chance occurrence produces a happy marriage beyond the conception of either our elders or ourselves.

The tone of these stories tends to be serious, ironic, nostalgic, even tragic, as we trace the destinies of mostly female characters. But Grace King was capable of writing humorously if the subject inspired her. Among the balcony stories, "A Drama of Three" is not without humor, but it is "Pupasse" that reflects humor more than any other in the series. In this story we return to the scenes of "Monsieur Motte"—the Institut St. Denis in the days of schoolgirls in hoop skirts. It is likely that Grace King remembered the tall, ungainly Pupasse, the perennial dunce who constantly complains about the injustices imposed on her by her teachers. The humor in the story flourishes when Pupasse loses her enviable long list of sins that she has recorded in preparation for her first communion. When she threatens to accuse her fellow schoolgirls of stealing her list, they contribute their own sins to Pupasse, whose new list then becomes the longest of all. Here Grace King the Protestant looks back with affectionate satire on the rigid customs of the Catholic school of her girlhood.

Several of the less dramatic balcony stories tempt one to categorize them as failures because they are little more than sketches. Among these are "The Miracle Chapel," "The Story of a Day," and "One of Us." These three are fictions that partake of the essay, that stress the author's idea over her dramatization of it. For this reason it is easy to reject them, but on a second or third reading their slightness comes to seem entirely intentional. "The Miracle Chapel" is more essay than story. The author ponders the human characteristic of praying for miracles, analyzing the human heart, certainly, rather than the truth or impossibility of miracles. She tells her little story from the point of view of the thinking person who sees miracles as a sign of God's veering from the rules of logic and reason so as to help the poor in their distress. A small blind boy hopes for sight and receives it through the help of a benevolent person who takes him first into the miracle chapel and then to a hospital, where a physician cures him. The final authorial comment implies that the Virgin did indeed hear his prayer and helped him. But where does

Grace King stand on such a matter? She had a strong Protestant upbringing which gave her faith, but her love of Catholic New Orleans reflected in the story would hardly approach the point where she would believe in the un-Protestant miracles of the Virgin. Throughout the story she implies that life is conducted by rules of logic and reason, though sometimes the elements of chance and the goodness of the human heart are the true catalysts that bring about what are called miracles. The boy's blindness is cured by modern science, but without chance and kindness he would never have been brought to the hospital. Thus the miracles performed by the Virgin are indeed true in a poetic or metaphorical sense.

She was more successful with this sub-genre, if it can be called that, in "The Story of a Day," which is more poetic than meditative. This story has a rather precise local background—the sea marsh and bayou country of Acadian Louisiana. Here the author uses the charming world of nature to produce a metaphorical, poetic effect. Grace King gives the reader a hint of her concept of the story at the beginning by saying, "It is really not much, the story; it is only the arrangement of it, as we would say of our dresses and our drawing rooms."[13] This observation suggests her mature knowledge of what art was from the point of view of advanced artists of the late nineteenth century; the very word "arrangement" echoes the titles of several of Whistler's paintings.

Her "arrangement" in "The Story of a Day" consists of two apparently unrelated parts placed in juxtaposition. In the first the narrator is proceeding with others by small boat to a remote Cajun farm at dawn in the spring of the year. Her poetic word picture is one of lyric exultation as the dawn gradually reveals the natural magnificence of the bright blue and white water lilies that lie upon the water in profusion. Other details make the first part one of the most spectacular of Grace King's prose passages—the vision of alligators, huge live oaks, birds and cattle—to such an extent that the Cajun world seems almost demi-paradise. But in this watery Eden of the sea marshes, there is also the element of chance and the constant danger of catastrophic death. On occasion a pretty heifer, going to the bayou to drink, is sucked into the

13. Grace King, "The Story of a Day," in *Balcony Stories*, 69.

mud and drowns. External nature is a pattern of abundance, proliferation, strength, inexpressible beauty—and catastrophic death. In the midst of this world of nature the human comedy plays a varied drama, as the second part of the story blends into the first. Love is the major phase of the drama, here at best a precious but temporary experience. The narrator then hears the pathetic story of the young woman of the farm who, at thirteen, was engaged to marry an eighteen-year-old neighboring youth. Their period of love before their wedding is full of exuberance and the highest joy, like the symbolic blossoming of the blue and white lilies at dawn. The portrait of the young woman in love is reminiscent of Wordsworth's Solitary Reaper—the young woman who works with her hands and sings out of some unspeakable sense of joy and sorrow in her life. Grace King did not often describe the high passion of young love at its height; she may have hesitated because of the limitations of her own experience. In this story, however, by mere suggestion she shows her profound understanding of the experience of country lovers or any kind of lovers. The Acadian peasants know that marriage is the only cure for love and they encourage their daughters to marry early—even at the age of thirteen. But if the young woman knows joy and despair alternately during the final weeks before the wedding, the young man cannot suffer the final week in such silence. He goes on a short journey up the bayou in moonlight, maddened with his passion. Somehow he drowns in a prairie thick with lily roots and is not found until the next summer drought.

The tale is a subtle one in which the actual love story is built up only by conjecture and in the imagination of the narrator. We never learn how the lover died, and we do not need, or get, an explanation of the girl's despair. We see her as a woman of twenty-five, twelve years later, the best cottonade-weaver in the parish, a woman who seems to have taken some "irrevocable vow of old maidenhood." One might ask what the connection is between part one (the background of Acadian nature) and part two (the love story re-collected). The connection is of course the "arrangement" as Grace King sees it. Man and woman play their vital role in the world of nature, and what happens to them is closely connected with the world of the bayou, the alligators, the cattle, and the lily roots. All creatures of nature are subject to similar rules involving beauty, joy, sorrow, and catastrophe.

"One of Us" is another portrait sketch of a woman, though her story is far less romantic than that of the cottonade-weaver. She is a type Grace King might have met at the old French Opera House—a *dugazon manquée*, a one-time aspiring singer who, because of her inadequate voice and her thin, bony appearance, failed to be cast in any role but that of the confidant of the prima donna. She has also failed in the more natural female role, never having been a wife or mother. The disappointed opera singer lives a life of frustration in which her one desire is to care for little girls. She would like to work in chari-table orphan asylums, where the joy of contact with children is an everyday occurence. This sketch was Grace King's way of writing a fictional essay on "the gulf between the real and the ideal, the limitations between the natural and the romantic."[14] It was a problem that she probably spent much time pondering. She thought of herself as being on the side of the real and the natural as opposed to the ideal or romantic. But she came to the ironic conclusion that in New Orleans and in Louisiana generally the romantic sometimes *was* the real. This principle might apply to "The Story of a Day" more than to "One of Us." The first exalts the poetic and romantic in the real setting of exotic rural Louisiana; the second places almost no emphasis on local background but comes to the conclusion that the "real" or "com-monplace" life would bring the greater fulfillment to the singer, not the supposed glamour of an operatic career.

It is impossible to say whether the balcony stories stem from actual tales told by such ladies as Grace King's mother on the galleries of their New Orleans homes. At least two of the stories—"Grandmother's Grandmother" and "Grandmama"—have the undoubted ring of authenticity. The first is authentic in its lack of point. It is the kind of story that might have been handed down in a family—the chronicle of the murder of a young husband in pioneer days. The second is a relatively important story disguising itself as a mere family story. Its quality lies in a subtle humor that tells us much about the social history of early Louisiana. Essentially it is a contrast between the Puritan and the Creole way of life. "Grandmama," an heiress who has had the strictest of upbringings, marries Middleton, a Virginian who believes in the

14. Grace King, "One of Us," in *Balcony Stories*, 127.

relaxed life of pleasure. They settle in New Orleans and visit the resort town of Mandeville across Lake Pontchartrain from the city. Because "Grandmama" believes that M. Populus, an elderly and self-indulgent Creole, is a bad influence on her husband, she insults him at dinner by ignoring his gracious toast to her. Other members of the party expect that a duel will ensue, that Populus will demand satisfaction from Middleton for his wife's insult. But when the two men meet again the elderly man proves to be the magnanimous hero who waives the rules of honor in favor of his own respect for the virtue of the pious "Grandmama." " 'Wives always think that some one else corrupts their husbands,' he says. 'It is a pretty illusion, and one that I would not destroy.'" M. Populus smoothes over an incident that might have produced a duel, and his final gesture is to drink a toast "To the good women. We are not good enough for them. She ["Grandmama"] . . . is the kind we like our mothers to be—our fathers being what scamps they please."[15]

Much of the charm of the story lies in Grace King's deftness of touch, her restraint in keeping her dramatic scenes short, and in the tone of humor and wisdom that controls the springs of action interpreting an incident of the past. When we complete the reading of the story we realize that the simple incident suggests a universal juxtaposition of attitudes in the formation of the American character. The wife represents the Puritan rigidity of behavior in the South or in New England. Her Anglican, Virginian husband is the middle way, and M. Populus is the aristocratic Catholic Creole. No one wins in this historic struggle between the followers of the straight and narrow as opposed to the pursuers of pleasure. But M. Populus shows the greater wisdom in the end in paying his compliment to womankind, thereby leaving us with the well-worn idea of the double standard between the sexes. It is all right for the men to do as they please, but we want our mothers to maintain standards of propriety and virtue. Mrs. Middleton, of course, would never be convinced of the appropriateness of such a standard.

Like "Grandmother's Grandmother," the story "Joe" was written for the 1925 edition of *Balcony Stories* and continues the lives of the Middletons; it is probably based on the life of a slave in the household of Grace King's maternal

15. Grace King, "Grandmama," in *Balcony Stories*, 266.

grandmother. In the story the early death of the grandfather—a pleasure-loving husband who is careless of his health—is recorded. He has had a young Negro slave named Joe, whom he spoiled by taking to the theater. After the master's death Joe is lazy until he asks to be hired out to a virtuous, church-going Presbyterian. He improves with the change and is eventually sold to the new master. Joe then escapes by stepping on a vessel in the harbor and traveling to a northern port and eventually to Montreal, where he spends the remainder of his life.

The story is one of Grace King's more important fictions about the relations between blacks and whites in antebellum times. She now deals with the life of a male slave, an educated one trained to be the personal servant of a gentleman. She preferred to write about this kind of servant rather than the field laborers whom she remembered as a child at l'Embarras Plantation. The intelligent slave was interesting to her because of his closeness to the master and the likelihood that he had lived a fairly genteel existence, perhaps even receiving the rudiments of education. She could then show the complicated bond between master and slave that involved those loyalties she preferred to remember. This is not to suggest that such loyalties did not exist. They must have existed within households where decency reigned and where the master and mistress lived by Christian principles. Mrs. Middleton, as the pious "Grandmama," assumes the old duty of training her slaves in biblical lore even to the point of giving Joe a Bible with her recommendation of him in it when she reluctantly sells him. That to the end of his life Joe should read daily the verses his former mistress wrote in the Bible for his moral improvement does strain our credulity, but that he should maintain an affection for his former owners was of course Grace King's stock belief, one of the historic facts she wished to record in her fiction when she began to write in the 1880s. Because of its element of humor, the story "Joe" is less intense than "Monsieur Motte" of the earlier period, and it is less important than the chapter "Jerry," the story of the freedman of the Reconstruction period in *The Pleasant Ways of St. Médard*.

Critics of the first edition of *Balcony Stories* varied in their appreciation of the new volume. A popular word in the 1890s was "impressionistic." Some saw this quality as an asset in Miss King's work, others a liability. A critic for

The Nation wrote that these new stories "resemble an exercise in composition for the abolition of the verb. . . . Miss King appears to have taken great pains to achieve the unintelligible. Her compositions are not stories but hints and most of the hints are so vague, so mysterious, that to take them with certainty would need phenomenal acuteness. Miss King is an impressionist; her observation is colored by her temperament, and she aims at the production of effect by suggestion."[16] The reviewer for the *Atlantic Monthly* came to more complimentary conclusions: "For the most part, these sketches are mere hints of stories; sometimes one has but the fringe, and no garment at all, but now and then the story teller rises to dramatic power as in Grandmother's Grandmother, or passes into pathetic beauty as in The Little Convent Girl and A Crippled Hope . . . but always the stories conform to one artistic type, and that a very noticeable one, because it has the note of personality without being insistently individual."[17] Today these comments suggest that the reviewers were unaware of the impact of Maupassant on the contemporary short story. The volume sold well enough to justify the subsequent editions, and the editors of *Century Magazine* continued for years to urge Miss King to write more stories for them like these.

*

After 1893 Grace King proceeded writing her volumes of history, which consumed much of her energy until the end of the century. Her publication of short stories was thereafter sporadic. She published four short stories in *Harper's Magazine* in 1894, one in 1895, one in 1898, and one in 1901. *Outlook* published her "A Quarrel with God" in 1897. After the 1901 publication she ceased to place her short pieces in *Harper's*, and only a handful of stories were written or published at all. Among these later, uncollected stories perhaps half are less than successful, but several are important and rank among her best.

"An Affair of the Heart" and "At Chenière Caminada" (both 1894) are love stories with rural Louisiana settings. In both the setting succeeds but the love story fails. The first is a good picture of the perils of life on a sugar plantation

16. Review of Grace King's *Balcony Stories*, in *Nation*, LVII (December 14, 1893), 452.
17. Review of *Balcony Stories* in *Atlantic Monthly*, LXXIII (April, 1894), 557.

in Mississippi flood time. In "At Chenière Caminada" Grace King attempts a story of tragic young lovers with the background of Barataria—the coastal Louisiana area once settled by pirates. She may have been influenced by Lafcadio Hearn's short novel *Chita* (1889), where innocent young beauty is pitted against the terrific power of the hurricane. Her story begins like an essay. Too much of it is devoted to undramatic preparation for the second half when the fiction begins. Perhaps she was ashamed of the sensationalism of her story in an area that she was not intimately familiar with. A young novice, about to take her vows as a nun, has avoided Claro, only to die in his arms when the two are swept into the flood waters.

In the July, 1894, issue of *Harper's* appeared a fourth story for that year—"The Evening Party." This was more successful than the previous ones because Grace King began to render her scenes as dramatic fiction from the beginning; her social analysis here is implied more through action than direct comment. "The Evening Party" deals realistically with a subject she knew better than Barataria—the problems upper class New Orleans mothers had marrying off their daughters. The first seven pages are devoted to a panorama of New Orleans society at an evening dance for young people, where the parents are also in attendance. The affair has its charm—the grace of the young ladies, the chatter of the mamas, the music of Marron, leader of the orchestra. But through all the tinsel and the pleasure runs the basic motivation behind the party. It is a tense field of competition in which the fittest of the young ladies survive, that is, they find appropriate dancing partners and impress the guests with their acceptability. The papas are less in evidence: they have been pushed off to a room where they play whist. After we have learned the rules for the entrance of a daughter into society (which could be any American nineteenth-century society), there is a space break, after which the conclusion of the drama implies more than is stated directly, as we shift from the activities of the party to the mind of Louisette. She is the less-than-acceptable girl for whom the party has been a failure:

> The young girl struck a match and lighted her gas. What confusion round about! The event that had come, had passed. The gloves, slippers, muslins, ribbons, necklace, hair-pins, fan, and the most forgotten, but

bought at the last moment, the new handkerchief; for of course there could have been no party without a suitable handkerchief. They all went to add to the debris and confusion on floor, chairs, and bureau. And, like an edifice falling down amidst all its carpentry and masonry, she fell on her bed.

She could hear her mother trying to keep her father awake long enough to hear the account of the party. All the rest of the family were asleep, still asleep, with anticipations of it. What feats of expectations, what feats of labor and patience and financiering, during the past ten days! What worlds and worlds of strangers! What heights of beauty and finery! What roulades and crescendos of Marron! What moments in the dancing-rooms! What—what hours in corners of parlors, with the mamas talking! She turned on her face to cry noiselessly.[18]

Social rejection was a subject about which Grace King felt keenly. Her mother, with four attractive daughters, had married off only one of them. The daughter may have felt some of that failure as she looked back on her youth, but she had compensated for it in creating in herself a relatively new thing in the South—the intellectual woman who could hold her own in society without having to worry about the marriage market.

"A Domestic Interior" (1895) is an unassuming work that fully succeeds in accomplishing what it sets out to do. It is a genre piece that might be discovered like a Hopi pot, coming out of the earth to stir the imagination about what life was like at a given time and place in human history. Reading it, buried as it is in the February, 1895, issue of *Harper's*, is like coming upon a dusty genre painting of Eastman Johnson. It is the portrait of a large nineteenth-century New Orleans family, in which a new son has just been born, the Negro nurse has been rehired, and the mother's sister has taken charge of the other children, seeing that they get fed and put to bed. The simple scenes preserve customs, cultural memories, and feelings that might be lost by the author who concentrates solely on plot or action. The drama is commonplace life itself, depicted with well-selected detail. There are three scenes in the

18. Grace King, "The Evening Party," *Harper's Magazine* LXXXIX (July, 1894) reprinted in Bush (ed.), *Grace King of New Orleans*, 164–71.

story: the mother's conversation with her nurse and the entrance of the children to see their new brother; the young aunt serving dinner to the children; and finally the midnight entrance of Alfred, the husband, returning from his club aglow with wine and good spirits, to join his wife and relate to her all the gossip of the day. The story's only motivating action is the spur of daily living from morning to night. The feeling of the women for their daily routine is what gives the story its meaning, and that meaning manifests itself through the minds of the mother and her sister as the day passes.

"A Quarrel with God" appeared in *Outlook* in 1897. In *Balcony Stories* Grace King had shown her compassion for the aged and had satirized their weaknesses as well. Here she deals with a subject Sarah Orne Jewett frequently used—the ladies of the old women's homes, a place where indigent and genteel ladies were able to live in some dignity and avoid starvation. In the early part of the story, we learn that it is entirely respectable to live at Madame B_____'s home for the aged, but it is almost disgraceful to die there. Mademoiselle Herminie, an aged spinster, is in danger of doing just that. Even more disgraceful to the other ladies in the home is the fact that the dying lady has a quarrel with God: she has never submitted to Him in accepting the misfortunes of her unhappy life. She is described, when in health, as "at one moment, haughty, stiff, and reserved; at another, nervous, irritable, and cross, acrid, bitter, sarcastic, skeptical in speech, defiant in manner, shocking in impiety." The ladies of the home form a kind of Greek chorus in introducing the problem and avowing that Mademoiselle Herminie should make her confession to the priest and submit to God's will before her death. The ladies are not individualized, but their brief comments suggest how society maintains its rules even at the humble station of the poor house. Some of these comments illustrate Grace King's analysis of society and her satire of it: "For a man to die so, one can imagine it; but for a woman!" "Ah, yes! Men imagine that religion is only for women!" and "Women expect too much of God." The ladies come to the conclusion that the priest must not let Mademoiselle Herminie die before she makes her submission, and that he must do this by touching her heart.

The story then focuses on Florestine, the black servant of the house, who is developed as a major character. She is one of those selfless black women who have been reared to accept the rules established by white society. Closely related in type to Marcélite, the hairdresser of "Monsieur Motte," she is devoted to her white ladies because she knows they need her. Again we have a champion of Grace King's belief that domestic black women were devoted to their mistresses both before and after the Civil War. Florestine's function is to convince the priest that Mademoiselle Herminie endured many misfortunes. Her argument is based on the old woman's loneliness throughout life: "Well, God did that to Mademoiselle Herminie. . . . And it is not with white people as with negroes. You cannot take away every one from negroes; there are always so many left; and, anyhow, they are all black together. And, then, they can always go to the white people. Who have the white people to go to?" She is a kind of advocate of the dying lady, not to ask God's forgiveness for her stubbornness, but to prove through the priest that God treated her badly and her "quarrel" is justified. The final paragraph tells us that the old lady "performed her religious duties, and died at peace with the world or God—whichever she had been at war with."[19]

The submission actually pulls the rug from under Mademoiselle Herminie as a character. She was interesting in her quarrel with God; giving in seems sentimental and not entirely convincing. There would have been more drama in a refusal to submit even at the last moment.

The seriousness of this tragi-comic story adds to Grace King's constant theme of the destiny of women and the feeling that even obscure destinies have their importance and their mysterious meanings. One of the most engaging of her stories on that theme, "Destiny," was published in *Harper's* in March, 1898. Echoing situations the author had used before, it presents two old ladies looking back on their relatively happy lives. The two had much in common in their childhood when the directions of their lives seem to have been determined: "There is no greater truth than that our childhood furnishes us our fatalities for life." The planter-father of one girl was the godfather of the other, and the planter's nephew, Belisaire Martin, becomes the central force in the story. Martin knew how to treat young girls, not only by showing them how to get by in their studies but by giving them as well a

19. Grace King, "A Quarrel with God," *Outlook*, LV (March, 1898), reprinted in Bush (ed.), *Grace King of New Orleans*, 172–83.

sense of the romance of life, which their convent education was incapable of providing. Bibi, as this man of the world was called, had the genius of creating illusions, which were what young girls of their sort needed. The background planned for them by the planter-father was the conventional practice of grammar, catechism, French history, and etiquette. Minerve, the elderly narrator, commented to her friend Théodora, "your father is preparing us for a heaven presided over by Louis XIV, as God."[20] Louis XIV represented a rigid classicism in French civilization, and Bibi was to them the supreme romantic, the young man who cared nothing for religion or convention.

On the positive side he showed them values they could never have discovered in the convent school—the imagination and illusion that made their young lives meaningful and provided them with emotional resources for years to come. While the two friends were spending the prescribed four years in the convent school, Bibi wrote to each of them a series of letters from imaginary correspondents. Gentil Gallant was Théodora's correspondent, for she was at the age when she could adore a youth who was "timid, hesitating, and bashful, of the kind that would have most influence upon Théodora." On the other hand, Bibi wrote to Minerve through the personality of Preux Vaillant, "a bluff, brusque, battle-scarred warrior." Bibi was of course a psychologist who had the imaginative principles of a first-rate modern educator. To each other the two girls pretended not to take the letters from Bibi seriously, but to destroy them once they had been read. After the death of Théodora, Minerve finds the pack of letters from Gentil Gallant in her friend's desk and reads them with pleasure. Bibi died at a young age during a siege of the cholera in New Orleans. Neither of the girls ever married, and most of life was a conventional bore after the romantic Bibi. "Destiny" is a story of great charm that hides its profundity under a cloak of nostalgia, old friendship, and memories of youth. It provides us with a Grace King "philosophy" of sorts: that we are marked for life by our girlhood or boyhood experiences; that religion and education may form the solemn, necessary basis for our lives, but that the real joy comes from illusion and romance.

"Making Progress" (1901) was the last short story by Grace King to appear in *Harper's Magazine*. It has none of the charm of "Destiny" and little of the

20. Grace King, "Destiny," *Harper's Magazine*, XCVI (March, 1898) reprinted in Bush (ed.), *Grace King of New Orleans*, 184–96.

commonplace realism of "A Domestic Interior." Its power depends on its irony, its stab at the fact that in the eyes of some people making progress is making money. Technically, "Making Progress" is poorly executed. Scenes are reported from a distance rather than rendered in selected detail as they are in "Destiny" and "A Domestic Interior."

During the span of six years from 1901 to 1907, Grace King published only three short stories: "The Flitting of Sister" (*Youth's Companion*, June 25, 1903), "On the Prairie" (*Appleton's Booklover's Magazine*, March, 1906), and "The Clodhopper" (*McClure's Magazine*, March, 1907). Except for the two additional stories written for a new edition of *Balcony Stories*, and "Annette" (1930) these were her last stories, published when she still had over twenty years to live. All three are about humble country people, and the first two have a specific Louisiana setting. All are written in a style that is unobtrusive, with characterization that is both credible and memorable. They begin well, but in each case the denouement leaves something to be desired, and meaning verges on the sentimental. In spite of what may be weaknesses in plotting and total meaning, the rendering of characters and scenes is among the best of Grace King.

"The Clodhopper," a curious blend of naturalism and romanticism, was the final story of any importance to appear in print. The author had often pondered the idea of destiny, but seldom if ever had she dealt with the problem of heredity and environment. Although she had read Herbert Spencer with enthusiasm in the 1880s, Zola had never been a favorite novelist. In "The Clodhopper" she creates an interesting character in a black field worker, Maria, who has the toughness to do a man's work and the motherly affection to pamper her infant son by suckling him until he is three. When the spoiled child becomes a youth he is drawn to the city ("the devil's plantation"), where his selfish nature leads him to thievery and the penitentiary. The concept of the city as the mecca of rural youth and their ruination echoes Wordsworth's narrative poem "Michael," and that idea is blended with the suggestion that the mother's excessive care has spoiled her son for life. Grace King seems to be posing the old question of whether people's destinies are determined for them by their inheritance of good or evil character or whether environment plays the stronger role. The question is left as much a mystery in the story as it is in human life.

In her lifetime Grace King wrote only about thirty-five stories. What is probably her final one is "Annette: A Story of the Street," which appeared in *The New Orleanian* for September 20, 1930. This pathetic story of a young woman who makes her living embroidering baby clothes has character delineation but little plot or even point. It is a weak story by a tired writer who has long since exhausted her rich vein of ideas and now has nothing more to say.

Eight

The Historian, 1892–1899

W hen Grace King returned from Europe early in December, 1892, she assumed that she might never go there again, but she was to return in 1906. The two dates conveniently frame a long and important period of her mature life. On her return home she resumed what was for the cultural life of New Orleans the important role of hostess for the prominent writers who visited the city. Over a period of years the list was a distinguished one. Besides continuing to entertain Charles Dudley Warner and Henry Mills Alden the Kings' guests included Madame Blanc, the Frank Stocktons, the Ernest Fenollosas, F. Hopkinson Smith, Clarence King, Joaquin Miller, John Fiske, and J. M. Barrie.

During the 1890s she would prove that she could be both a prolific writer and one of quality. In that decade appeared her two volumes of fiction, *Tales of a Time and Place* and *Balcony Stories*, the biography of Bienville, her *History of Louisiana* for schools, *New Orleans, The Place and the People*, and *De Soto and His Men in the Land of Florida*. In addition to the six volumes she published a series of new stories in *Harper's* and several historical articles. It was the most confident period of her professional life.

The shift in emphasis from fiction to history may be explained in a number of ways. In fiction Grace King had begun as a local colorist (although she seems not to have used the term at all), but the demand for local color was beginning to wane during the 1890s. Early in the decade she began to write her shorter "balcony stories," in which the details of regional background were kept at a minimum. Another reason for her emphasis on the writing of history was the obvious fact that publishers wanted the kind of sound, attractive history that she proved capable of writing. She was a scholar as well as a popularizer, tireless as a researcher but also a graceful stylist whose histories would appeal to the general reader and qualify as literature.

As much as any fiction writer of her time she was conscious of the brotherly relationship between history and fiction—as much as Henry James, who was not a historian. There was little nineteenth-century precedent for a woman to write history. Federal New England had produced two interesting women historians in Hannah Adams and Mercy Otis Warren, but American women tended to leave the profession to the men, as if they had taken seriously the ungallant remark of John Adams to Mrs. Warren that history was "not the province of the ladies."[1] Grace King and Ida M. Tarbell both began their careers as historians in the early 1890s. During the final decade of the century they and Agnes Repplier were the only prominent female historians in the United States. And since southern women had never produced history at all, Grace King might have claimed to be the first historian of her sex in the South.

Because there was a demand for the kind of history she could write, many of her historical works were produced after a publisher requested them. She had met Hamilton Wright Mabie, editor of the *Christian Union* and later of the *Outlook*, on one of her trips to New York, and they became friends through a steady correspondence. At some time before 1890 Dodd, Mead and Company, through Mabie, proposed that she write a study of some Louisiana figure who would fit into their series "The Makers of the Nation." Mabie encouraged her to accept the offer, although Grace King would admit that her knowledge of Louisiana history was at that time decidedly sketchy. She knew little state history beyond the stories of Gayarré and the references made by her father.[2]

1. See Michael Kraus, *The Writing of American History* (Norman, Okla., 1953), 79.
2. Grace King, *Memories of a Southern Woman of Letters* (New York, 1932), 69–72.

But even though she had not intentionally prepared herself to be a professional historian, many aspects of her early education contributed to this newly discovered talent for historical writing. William Woodson King did not believe in bringing children up on fairy stories or encouraging their imagination excessively. He told them about Washington and other famous generals, and the favorite family hero was William Tell. He made them read history aloud, beginning at a very early age. Grace was barely twelve years old when she was reading David Hume's *History of England*, and after that came Macaulay and Plutarch. She remembers her mother, appropriately a devotee of Walter Scott, reading *Ivanhoe* to her at an early age.[3] History had been an essential part of the family education, although American history itself was not a part of the curriculum of the schools she attended. The habit of reading the historians continued, probably largely abetted by the influence of Charles Gayarré before she was twenty. At one point in her twenties she was deep in the reading of Gibbon. Gayarré urged her to study Tocqueville before she was ready for him, and she read *Democracy in America* with difficulty.[4]

She began to study Gayarré's history of Louisiana in search of the figure whom she would write about as a "Maker of the Nation." Bienville, the founder of New Orleans, was then no more than a blank page in her mind, but she chose him because of her curiosity about her own city and also because he had been neglected: there was no biography of him. After she had signed a contract with Dodd, Mead, she went to Judge Gayarré to ask his opinion and to seek advice on research. Gayarré was unenthusiastic about Bienville because the man himself was insignificant and there was little material about him for a book. He did direct her to the historical collection in the state library, which he himself had formed during his term as secretary of state; he also told her to look for a manuscript copied from the Archives of France by an editor named Magne.

The state library in the old medical building on Tulane Avenue was the setting for Grace King's first real experience in research. There on the top floor she was introduced to such basic works as the Louisiana history of

3. Grace King Journal, undated, in the Grace King Papers, Department of Archives and Manuscripts, Louisiana State University, Baton Rouge. Unless otherwise noted, all manuscript material is in this collection.
4. King, *Memories*, 70.

Antoine Simon Le Page du Pratz (1758) and the famous Jesuit Relations. Next she was directed to the new Tulane Library, where she found the manuscript copied by Magne—the first great revelation to her of the subject she would be writing about. In it were excerpts of Bienville's reports, and she then began to fear that she would have to go to Paris to consult the complete documents from which the excerpts had been made. The solution to this problem came in a suggestion made by her brother, Frederick King, that Edgar H. Farrar might have in his private library many of the works she needed. Happy to see his collection used by a novice historian, Farrar sent her a basketful of material—the richest collection relating to her subject that she had yet come across. Not only did it contain the works she had consulted in the state and Tulane libraries, but in it was the great edition known as the Margry documents, with Bienville's complete reports which she had only seen excerpted before. Now Grace King could write the Bienville book without making an expensive trip to France.

She was writing her first history in her late thirties, a rather advanced time to set out on a very different kind of writing from the imaginative fiction she had so far done. But the development was a healthy one. She was experiencing a thrill that she had never known—the thrill of historical research. And she was the more excited because she was doing the work quite independently on a figure whom other historians had ignored and of whom even Gayarré had disapproved as a subject. It was for Grace King the beginning of the first long, painstaking task that would consume several years, but the passion of research was now with her, and throughout her life it would be a major drive that would keep her productive energies in action.

When she visited Paris in 1891 and 1892 she attempted to trace the later life of Bienville after he left Louisiana. But the records of the Hotel de Ville having been burned, little information was to be found, nor was there any trace of Bienville's grave in Montmartre Cemetery. The manuscript had been virtually complete when she left home, and she found little in Paris to add.

Her book appeared in 1892 with the rather pompous title, *Jean Baptiste Le Moyne, Sieur de Bienville*. The edition was small, and the distribution primarily to libraries, which suggests the kind of book it is. Because no biography of Bienville had been written before, it filled a large gap in Louisiana history. Grace King's role as historian was largely that of compiler of the many facts about Bienville's career to be found in manuscripts and in early printed histories. It is clear that in this first scholarly work she was highly conscientious, that she used all available sources to put together the chronicle of a man almost ignored in American history. Much of the first part of the study deals with Bienville's older brother Iberville, founder of the French settlement at Biloxi. Bienville succeeded his brother and became the sole important leader of French colonization on the Gulf of Mexico in the early eighteenth century.

When Grace King began her work she thought Bienville had left no tracks on history, but her preface indicates that his career is well documented in French archives and in the more obscure histories. If Gayarré considered Bienville insignificant, his protégé's labors made him indeed significant. For a series entitled "The Makers of the Nation" one might expect a book of popular history, but *Bienville* makes little attempt to popularize; it is scholarly, sound, factual, frequently somewhat dour. The author is strongly controlled by her sources and somewhat timid about commenting on them herself. The compilation of many facts about the founder of New Orleans as his career develops from early youth to middle age causes the reader to infer that he was a man capable of suffering infinite hardships and disappointments, that he was heroic in his tenacity as leader of the settlement so long as he could maintain the approval of the authorities in Paris. The emotional power of his long heroic career ended there as he grew old and his reputation faded. Grace King may have been too scholarly in the depiction of Bienville's character, if, indeed, she wanted her book to produce a greater emotional impact.

In the earlier passages she shows considerable originality in contrasting the historic area of Biloxi as it must have been as wilderness with her own knowledge of the Gulf Coast. Here she shows a literary tendency and here the imagery of her prose gives the work a certain poetry. After detailing the authentic account of Iberville's exploration of the harbor of Biloxi, she digresses with her own picture of the harbor view of her own time:

> A railroad trestle now spans the deep embrasured little recess, and the eye of the speeding passenger can note on the eastern side the eminence upon which Iberville camped nearly two centuries ago. Now, as then, guns, planted upon it, would sweep three fourths of the limited horizon, arbitrarily commanding the channel in all its length and breadth. The

channel now is ever white with sails of business or pleasure boats, and the fanciful gaudiness of summer villas studs the sombre, heavily-wooded beach. Opposite the island, under the wide-spreading branches of the great oaks where once the fishing and hunting parties of Indians lighted their fires and swung their cauldrons, a quaint assemblage of French and Spanish houses forms a town,—a town picturesque and redolent of an indefinable charm, despite the sordid vulgarities of competing summer-resort hotels.[5]

Little notice was taken of *Bienville* in the United States, though because the Le Moyne brothers were Canadians the book achieved some recognition in Canadian periodicals. When Grace King returned from Paris late in 1892 she probably expected some kind of encomium from Gayarré on entering the field of history, but he was still convinced that there was no real book in the career of Bienville. "What could anyone of today write about Bienville?" he asked. "A very ordinary man, not worth writing about." Grace King may have been somewhat crestfallen to know that Gayarré had not changed his mind, but the stubborn old judge had not read her book, and the reading of it might have changed his opinion.[6]

Her article on "Iberville and the Mississippi," published in *Harper's* for October, 1894, is a companion piece of the Bienville biography and, like the earlier work, came at the request of an editor. In each case the request had been for a book or article on a single man. It is obvious from reading *Bienville* that Grace King was inclined to look on the exploration and settlement of the lower Mississippi Valley as the work of a combination of leaders rather than that of a single one. She had felt it necessary to write at some length about Iberville, the older brother, before she began the life story of her subject, the younger one. Similarly, she was most conscious in her article on Iberville that his story was somewhat truncated without some explanation of the great accomplishments of La Salle and Henri de Tonti in descending the Mississippi to the Gulf. La Salle's failure was not that he did not know the river from its source to its mouth, but that he failed to find the mouth when he approached it later from the Gulf. It was left for Iberville to do that and to claim the

5. Grace King, *Jean Baptiste Le Moyne, Sieur de Bienville* (New York, 1893), 70.
6. King, *Memories*, 133, 181–82.

historic distinction of succeeding in the final act where the greater man had failed. We might come to the conclusion, then, that the entire early exploration of the Gulf Coast and the lower Mississippi was the work of four men— La Salle, Tonti, Bienville, and Iberville. Would it not have been a more unified conception for Grace King to have written of the entire accomplishment as history rather than to try to deal with it in pieces? But Dodd, Mead and Company needed an individual hero in their "Makers of America" series, and Henry Mills Alden had determined the hero-subject for the Iberville article.

The article, nevertheless, is probably Grace King's best in the field of history. It was well researched in Paris, showing her knowledge of the available sources—the *Relations* and other works, such as Saint-Simon's memoirs and Francis Parkman's *Frontenac and New France under Louis XIV*. Her article is well planned, its opening paragraphs sketching the late seventeenth-century rivalry in North America between France, England, and Spain. She then introduces the young Iberville as a Canadian hero, willing to risk everything in a series of exploits against the English in North America. The first is the expedition made with two of his brothers to chase the English out of the French possessions on Hudson Bay. And the Le Moyne family legend begins to grow.

> It was an expedition that demanded the full equipment of Canadian hardihood and vigor. Setting out from Montreal in the depths of winter, they marched over the frozen country on raquettes, dragging their provisions in sleds, stopping to make canoes as they needed them to cross lakes and shoot rapids. Iberville's canoe upset in one of the most dangerous of the rapids; two of his companions were drowned, but his coolness and presence of mind saved his own life and that of his other two companions. In June he arrived on the field of campaign, where the surprise of the English and the success of the French was complete.[7]

Ardent Francophile that she was, Grace King took great satisfaction in recounting her Canadian's successes against the English. After describing Iberville's many exploits, she proceeds in the second half of her article to chronicle his major claim to fame—his departure from Brest with a fleet of

7. Grace King, "Iberville and the Mississippi," *Harper's Magazine*, LXXXIX (October, 1894), 724.

four ships to sail to San Domingo, his encounter with many difficulties as he explores the coast and enters the mouth of the Mississippi. At this climax of her article and of his career, she makes the event the more immediate by quoting Iberville's own words:

> In approaching the rocks I perceived there was a river there. I passed between two of the rocks in twelve feet of water, the sea was very heavy. Nearing the rocks, I found the water fresh, with a strong current. These rocks are wood, which, petrified with slime, becomes rock that resists the sea. They are innumerable, standing out of the water, some large, some small, separated twenty, one hundred, three hundred, five hundred paces, more or less, one from the other, which made me recognize that it was the Palissado River, which appeared to me very well named, for the mouth appears all barricaded with rocks.[8]

This was a European's first recognition of the Mississippi's mouth, an accomplishment that much outshone his success over the English in the North. It led to "the veritable ownership of that magnificent territory of the Mississippi River affixed on parchment to the crown of France by La Salle seventeen years before."[9]

Grace King's second volume of history was the textbook *A History of Louisiana* (1893), written in collaboration with Professor John R. Ficklen of Tulane University. She wrote the first half, from the colonial through the antebellum period, and Ficklen wrote the concluding half from the Civil War to the end of the nineteenth century. The State Board of Education accepted it as a text for Louisiana schools for four years. In 1905 the same collaborators wrote a companion volume, *Stories from Louisiana History*, which was also used in elementary schools—gauged, as Grace King wrote later, for the ten-year-old brain. During the years when the first text was in official use she earned a considerable royalty on sales, and she was greatly disappointed when the book was withdrawn from the schools in favor of another. Besides being intended to earn money, the joint effort was regarded as a production of the Louisiana Historical Society, of which she and Professor Ficklen were both officers. For her, writing the Louisiana history was also a preparation for the

8. *Ibid.*, 730.
9. *Ibid.*, 732.

two more important volumes that were to follow—*New Orleans, The Place and the People* (1895) and *De Soto and His Men in the Land of Florida* (1898).

In 1893 or 1894 Hamilton Wright Mabie again played intermediary between Grace King and a publisher by suggesting to the Macmillan Company that she be asked to write a book on New Orleans as one of a series being planned on great American cities. Elated by the commission, she was quick to accept it, at the same time realizing that she was probably taking what Gayarré himself should have had. She explained in her memoirs that the series was being prepared by younger writers, but there is little doubt that she was aware that for this particular kind of history she was now better equipped than he. Gayarré of course had a greater knowledge of the subject, but privately she believed that both he and François Xavier Martin had used for their dull histories of the state materials abounding in excitement and beauty.[10]

The broad subject of New Orleans was much more congenial to her talents than the more limited topic of Bienville, and she was much more successful with it. Her research had prepared her for the new book; now she could call into use all the recollections she had of the old city and those of the past which her mother and Gayarré could give her. Gayarré's memory went back to the time before the War of 1812 and the Battle of New Orleans, and Mrs. King's parents had settled in the city not long after. If Gayarré knew the educational and political history of the city first hand, Mrs. King knew the social, cultural, and religious history. The book proved to be much more a labor of love than the *Bienville*. If Grace King enjoyed the thrill of discovery in doing research for her first histories, she now felt that she was writing her own family background, the life of the city that had had as varied a career as any in the United States.

The author of *New Orleans, The Place and the People* had full command of her subject, and the writing of the book seemed to come as a joyful experience in which her interest and her affection were fully involved. Her style is highly sophisticated and relaxed, replacing the earlier scholarly tone with one of urbanity. It is never heavy and there are occasional sallies of wit or humor. Always one senses that what has happened in the past fascinates the author. A specialist would not read *New Orleans, The Place and the People* as a conventional

10. King, *Memories*, 182.

history in which dates or economic facts might be of importance; she ignores them unless they are interesting for her purpose of vibrant interpretation. New Orleans becomes a feminine personality in the book, and the reader feels the spirit of the place through this woman symbol.

The historical facts were of less importance than the "atmosphere, the glamour that invested the early city in the memory of the descendants of its first citizens."[11] In her word "atmosphere" we can read the word "romance." She did not wish to join the dry-as-dust school by being overfactual or by dwelling on uninteresting phases of the city's development; so she limited her subject to the interesting, the phases of local history that showed vitality, beauty, drama, and even tragedy. She had little to do with the statistical or the more pedestrian developments of New Orleans life. If she had done her duty to fill a scholarly need with *Bienville*, she was determined to convey her own enthusiasm in *New Orleans*, to write a partially popular book that would at the same time be of literary value. This had been the ideal of the major American historians of the nineteenth century.

Recognizable, then, as a labor of love, the book follows an ardent New Orleanian's affection for her city's history. When she describes an event like Jackson's victory at Chalmette, she conveys the full memory of the city's response to its own heroism, looking back to her forebears' accomplishment with pride. Conversely, she strongly feels the humiliation suffered by the city when it was occupied by Federal forces in 1862 and then endured the very difficult conditions of Reconstruction. The happy chapter on "The Glorious Eighth of January" draws graphic pictorial imagery that characterizes the book's style and makes the event attractive. But in the untitled "Chapter XIII" concerning the rule of New Orleans by "Beast Butler" and the carpetbag government the citizens endured until 1870, little of that ingratiating style remains. Rather, having been one who herself suffered and endured that period, Grace King accumulates her various facts with understandable emotion to make her point against the shortsightedness of Federal policy.

After reading what he considered her biased account, a former Union soldier who was one of the occupying forces in the city wrote her to defend the actions of the Union army as entirely within the logic of occupational

11. *Ibid.*, 183.

forces. She saved his several letters, indicating that she had written him more than once in answer to his criticism.

Grace King was indeed close to the experience of the occupation of New Orleans, but she was close as a child rather than an adult, and she chose to maintain her resentful attitude throughout life. In passages like the following we can be sure that the memory was colored by the child's personal fears as she describes the scorched earth policy of the city when Federal forces approached:

> The sky was hidden by a canopy of smoke, streaked with flames. Heaps of burning cotton, sugar, salt meats, spirits, provisions of all kinds lined the levee. In the river the shipping, tug-boats, and gun-boats, floated down the current in flames. Molasses, running like water, flushed the gutters. All night the city had glowed in the lurid light of her own incendiarism. The little children, seeing the gleams through the closed windows, and hearing the cannons from the forts, trembled in their beds in terrified wakefulness. Deserted by their parents, and shrinking instinctively from their negro nurses, they asked one another in whispers: "Will the Yankees kill us all?"
>
> The next morning, from old Christ Church belfry, on Canal Street, the bell tapped the alarm. Mothers called their children to them, and, sitting behind closed doors, listening, counting, cried, "The Yankees are here!" The children, horrified to see a mother weep, cried aloud, too, despairingly, "The Yankees are here!" Slaves, rushing out, leaving the houses open, disordered, behind them, shouted triumphantly to one another, "The Yankees are here!"
>
> The rabble, holding riot in the streets; men, women, and children, staggering under loads of pilferings from the conflagration, cried, too, "The Yankees are here!"[12]

When she later describes without sympathy the taking over of the city administration by the Federal officers, representatives of Admiral Farragut, we can only contrast her historical view of the scene, which she did not personally observe, with that of George W. Cable, then a young man, who did

---

12. Grace King, *New Orleans, The Place and the People* (New York, 1895), 300.

observe the approach of the two Federal naval officers walking unarmed through a taunting mob to City Hall to demand the surrender of the city. In compliment to them he wrote, "It was one of the bravest deeds I ever saw done."[13] Cable, of course, did not favor Federal occupation; he was later to join the Confederate army. However, he was able to observe a scene with objectivity.

Curiously for Grace King, whose fiction conveys a woman's attitude toward her subject matter, her style in *New Orleans* is neither masculine nor feminine. Formal as the tone is, it has much of the speaking narrator about it, especially in its discursiveness. She allowed herself the luxury of digressions, which are usually interesting and attractive, although some of them (St. Denis and Pennicault) are overlong and pointless. In one passage she quotes from *Manon Lescaut* at length and comments on it with obvious exaggeration: "Never has author breathed upon his creatures of romance the breath of such reality, if not of life."

Occasionally an interpretation of French or colonial history reflects the wisdom she has gained from a knowledge of herself. When she discusses the role of the French prime minister, the Duc de Choiseul, she introduces his sister, Madame de Grammont, who was known as the "man of business" of Madame de Pompadour and "La doublure" or "the lining of her brother." Commenting on this woman's role in life, Grace King remarks, "Her ambition, it seems, was that purely feminine one, of repairing the impoverished fortunes of her family, and in this ambition women can be inflexible, inexorable, and unscrupulous."[14] Was this not giving profound insight into such proud women in all societies who dedicate their lives to restoring their ruined families to their former status? The family of the Duc de Choiseul or that of William Woodson King—it is all the same. Grace King was throughout her life inflexible and inexorable in her major purpose. She might also be capable of a touch of the unscrupulous if it were necessary to help the cause of the King family fortunes.

Reviews of *New Orleans, The Place and the People* were almost unanimous in their praise; the book was thereafter accepted as the best general book written

13. George W. Cable, "New Orleans before the Capture," *Century*, XXIX (January, 1885), 922.

14. King, *New Orleans, The Place and the People*, 40, 90.

about the city. In a comment in a letter to Grace King five years after the book's publication, William Dean Howells said, "I should like so much to tell you that your history of New Orleans is almost the most perfect book of its kind that I know."[15] The Macmillan Company brought out later editions in 1907 and 1912; it was a book that the city would not let die. As late as 1926 Edmund Wilson, who had met Grace King in New Orleans, wrote her on his return to New York: "I can't tell you how much I enjoyed your book; I believe I learned more about the South from it—not merely from the point of view of information but from that of dramatic communication of the spirit and ideas of society—than from any other book I've read."[16] Agnes Repplier wrote in 1932 after the recent death of Grace King that *New Orleans* was "as good a piece of municipal history as any American writer has given us. It has never been superceded, and is not likely to be superceded by anything better."[17]

*

While *New Orleans, The Place and the People* was being written, Madame Blanc made her promised trip to the United States in the winter of 1894. Her purpose was to write a series of articles on American women for the *Revue des Deux Mondes*. Anxious to give her friend the best possible impression of New Orleans, Grace King urged her to come first to Louisiana as a house guest of the Kings. This was in February, Mardi Gras time, when the French lady could be taken to the Mystic Krewe Ball and observe how the traditional revelry of the city followed some of the customs of an earlier France. She was guided by the Kings throughout the old city to help her prepare material for what would eventually be her chapter on New Orleans in her book *American Women at Home*.

The Kings arranged in her honor an elaborate musicale with performances by several of the best singers and pianists they could engage. Madame Blanc thought one of the musicians was good enough to be singing at the *Opéra*

15. William Dean Howells to Grace King, December 7, 1900.
16. Edmund Wilson to Grace King, April 11, 1926, in Robert Bush (ed.), *Grace King of New Orleans* (Baton Rouge, 1973), 30.
17. Agnes Repplier, review of Grace King's *New Orleans, The Place and the People*, in *Commonweal*, XVII (November 16, 1932), quoted in Bush (ed.), *Grace King of New Orleans*, 31.

Comique. And Grace King was thoroughly satisfied with the occasion as one that reflected her family's great pride in the city, showing itself off to a genuine literary light of Paris.

Madame Blanc had made plans to visit Octave Thanet (Alice French), who lived on a remote plantation on the Black River in Arkansas. Grace King was anxious to have her French friend experience some of the glamour of old times on the Mississippi, even though the days of the great steam packets were now a part of the past. She arranged passage for two on one of the most picturesque of the packets that still plied the river and took the greatest satisfaction in seeing Madame Blanc's eyes open as the charms of leisurely travel were revealed to her. Grace King felt particularly proud of the service on such boats and the captain himself escorted the literary ladies up the gang-plank of the almost palatial steamer as it lay at the levee in the bright sun of a late winter afternoon. The red-carpeted saloon glittered with white paint and gilding, the chambermaids were immaculate in black silk dresses and white lawn aprons, and the little rooms were quaintly equipped with such comforts as armchairs, toilet tables, and four-poster beds with mosquito bars. Grace King occupied the bridal chamber, much to Madame Blanc's amusement.

The literary mind and the leisure of a trip on a Mississippi steam packet—the combination was quite perfect; the artist needed time for contemplation and the river voyage provided it. They sat high in the pilot house and watched the wooded bluffs pass by at a distance, saw the bright sun on mostly deserted plantation houses with Negro shacks close to the levees. They talked for hours about the matters that interested them in both France and the United States. The parade of celebrated personalities whom Madame Blanc either knew personally or was conversant about was prodigious—the Empress Eugénie, the Prince Imperial, Alphonse Daudet, Paul Bourget, Émile Zola, Ferdinand Brunetière, Jules Lemaître, Paul Verlaine, Victor Hugo, Robert Browning, Alfred Lord Tennyson, Henry James, Mrs. James T. Fields, and Sarah Orne Jewett. Their close friend the Baronne Blaze de Bury had recently died, and both ladies were moved as they thought about that extraordinary woman who had known so many of the great men of Europe for a generation but who had died in a state of despair, feeling herself deserted by her own relatives in her later years. Grace King had wondered about Madame de Bury: with all her exposure to the loose literary people of her times on the Continent, had she not been like the others, a little dissolute, given to the easy affair in her youth? Not so, according to Madame Blanc; the baronne, as far as she knew, had followed the straight and narrow path. Grace King was reassured. Even after her initiation into the mysteries of literary life in Paris, she could not escape her Presbyterian background. She read French novels in search of their advanced technique, but she was always somewhat squeamish about their treatment of sex. Madame Blanc had led a blameless life, and her good reputation was one of the attractions for the respectable American. On the Mississippi voyage, however, Grace King discovered that the French lady's views about sexual life were not so rigid as her own. It was reassuring that no breath of scandal touched the name of Madame de Bury, but Madame Blanc pointed out that "we should not judge a woman because she happens to have lived & lived up to the precepts of the sentiment." Grace King later commented significantly, "She about convinced me that the honest women of Paris were those who did *love*—i.e. that did not rest satisfied with the cold barren sentiment inspired by their husbands." The comment suggests that Grace King was capable of a liberal, almost feminist attitude toward sex. When her sister May married in 1884 she had considered women the victims of the system, inescapably bound to their lot. Now the influence of a protégé of George Sand and a French expert on her sex showed her that they might be honest when they rebelled against the conventions of marriage.

Grace King admired most of her friends with reservations, and so it was with Madame Blanc. She thought of her as "a very charming, interesting woman & full of good sense. I got a great deal of profitable advice out of her, and think she is going to do me a great deal of good in France by having my books translated & perhaps getting Bienville adopted as a prize book for schools." But she was amused that Madame Blanc was inclined to offer complete advice on what the King family should do with their lives—Nina should marry, Nan should write short pieces for newspapers and do translations. Their friend Louise Sullivan should be brought to New Orleans and married to their brother Branch. There was no end of her urgings and suggestions. As a traveler she reminded Grace King of Judge Gayarré himself, who was always complaining; she was always asking questions "in her slow, laboured, high flown mispronounced English, which no one understood, and which I had constantly to translate." Madame Blanc left the packet at

Vicksburg much to the amusement and perhaps relief of her guide. She was accompanied by two Negroes who carried her boxes, men "whom she suspected of any and all villainy & herself in a broken down vehicle with a most rascally Jehu." From the deck Grace King watched the equipage winding up the bluff at Vicksburg, "stopping every twenty paces for, I was confident, a hot altercation." On the return trip from Vicksburg a minor cyclone caused everything on the boat to crack and squeak. Grace King was driven from the deck and the pilothouse and feared that for the voyage home she would be confined to her quarters—the bridal chamber.[18]

*

The years of the writing of *New Orleans, The Place and the People* were concurrent with the decline and death of Charles Gayarré. As he grew weaker in his ninety-first and ninety-second years, Grace King began visiting him regularly on Sundays, not only to reestablish the old friendship after the rift of the late 1880s but also to record anecdotes and opinions that he wanted to pass on to her before his death. She wrote much of this material in her notebooks—recollections of the battle of New Orleans, the character of Jefferson Davis (whom Gayarré did not admire), and the scandals in the life of Madame de Pontalba. On January 13, 1895, she went to pay him her usual Sunday visit, finding him in his dressing gown with his wife's crocheted shawl over his shoulders and his derby hat on his head. His mood was at first irritable as he grumbled about his loss of memory, his inability to remember where he put things. He told her how he had burned most of his papers because his eyesight did not permit his going through them to keep from the world what he wanted concealed. He never said what it was that he wished to conceal; he had in fact led an exemplary life, but he may have had on his mind the siring, in his early youth, of an illegitimate son by a Negro woman.[19] He then began to muse on his own boyhood in the early years of the century. Grace King recorded much of his monologue either by taking notes or through her own memory:

18. Grace King to May McDowell, February 17, 1894.
19. Earl Noland Saucier, "Charles Gayarré, The Creole Historian" (Ph.D. dissertation, George Peabody College for Teachers, 1933), 43–44.

Charles Gayarré, about 1895, at his desk, Prieur Street, New Orleans

It is ridiculous to think I was ever a boy—it is so long ago. It does not seem to be a reality at all. More & more it seems a dream. Ninety-one years! Great heavens what a length of life. They speak of the trials of old age. No one but the old knows what they are! To live, but live past everything! The fairies, the illusions of my youth have become hags. No man knows how much we live in the future, until we have used up our future—how much our life is made up of projects—until we project no longer. How uninteresting life is, without future, without projects. Never grow old. Try never to grow old!

The old man described to her the illusion of music in his ears at varying intervals, music that was unwelcome because he had never liked music. And people passed before him in visions—always men and Negroes, never a woman to make it interesting. Then he pondered the possibility of consciousness after death:

> It would be interesting to know what is going to happen to me when I die. Any moment, I may pass from this life to the next. You know I have a great curiosity to see what will happen. Will it be the néant? Have we gone through life only to arrive at the néant? And if there is something else, I wonder what it is! They tell us to hope. Well, we can hope when we can do nothing else. . . . What an absurdity to make us go through 91 years of life to end in the néant. It seems such a waste!

Grace King made her final Sunday visit on February 10, 1895. Gayarré was near death, but his wife kept up the pretense that he would recover. The old conservative on this occasion inveighed against the horrors of woman suffrage: "What do you think of all this woman suffrage? Isn't it the greatest nonsense, the greatest nonsense you ever heard of? I tell you it's impossible for women to be free—the men have subordinated them, and will always keep them in subjection—always. Women must submit. *They are not mistresses of themselves*—No! No!"[20] The woman he was speaking to must have smiled inwardly; of course she could not debate the point with the dying man. But

20. Grace King Journal, 1886–1901, January 13, 1895, and February 10, 1895, in Robert Bush, "Charles Gayarré and Grace King: Letters of a Louisiana Friendship," *Southern Literary Journal*, VII (Fall, 1974), 128–29.

who in his long acquaintance with women had been more the mistress of herself than she?

When Gayarré died on the following day, Mrs. King and Mrs. Gayarré decided to have the funeral as soon as possible. But Grace, conscious of the judge's importance to the city and the state, would not hear of such haste. "We did want a little pomp & ceremony over the poor old Judge," she wrote her sister May and then proceeded to describe the funeral that took place three days later:

We were all there at half past nine. The archbishop sent three carriages of priests & acolytes to escort the body—& we all drove to the Cathedral. The weather was clear & cold, as we filed so slowly through the dirty, foreign-looking streets—past so many of the houses the Judge had known and illustrated—it seemed to me we were burying all the early cultural history of the state. When the coffin reached the vestibule, the great doors of the Cathedral were thrown open—& the dead march pealed out. It was indescribably solemn. The altar was one magnificent blaze of candles. The archbishop & his priests were waiting & the catafalque was most impos-ing—but the church *simply empty*. Well—it seemed all of a piece—with the whole of life.

The full service of the dead was chanted—the Miserere—the most beautiful burial service that there is. An exquisite contralto voice sang Requiescat in Pace—& the archbishop came out and pronounced what was to me a most touching eulogium of the Judge. . . . he was deter-mined that he and his church should do the best they could by the old man who had died in poverty and misery.

A good many people had drifted into the church by the end of the service. Gayarré was then buried in the old tomb of the De Boré family in St. Louis Cemetery.

Grace King regretted that there were no representatives of the literary circles and reading clubs of the city at the funeral. And she, who in her time would do much to bring together the social life and the intellectual life of the community, remarked with some acerbity that on the day of the funeral, "the coldest, bleakest day of the last ten years in N. O. the street was blocked for squares with carriages & people going to the Morris tea."[21] The remark is significant because it reflects the estrangement between Grace King and the family of John A. Morris, whose wealth was in part the result of his association with the Louisiana Lottery, which the King family strongly opposed. Grace King's old association with millionaire families for the sake of meaningless ease was now dead forever. Her comment also reveals her misgivings about the society of her city. Social life was indeed flourishing, but what of the cultural life with which she was identified? Was not the funeral of Gayarré one of the most important events of the century in the city? Of course it was to her, and she took some pride in having arranged to have a death mask made and in helping to plan the funeral. Throughout much of her life she felt that the city's social circles were rarely intellectually oriented. The genuine intellectuals of New Orleans were a very small group, and their influence was not felt far beyond their own circles.

When Christmas came in 1895 *New Orleans, The Place and the People* had just been published by Macmillan. Here was a product of New Orleans cultural life that Grace King was justifiably proud of. She had appropriately dedicated the book to the memory of Charles Gayarré and concluded it with an account of his funeral—the event that seemed to sound the end of Franco-Spanish culture in the city. Gayarré had passed some kind of a torch along to his friend's daughter, a Protestant and an Anglo-Saxon of sorts with a touch of Huguenot mixed in. The action was symbolic since in the twentieth century the French language would become only a scholastic memory in the city. New Orleans, nonetheless, was to be a large American city that would strive to hold onto its Creole heritage against the inroads of what were once called the *Américains*. Gayarré's many projects in the long period of his poverty all seemed to have failed, but one of his activities, hardly a project at all, was his sponsorship of Grace King. Their friendship went back to Reconstruction days. She and her sister May had been invited to his country home Roncal, filled with the furniture and paintings and books he had brought from the France of his youth. And although she had studied in a Creole school, it was at Roncal that she felt the spell of French culture that dominated Gayarré's life and was so to mark her own. From 1885 to 1895 the star of her career had risen

21. Grace King to May McDowell, February 13, 1895.

while his own had fallen. But he had been the great professor to her in a way, she the bright and willing student whom he had imbued with a greater love of history than even his own books could provide. Sometimes she had felt utter boredom with the old man, sometimes pique and anger and disapproval, but in the end she had more admiration and affection for him than for any other cultural figure in the city or in the state.

*

In 1896 Grace King signed a contract with the Macmillan Company to produce a sixty-thousand-word book on De Soto to be completed for publication for the Christmas trade of 1898. It was to be a book for the young for which she hoped to get an annual royalty. She chose the figure of De Soto from a series of suggestions of early Spanish explorers in whom Macmillan was interested. The library of Charles Gayarré by now had been transferred for safekeeping to the King home, and she could begin her work by reading in the original Spanish Gayarré's copy of the narrative of Garcilaso de la Vega. She developed a strong enthusiasm for this story of De Soto's conquest of Florida and his discovery of the Mississippi. She remembered that as she proceeded with the research and writing of the book she was "too elated with the idea of putting the wonderful narrative in shape for the young student to linger over a question of style or original contribution." She also wrote that she was determined "to avoid moral and pedagogic comment."[22]

De Soto and His Men in the Land of Florida (1898) appeared with a colorful stamping of a Spanish galleon on the cover, confirming Grace King's apparent belief that she was writing a book for the young. True, it might be read by high school students of American history, but she had made no attempt to write down to her readers. She had instead put together the story of the De Soto expedition based on the several versions and retold it clearly and interestingly for the general reader. It is a book that an adult would find entirely mature, but since it delves into no profundities of politics or psychology, no intelligent high school student would find it difficult. John Fiske, in acknowledging the copy Grace King sent him, agreed that there was no reason why it should not delight and instruct older people as well as the young.[23] As she herself said,

22. King, *Memories*, 204.
23. John Fiske to Grace King, November 4, 1899.

the book is not a critical one; it is an objective narrative presented without comment on the part of the author. The style is clear but not so distinguished as that of *New Orleans, The Place and the People*. Much of the character of the style was determined by the original sources with which she worked. The book resembles her *Bienville* because of its fidelity to the original narratives; but her enthusiasm for the subject, rather than her opinions, pervades the narrative.

Hamilton W. Mabie wrote Grace King enthusiastically in praise of *De Soto*:

> You have done nothing of its kind so well before. The narrative *lives*. What more can I say? It is all movement, vivacity and color. Your temperament is a perfect mine of literature; and I am glad to find that all the people who know have the opinion which I hold—that you have the real thing in you, and that whatever comes from you brings the muse of art with it; the elusive quality which cannot be acquired & cannot be imitated: the quality of the born writer. This piece of work has admirable construction; it is clear, well proportioned and firmly held together. It will keep its place long.[24]

The volume was recognized as a worthy one by certain learned journals. If we place in juxtaposition the literary comment of Mabie with that of the professional historian, Frank W. Blackman of the *American Historical Review*, we have a fairly complete analysis of the worth of *De Soto*. Blackman asserted that Miss King's attempt had "resulted in presenting the history of the conquest of Florida in the most attractive and readable form in which it has yet appeared in English. It makes it read like a romance—a romance tainted with the rapacity and cruelty of the Spanish conquerors." He correctly saw the author's purpose—to popularize in a graceful way so that it would appeal to the layman more than to the professional historian. He praised her for thus leaving out "the tedious details of historical criticism on controverted or unsettled questions." To Blackman, "The cruelty of the Spanish conquerors toward the natives was never made more prominent than in this little story. Without intending to be so it is one of the best descriptions of the habits, customs and

24. Hamilton W. Mabie to Grace King, October 30, 1898.

character of the natives of the early discovery. The history of no other expedition has brought out these characteristics so well."[25]

*

Although Grace King never attended a woman's college, at an early age she acquired the habits of learning that sustained her as a learned woman for the rest of her life. In a later generation she might well have become a graduate student in history or literature and taught on the college level. Throughout her career she had an interest in teaching and was unofficially a patroness of Tulane University and Newcomb College. As a long time officer of the Louisiana Historical Society she contributed heavily for more than thirty years to the vitality of that group. In 1886, when she was writing with fresh energy and confidence, she worked with the English Department of the University of Louisiana in a correspondence program. She corresponded with at least one student on questions of writing during the summer months, and after the success of the program she was asked to continue her tutelage for a second year in 1887.[26]

In 1896, with her books *Bienville* and *New Orleans, The Place and the People* added to her varied bibliography, she was asked to give a series of lectures on the history of Louisiana at the Chautauqua Summer School, held at Ruston in northern Louisiana. She accepted this commission almost as a duty, encouraged by her friend Dr. James Dillard, professor of Latin at Tulane. Dillard was an educator who believed it his duty to be concerned about rural education for all people, and his contribution to the state was later to be recognized when Straight University for Negroes changed its name to Dillard University. Grace King's lectures were welcomed enthusiastically by the men and women who were taking courses to improve their abilities to teach history in the state's public schools. In her first lecture she conveyed the reasons that brought her to the study of Louisiana history.

In July of 1898 she was again at Ruston, this time with a batch of *De Soto* proofs to read, a task she worked on at five o'clock each morning. This time

25. Frank W. Blackman, review of Grace King's *De Soto and His Men in the Land of Florida*, in *American Historical Review*, IV (April, 1899), 541-42.

26. Evelyn Ordway to Grace King, September 21, 1887.

she was rather more satisfied with her accomplishment as a lecturer. There were sixteen in her class, which was given in the late morning hours. She was pleased with the opportunity to meet the young men and women teachers from various parts of the state and was convinced that they had read next to nothing about history, let alone Louisiana history. She spent one class period giving them a reading of her proofs of *De Soto*. Other lectures were on the cartography of the Mississippi, and on the individual figures La Salle, Iberville, and Bienville. She then concluded with a general talk on the three.[27]

*

In January, 1899, Henry Mills Alden, who made a habit of introducing *Harper's* authors to each other, wrote Grace King to tell her that his friend William McLennan was coming to New Orleans with his wife and was looking for a place to stay. McLennan (1856–1904), somewhat younger than Grace King, had interests similar to hers. He was a Montreal Canadian with an appreciation of Quebec province's French background as passionate as Grace King's feeling for the background of Louisiana. As poet, romancer, and historian, he had labored long to publicize the history of Quebec, and among other volumes had written *Spanish John* (1898), an historical romance about the life of John MacDonnell. Shorter works of his appeared occasionally in the regionally oriented *Harper's* of the 1890s. Grace King, always willing to do her duty when a letter of introduction arrived, went to the St. Louis Hotel and met Alden's friends in a living room opening on a wide balcony through which came the picturesque sight of Creole street life and the sounds of Creole patois. She stayed over an hour, a sign that the Canadians interested her. McLennan was a tall, thin, bewhiskered man, somewhat emaciated by the illness that had brought him south; his wife was contrastingly tiny. Unlike her friend Madame Blanc, McLennan had read most of the historians of Louisiana. As a Canadian he didn't have to be informed about Iberville or Bienville. And he and his wife, on their first visit, took great pleasure in the charms of the old city. They were entertained frequently at dinner at Mrs. King's home, after which they engaged in good talk, with much animation and humor. Many couples and individuals had visited the Kings in the past, but this couple

27. Grace King to May McDowell, July 20, 1898.

was very special, their company always a pleasure. Grace King saw such after-dinner gatherings as among the most satisfactory pleasures of life.[28]

She was happy to accept the invitation of the McLennans to come to Montreal the following summer (1899). Her younger sister Nina, as she put it, "was deputed to accompany me." Traveling with Nina, like living with her, was somewhat trying for the elder sister. They sailed from New Orleans to New York, arriving there early in July, and then continued by train to Montreal, where the splendor of the McLennans' town house and garden so pleased Grace King that she thought they put to shame the estate of the Morrises at Throg's Neck. The library especially attracted her. Here she found many of the source books that she had searched for in Paris. Had she known Montreal and McLennan's library when she was writing *Bienville*, the task would have been an easier one. The tall, cadaverous McLennan himself was as fascinating to her as his books. He was the least boring of men—a man with something of interest on his mind always and a personality interesting in itself. He never seemed to tire of his guests, keeping them up with him in the late hours of evening, insisting on reading some fragment of poetry he wanted to discuss with them. All this was a treat for Grace King, who, prose writer that she was, tended to neglect poetry until someone imbued with it read some to her. So she could escape momentarily from a prosaic world and be reminded of attitudes that the prose writer sometimes forgot. Poetry was also a way of friendship, a pleasure that sometimes bound her to men and convinced her that there was consideration and sensitivity in the male sex when she was inclined to doubt it. So she enjoyed Mark Twain and his readings of Browning, and she had been introduced to the delights of Chaucer by Thomas R. Lounsbury.

As the month of July wore on, the sisters took several trips in the environs of Montreal—a boat trip to the seignory of La Salle, for one, in the little village of Lachine from which he set out to find the Mississippi. From there they took a steamer for an hour's ride down what she was convinced was the most beautiful river in the world.[29]

Because she was so well versed an authority on early Canadian figures herself, this trip was a kind of revelation to her—"more bewilderingly

28. King, *Memories*, 219–23.
29. Grace King to May McDowell, July 24, 1899.

strange to me than even the trip to Europe." After about two weeks with the McLennans she and Nina took the morning boat for an all-day journey to Quebec, where they stayed at the Hotel Frontenac. Here especially Grace King's sense of history came to life in the atmosphere of the old city. And her great preference for the French over the English also took hold of her as she relived the tragedy of Montcalm's defeat. She became as furious about that defeat as if it had happened yesterday. After her visit to the Plains of Abraham she wrote that "they never would have been beaten if Montcalm had stayed inside the walls instead of going out against Wolfe." As she and Nina turned to leave the battlefield, a gun fired from the Citadel at half past nine and the band played first the Canadian anthem and then "God Save the Queen." Grace King's indignation rose as she realized the irony of history: "I do not know which I hated most—the French for giving up this magnificent country—or the English for carpet-bagging it. And to think how easily we in New Orleans whipped a finer and better army with a handful of backwoodsmen & militia."

That night the historical pictures continued to fascinate her as she tried vainly to sleep: "I tossed on the billows of my historical emotions." [30] It is easy to see that a sensitive historian with a New Orleans background would have developed a healthy contempt for British overseas policies. She had once lived very near the site of the Battle of New Orleans. And it is easy to see that she would equate British rule in Quebec with "carpet-bagging," since she had also some knowledge of that. At Beaupré, their next stop, they roomed near the old marble church of St. Anne; there Grace King worked for several weeks in an atmosphere that continued to nourish her historical emotions. "As I am sitting here," she wrote May McDowell, "writing on my lap, the bells from the convent & churches all around are ringing to service. . . . Sometimes I think that it must be a dream—that I shall awake presently & find that I have fallen asleep over Parkman." [31]

The summer had been exhilarating. Her health and vigor and even her confidence in her abilities were restored. It had been years since she had felt so self-confident. She didn't mind being taken for Nina's mother, even though Nina was only nine years her junior. She felt a new vitality that made her hope for a productive winter ahead. In mid-September she and Nina made prepara-

30. Grace King to Sarah Ann King, July 30, 1899.
31. Grace King to May McDowell, September 17, 1899.

tions to return to Quebec, where they would take the train south. Grace King hoped the McLennans might come from Montreal to see them off, confessing to her mother, "I am so mean spirited a woman that I prefer having a man to buy my ticket & check my trunk than not." Nina persisted in saying she gave people trouble, but her rejoinder was usually the same: "I tell her, that from my observation it is only that kind of woman that gets anything out of men." She and Nina had little conversation together for the fun of it; Nina had little sense of humor. Grace on this trip rather longed for her sister Nan, who had been so pleasant a companion during the European trip eight years before:

> I feel with Nina as if she were an English governess & I an unruly, ill-mannered little girl who must be kept severely snubbed. I think she hates to scold and snub so much, but she feels that it is her duty—& she has a despairing hope that I may still turn out to be a prim, well behaved little lady some day. I know that her hope is vain & that on the contrary I am going on doing more & more as I please & what I please & I do not care if my dress does stand open at the back because I forgot to hook the placket or that my wash rag—I beg your pardon—cloth—does get dark because I am not laundress enough to know how to wash & rinse & dry it—etc. etc.[32]

By September 23 there was ice in the morning and a few flakes of snow. The McLennans arrived from Montreal and met the Kings in Quebec to see them off on the three o'clock train. Grace King now believed them to be "the nicest friends I have ever made."[33] William McLennan was a perceptive and humorous man, no doubt, one of the few who left what is perhaps an accurate sketch of the two sides of his friend's complicated character. While her sisters were in Montreal he wrote to Nan, who had remained at home, telling her what a pleasant summer he had had with Grace and Nina:

> It has been a rare treat & I am sure was a most beneficial experience for me in many ways beside the keen pleasure—for me no one cn be dull with Nina about and if anyone cn not be kept from thinking too much of himself & his own condition with such a generous unselfish woman as

32. Grace King to Sarah Ann King, September 14, 1899.
33. Grace King to May McDowell, September 17, 1899.

Grace in the same house, I wd have serious fears that he was in a perilous state. Few good women are selfish I grant you, but she wd rank high amongst the most blessed if unselfishness constitutes degree in the upper circles. She was a great consolation to me also in another particular i.e. my family have been under a delusion that I have prejudices. I have sometimes thought they were possibly right, but now I know I have none. When I sat back in my chair and listened to Grace smiting her pet aversions hip and thigh, I knew what "terrible in battle" meant, and better still I knew what my family chose to style *prejudices* in me were gentle predilections.[34]

Since Grace King's pet historical aversion in Canada was British rule and since McLennan as a graduate of McGill and an established author represented the best of the cultural side of that rule, the two friends must have found considerable grounds for disagreement.

After the parting at Quebec she was not to see McLennan again. He and his wife spent much of the four years left to him in Europe; he died in Vallambrosa in 1904 and was buried in the Protestant Cemetery in Florence. The impact on Grace King of this "tenderest of all our friendships" was the more poignant because it was so brief. They corresponded with some frequency, but their actual association together was only a few weeks in New Orleans and a few weeks in Montreal and the farewell in Quebec. McLennan's sisters found a poem of his among his papers after his death and sent it as a souvenir to Miss King:

> Take heart of Grace! Love never dies—
> Youth wanes, Youth goes. Death's shadows fall
> Yet Love if from the grave he rise
> Shall rise exultant over all!
> Youth cannot hold—nor Beauty stay
> His going, but the faithful heart
> Claims Love, its heritage for aye
> And chooseth this the better part.[35]

---

34. William McLennan to Annie Ragan King, September 10, 1899.
35. King, *Memories*, 232.

She kept the souvenir, and although convinced that it had been written before he had met her, allowed herself to believe it might have reflected his feelings about her.

The sisters traveled south for a brief stop in Boston, in Cambridge calling on John Fiske, and then went on to Hartford to see the Warners—the Clemenses were then in Europe. Susan Warner was still giving her brilliant musicales, performing on the piano as she had in the past. Warner himself was now visibly in decline as a result of his heart condition. Grace King observed "an air of languor" about her friend and "an ominous sign of deadness" in his eyes. She feared that this might be her final visit to the genial bearded man who had responded with such enthusiasm to her writing as well as to herself.

They were met at Grand Central Station by Henry Mills Alden, who took them to Metuchen for a brief visit. Nina then decided to remain on her own in New York while Grace visited her publisher and made plans to return home alone. She rode in an automobile for the first time with Walter Hines Page, who took her to pay a courtesy call on George Brett of the Macmillan Company. This was her first meeting with the publisher who had brought out her *New Orleans, The Place and the People* as well as her *De Soto*. She saw him as a "kindly spirited despot," who frightened her in his grand office.

She spoke enthusiastically of her recent trip to Canada, and he, in the role of kindly despot, asked her what was next on her literary agenda. The too often modest Miss King had no book in mind and told him she believed she had come to the end of her little quiver. She could not have been entirely sincere in this since she had already written her sister May that she hoped the Canadian trip would leave her with a fund of energy and confidence for a productive winter. Her remark was Brett's cue to make a suggestion, which he did, calculating publisher-planner that he was. He told her he wanted a novel, a fiction about the Reconstruction period in the South—an era that had always interested him personally. Here was the publisher and business-man talking to a lady whose very childhood and youth had been marked by the sorrows of Reconstruction. She admitted to him her strong feelings about the period, and this must have encouraged him the more to urge her to write about it. Did he use the word "romance" when he asked her for a novel, meaning that he wanted a story with a soft spot in the center, a place for courtship between an admirable Yankee and a southern lady? With such a formula Thomas Nelson Page had been most successful in 1898 with *Red Rock*. Brett unquestionably had something like that in mind.

But he had no concept of the woman he was talking to, or he might never have started her on the task of writing a novel that would not be finished for years and would not be published until 1916, and then not even by the Macmillan Company. She let him know from the beginning, quite honestly, that Reconstruction to her meant the humiliation of unjustified defeat, the cruelty of an unjust occupation, and the hardships of making a bare living. There was no romance in the subject at all, no softening picture, no love story. Brett heard her out and encouraged her to go ahead with it. "Write as you know it," he said, "your own experience; and send it to us." Grace King could not have known what years of struggle, despair, and waiting lay in his apparently simple demand.[36]

As she had arrived in New York that summer, she set out for New Orleans by sea. She was forty-six years old and in a state of good spirits following an entirely pleasurable and intellectually stimulating summer. For good or ill there was the Brett commission that she would not forget. She was ending a long period in her career. She felt the exhilaration of the blue waters of the Gulf of Mexico, the sight of porpoises and flying gulls. There were new friends to meet on shipboard, and there was the deck, where she could sit and watch the sea in solitude and ponder the little acorn thought the kindly spirited despot of the Macmillan Company had planted in her brain.

36. *Ibid.*, 233–36.

Nine

Deaths in the Family, 1900–1905

The events of the summer of 1899 created in Grace King a brief illusory joy at the end of a decade of hard work and genuine accomplishment in fiction and history. The friendship with William McLennan was precisely the kind that she throve on, good-humored aristocrat and enthusiast for early Canadian history that he was. The tour of Montreal, Quebec, and Ste. Anne de Beaupré had given her the kind of spiritual renovation that she needed. It would seem that she was storing up ideas for another volume of history. But the interview with George C. Brett of the Macmillan Company gave her one of those commissions from publishers she had always taken seriously. Indeed, if Macmillan wanted a novel about Reconstruction, they would have it. Her brain was already teeming with ideas and recollections of the period, and she would begin to plan and research the novel on her return.

At home in the fall, her mood was a positive one: she was ready to play the old housekeeping role with an elderly mother and the other unmarried brother and sisters—Branch, Nan, and Nina. If there were often clashes of personality within the group, there were also joys through moments of amiable companionship. But for all the hopes generated by the summer of

1899, the immediate future, even the far future, held little joy. By the end of the year, when the century had run its course, Grace King's mood had changed from one of hope to one of almost abject despair.

New Year's Day 1900, a cold, dull, gray day, reflected her own inner temperament. She could not arouse any cheerfulness in herself or in those about her in the Prytania Street house. The five Kings were comfortable enough there, but she, and especially Nan, suffered from such domestic worry that the greatest pleasure they could enjoy was the simplest—a sound sleep at night. The family problems were the two youngest members, Will and Nina, both of whom would cause a great deal of tension and irritability within the household. The problem of each would gradually lead to a crisis that would shatter the emotional stability of the family group. Will would not survive his crisis, but Nina would recover from hers and outlive them all.

Grace's youngest brother Will was the handsomest and the tallest of the brothers. As a young man he was remarkably intelligent, but as a student somewhat lacking in the drive to achieve academic success. In boyhood and youth he had been his father's favorite, and as he grew tall and impressive his parents looked upon him as the male hope of the family. His grandmother had spoiled him as a child and perhaps his mother had as well. But for whatever reasons, he had become a heavy drinker by the late 1880s. Could this have been explained by his recognition of his own failure, especially his failure to honor the family name when his elder sister had made within the city a solid reputation as a writer? The Kings, brothers and sisters within a gifted and complicated family, felt strong competition among themselves. For a sister to outshine the males of the family—was that reason to feel discouraged with one's own abilities? Or was the reason for Will's drinking to be found in a family tradition, where the males in Alabama or in New Orleans had a free and easy way with the bottle? It was hardly ladylike to be seen drunk, but it was a thoroughly manly characteristic in the Deep South. The problem with Will was that as he became more hopelessly addicted to alcohol he could no longer hold a job to support his wife and four children. Eventually the family had to depend for help on his wife's family in Bladon Springs, Alabama, or on the Kings in New Orleans.

Mrs. King sympathized with her son throughout his ordeal, realizing that he was ill rather than self-indulgent, and rather than condemn his behavior she gave him money when he needed it. But his brothers and sisters saw Will as having fallen into a state of degradation that disgraced the family reputation. Well known in New Orleans society, they were deeply ashamed of a brother who was known to drink excessively. His mother would never refuse him his room in her house or money from her purse if he needed either, but such an attitude to Grace was pure indulgence, the parent spoiling the wayward child. This conflict of views had vexed the mother-daughter relationship for years. Grace King saw Will's behavior as a detriment to her mother's health since Mimi suffered greatly when Will disappeared for weeks at a time and then reappeared at home to recover from his drinking bouts. On New Year's Day 1900 Will occupied his room in the Prytania Street house—to his sister Grace an unreasonable kind of boarder who constantly put demands on the servants. On that day her mother was constantly waiting on him, looking upon her son not as a wastrel, but as a pitiful cripple who deserved her compassion. Mrs. King would not reproach him, but frequently she scolded Grace and her sisters for daring to berate him, or her other sons for failing to get him a situation.

Grace King pondered the irony that Will was now supported by the family, and his wife and children were staying with relatives. She could feel little sympathy for him because his own attitude was an arrogant one. She belonged to a period that was incapable of understanding the plight of the alcoholic, and she could not see that he was now incurably ill, that his former charm of personality had evaporated in the onrush toward catastrophe.

Mrs. King championed her son as her only response to the deep maternal worry she had for his plight. She and he were isolated within the household— a Hagar with her Ishmael. On that day Grace pondered her mother's elemental female characteristic as "pure unquestioning savage fierce maternal instinct"—an instinct that the younger woman could only know as an observer. Years later she would rethink these matters and see her mother differently, as a person driven by the greatness of her heart in contrast with her eldest daughter, the nonmother, the publishing author, the intellectual, whose behavior was under the firm control of her head. On that New Year's Day she could see only the indulgent mother and the spoiled son: "She would not be actively unkind to us for him. She would not put us out of the house for him. But she would drain us of our last cent. She would crush the life out of us by sheer pressure—day by day with her incessant worries, exactions, fault-finding, sighing & groanings at night—in our hearing—casting up her eyes when in our sight, at mention of Will's name. She would quarrel with the servants & turn them off for him. I think she even takes a pleasure in having him there with her, & would now mourn and grieve if he were to go away—even for his own betterment." The crisis of the problem of Will was to come within the year; all members of the family seemed to sense the foreboding nature both of the illness itself and the quarrels the illness generated within the family circle.

Almost as deep a source of unhappiness was the problem of Nina, who was momentarily expected to return from New York, where she had undergone an extensive physical examination. Nina's psychological problem—a tendency to be abusive and critical of others, especially of her sister Grace—was discovered to be caused by a fibroid tumor. This disease was suffered, possibly as a family inheritance, by May McDowell and Grace herself. The recommended treatment for Nina was surgery, and arrangements would be made for her to go to a sanitarium for an operation when she returned. Grace King dreaded the younger sister's arrival:

> She comes home fulminating anger & hatred against the family, does not wish us to meet her, receive her—no sentiment, nothing but endurance of her presence. Like Will she comes, because she has a right here—and she asks only her right of us with nothing more—gives nothing more. She attributes all of her failure in life to infirm health—all of her infirm health to our neglect of her. Our conduct, our tempers, our manners—our whole life, in short, have been detrimental to her—want of understanding, encouragement, & sympathy have blighted her intellect and killed her affection for us. Me she hates, hates purely and simply (I mean of course in her present mood). For me to sit by, as I have often done, and hear her give her version of my character, is a curious experience. Strange to say, I am to her what I most detest in woman. I listen to her marvelling, as she pours out with all the eloquence of righteous indignation, her earnest & solemn protestation against me and my influence at home. She converts me against myself. I see myself an unconscious Jekyll & Hyde.

Nina's train was already past due, and Grace King dared to hope it might not come until the next day so that the day could be their own.

Will King, youngest of Grace King's brothers, about 1890

Waiting for Nina in this solemn mood, she contemplated the struggles of the family in the past. Their idealism and their poverty had given them a nobility by which they felt exalted above the rich:

> In my childhood there were no set conventionalities of religion, duty—no maxims, no bending & cringing to the world. We had a few inflexible rules. We suffered poverty, hardships, slights. We rubbed against one another in temper. We all had sharp tongues & we were merciless in using them, but we lived on a plain from which we looked down in contempt upon the rich, luxurious world. I fairly despised the gilded domain of society as composed of inferiors. And when I should have felt proud & happy to have received the attentions of a wholesale grocer's clerk, I could not find a man great enough for me.

The heroic thoughts were interrupted. Nina had arrived, looking worn and tired, "rigid with her fixed purpose, on her guard, suspecting us all, with no scintillation of interest in anything we say or do." Some time later that day Grace contemplated the swift passage of time that she could do nothing about. She determined not to care about the past or the question of how much time might be left to her. She would live in the present, knowing that whether it happened to be sorrowful or pleasant, it would soon be a part of the past. She made one final resolution for the new century—

> To work, to endure, both cheerfully. But what is cheerfulness to me seems passiveness, callousness to the others. I must write my novel before this time next year. I have a fine idea before me & I believe I have every good impulse that can warm a woman's heart. If I can put my book, as I feel it, in print, it will be a strong book. Surely I cannot be mistaken in my strength! I have waited for my purpose to ripen. I have waited as I would have waited for the harvest—sure that it must come—making my calculations as to what it would be. The harvest time is here for me—all the harvest time I shall ever know. Let me now gather it.[1]

*

1. Grace King Journal, January 1, 1900; added information from family correspondence in the Grace King Papers, Department of Archives and Manuscripts, Louisiana State University, Baton Rouge. Unless otherwise noted, all manuscript material is in this collection.

The turn of the century brought a series of changes in Grace King's life for which she was not unprepared. In October, 1900, she received word that her old friend Charles Dudley Warner had died suddenly in Hartford. This was the first of a series of losses that were to distress her in the years that followed. The loss of Warner was no surprise; she had seen him during the previous summer and sensed his decline then. They were still good friends, but some of the enthusiasm they had had for each other in 1885 and the years of Grace King's early successes had diminished. Her disapproval of Warner's friend Isa Cabell had left an imprint on her; and on some of his later visits to New Orleans she was inclined to remark how ungenerous the man was: he had lunch and dinner frequently with the Kings, but although he asked Grace to help him shop for gifts for other friends, he rarely brought anything to the King household. Would it be correct to say that he became of diminished use to her as he grew older? And after her first year in Paris, did she feel a superiority to him? Such changes of attitude kept the old friendship from its early heights of mutual admiration and affection.

When a reporter for the *Times-Democrat* appeared at the Prytania Street house and told her the news, she was reported as being appropriately shocked, but she said that she had known that Warner would not live long. On some encouragement from the reporter she gave an interview of some length in which she outlined her long friendship with Warner and acknowledged his great assistance to her not only in getting her first story published, but in opening the door for her at *Harper's Magazine* as well. Probably because she was unprepared for the interview, it contained a few inaccuracies, and when it was published in the *Times-Democrat* she was vexed for having consented to the surprise interview in the first place. She was reported as saying that Warner had been the first to encourage her to write, which was not quite true since she had begun writing fiction after Richard Watson Gilder challenged her to write what she considered to be the truth of the Creole character to correct George W. Cable's interpretation.

Grace King's way of justifying her friendships with Yankees was to become convinced that they were in fact southerners at heart. She was quoted by the reporter for the *Times-Democrat* as saying that she "could never help but regard Mr. Warner as a Southerner. Although he was a Northerner, and a Republican, too, the sympathy of his whole heart was with the South."[2] The truth

2. New Orleans *Times-Democrat*, October 21, 1900.

is that he was a Yankee of Yankees who also happened to be a romanticist. The South delighted him, and his manners and his kindness appealed to southerners; his articles on the South in *Harper's Magazine* were genuinely sympathetic.

Warner had died of a heart attack, according to the account in the newspapers, after he had been seized while on a Sunday walk that took him to that part of Hartford where the black people lived. He had asked for refuge in a Negro woman's house and had died there before his wife could be informed. To Grace King these circumstances were disgraceful. She wrote May Mc-Dowell, "What an ignoble sort òf death it was," adding that their brother Branch said, "Mr Warner was fond of that sort of thing" and that he had nearly died in New Orleans under such circumstances years before. The implication, justifiable or not, was that Warner had not necessarily gone for a walk when he was taken by his fatal heart attack, but that he was in fact visiting the woman whose house he died in.[3]

But Warner was of course dearly loved by his friends, and his death marked the end of Hartford's literary Nook Farm. As a friend, Joseph Twichell called him "one of the very dearest God has given us in life."[4] Warner's neighbor and successor as editor of the Hartford *Courant*, Charles Hopkins Clark, wrote Grace King that "Mr. Clemens came up yesterday to the funeral with Clara, and he looked very natural indeed and was quite his old self. Talking over the changes in Hartford with me he remarked that the Monday Evening Club seemed to be holding their sessions in the cemetery."[5]

For Grace King the death of Warner spelled the end of her association with the friends of Nook Farm. Her friendship with Susan Warner was not the close one she had maintained with Warner himself. The Clemenses were now spending little or no time in Hartford after they had been shattered by the unexpected death of their daughter Susy of meningitis in 1896. Mrs. Clemens lost her very grip on life when Susy died, and in 1899 she had written Grace King an extremely intimate letter, divulging her own despair and telling her that she and Mark Twain could not bring themselves to go back to Hartford, where they had lived the happy and opulent life of the literary

3. Grace King to May McDowell, October 29, 1900.
4. Kenneth R. Andrews, *Nook Farm, Mark Twain's Hartford Circle* (Seattle, 1969), 228.
5. Charles Hopkins Clark to Grace King, October 24, 1900.

Gilded Age. She asked her friend Grace's opinion: should they return to their home in Hartford and try to pick up the pieces of their lives where they had left off before their tragedy? Flattered that she should be asked to help them make such a decision, Grace told Livy that she and Mark Twain should go back to the old house and provide a home again for themselves and for Clara and Jean. She praised the quality of their home life in Hartford in the highest terms: "We all saw your life there—the material luxury—the intellectual atmosphere—the good fellowship with all men—the beautiful devotion of husband and wife—the lovely children—radiant with future promise. . . . I never saw household in which there was a nobler striving towards what we all acknowledge as the best in life."

After a high compliment to Mark Twain and a strong urging to Livy to bring him back to Hartford, the tone of the letter changed from the consolatory to the critical as Grace King volunteered her observations of the Hartford society to which she had been introduced in 1887 and 1888. "I do not conceal from myself," she had written, "a moment—that Hartford is itself to me the most perfect expression of American Philistinism that I ever came across. I thought when I was there among your old friends that I never met more uninteresting people in my life—of a more boring form of uninterestingness." Even Charles Dudley Warner and his wife were now seen as examples of too much success and too much wealth: "Ah my dear! They show me, the want, the actual want of a grief in a loss in their lives. They have grown old in increasing prosperity—they have *succeeded*—and they are typically American in their enjoyment of it. As the children say, they 'show off.' I was carried hither and thither to see a new house here, old furniture there, the progress, the increase of wealth everywhere. But it did not interest me."[6]

The double tone of the letter suggests the ambivalence that Grace King had developed in many of her northern associations. She had great affection for the Clemenses, and Warner had done more for her career than any other person: he had in a way discovered her and had been the first to publicize her among his colleagues and literary friends. But once having suffered heroic poverty as her family had during the lean years of war and Reconstruction,

---

6. Grace King to Olivia Clemens, December 6, 1899, in the Bancroft Library, University of California, Berkeley, quoted in Robert Bush, "Grace King and Mark Twain," *American Literature*, XLIV (March, 1972), 49–50.

she could not then look on a prosperous northern city without a certain disdain. She had sympathy for Livy, a woman of heart who sought comfort from her strong-minded intellectual friend. But Grace King resented Hartford for its display of wealth. The fates had been unkind in choosing the wrong victor; the Yankees of the 1880s seemed to be reaping the economic rewards of what was to her the unjustified victory of 1865. On the other hand, beyond her undeniable bias she had been in a position to observe the Gilded Age in its very capital and in the very homes of the inventors of the name. Since she came from an atmosphere the very opposite of the Gilded Age, who was in a better position to judge Hartford society than she? But she would probably be the first to admit that she exaggerated her case to make her point to Olivia Clemens, who for all her great heart was rather complaisant about wealth. One can well imagine the boring characters among the rich and ostentatious whom Grace King had met in Hartford, but she also met men and women like Isabella Beecher Hooker and Joseph Twichell. Were they examples of the boredom or were they the exceptions? In her comments she wanted to emphasize her objection for the sake of asserting her moral superiority as representative of the South, and for that reason she took in the whole of Hartford as being representative of American Philistinism. Mrs. Clemens did not fully understand what she meant by her comments about Hartford society and said so in a letter that came in response.[7] Grace King was not to see her again: after a long illness she died in Florence on June 5, 1904.

In New Orleans during the first years of the century Grace King continued her scholarship and fiction writing as she had in the past, but publications for a number of years were to be of minor importance. Nothing of consequence was published in 1900; in 1901 only the story "Making Progress" and an article on "The Old Cabildo in New Orleans" appeared, both in *Harper's Magazine*. During these years she worked with some persistence on her novel in progress, which was eventually to be called *The Pleasant Ways of St. Médard*. Her intellectual and social life continued predictably but not with the intensity of earlier years.

Late in October, 1900, Professor Marion Baker of Tulane brought James M. Barrie to meet the Kings. Baker, proud of his city, wanted the visiting

7. Olivia Clemens to Grace King, undated, c. 1899.

celebrity to meet a literary lady who was a member of a hospitable family. Grace King was charmed by the Scotsman, whom she called "the nicest, shyest, most sensitive little piece of genius you ever saw. I liked him immediately. He is such a gentleman—so simple & so sincere. In fact he is through & through the little Minister." It was probably on the following day that Mrs. King, Grace, and Nan called on Mrs. Barrie, the former variety actress, at their hotel. "Well," Grace reported to May McDowell, "she is still perfectly theatrical. She would be common, but she has such a nice, sensible, good, beautiful face. . . . Her manners were very cordial & nice." When Barrie himself appeared, she presented him with a fresh copy of *Balcony Stories* and his friend Robertson Nicholl with her *New Orleans, The Place and the People*. She was quick to see that neither of them had ever heard of her before, and she "thought it only kind to let them know why Marion Baker brought them to call." Barrie's face brightened when she happened to mention George Meredith because she was the first American to discuss him with Barrie, who said he considered Meredith and Thomas Hardy the greatest English novelists. Even in Boston, he told her, neither of his favorites had been appreciated, although very inferior authors were highly admired.[8] The praise of her literary judgement above Boston's doubtless gave her the highest pleasure of the day.

*

A typical day of 1900 would be All Saints' Day or November 1, which was a Sunday. Grace King's historical respect for the memory of the past was such that she loved the first of November, when New Orleans people of all faiths decorate their families' graves with yellow and white chrysanthemums and candles. The ancient cemeteries bloom with bright flowers in the daytime and sparkle with hundreds of candles at night. If it is Catholic and Creole as a custom, it is also peculiarly southern in its unwillingness to let the dead past be forgotten.

The first part of the day was spent visiting the family graves, and it was the women who performed this rite. Mrs. King and her three daughters hired a carriage to take them to Métairie Cemetery, where they spent an appropriate amount of time decorating the graves. Then they proceeded by carriage to

8. Grace King to May McDowell, November 1, 1900.

ancient St. Louis Cemetery in the heart of the old city, where they wound their way through the rows of quaint tombs of plastered brick, finally discovering the tomb of their old friend Judge Gayarré. They had prepared for him a tribute in crossed palm leaves, which they placed where he is interred in the tomb of his grandfather, Étienne de Boré. Deserted, ill-kept, and forlorn, this crumbling tomb was as melancholy as Grace remembered the old judge himself. The four ladies drove home to Prytania Street and set out again, this time to church—Nina and her mother to Christ Church Cathedral on St. Charles Avenue and Nan and Grace to Trinity Church. The King ladies were reared in the Presbyterian faith, but as time passed they were drawn to the more formal liturgy of the Episcopal Church. The sermon that Sunday at Trinity was disappointing, a tame experience after the sensuous beauty of the cemeteries on All Saints' Day.

Coming from church, Grace and Nan met Henry Bristol Orr, professor of biology at Tulane and a particular admirer of Grace. He walked them home, where they had tea. Aglae Delery, Grace's former schoolmate, arrived with a copy of *New Orleans, The Place and the People*, which she asked the author to autograph so that it might be sent to a friend in Philadelphia. Other people dropped in, but the conversation thereafter was small talk.

At dinner Grace's single brother Branch was present but was irritable and worried about the coming election contest between Bryan and McKinley. He was in a mood to quarrel about politics since he favored the Republicans only because, involved in the sugar business, he believed he would fare better under a McKinley administration. Grace, favoring Bryan, did not pick up the quarrel.[9]

As an officer of the Louisiana Historical Society, it fell to her to arrange the details of a reception for the reelected President McKinley in May, 1901, about four months before he was gunned down by an assassin in Buffalo. The reception was held in the old Cabildo on Jackson Square. She had originated the idea of making permanent use of the Cabildo as a museum of Louisiana history because of its architectural interest and especially because it was the scene in 1803 of the transfer of the government of the old territory from France to the United States. As a kind of national announcement of that

9. *Ibid.*

project she had written her article on "The Old Cabildo of New Orleans," which *Harper's Magazine* had published in January, 1901. The preservation of the building was in anticipation of the celebration of the centenary of the Louisiana Purchase.

The McKinley reception was the kind of thing that she and her family knew how to do with proper style. Her role as the woman active in public affairs, anxious that her city put its proper face to the national personage, fitted her well. She directed all of the details of inviting the Louisiana dignitaries, and she decorated the interior of the Cabildo with such elaborate vegetation that one wonders if the details of the building itself were not obscured. She was a woman for whom appearances and correctness of official behavior were paramount. Her own appearance had to be correct as well—a dress of white *point d'esprit* trimmed with lace, black velvet belt and choker, a black hat trimmed with white lace and black and pale blue ribbon.

The reception in its historic setting was almost regal—crowds of people, the Continental Guards lining the stairway, the approach of the presidential party with the governor of the state. Miss King was introduced but was rewarded with only a smile and a handshake from McKinley, whom she later described as "the unhealthiest & unhappiest looking man I ever saw, who nevertheless had an impressive face and fine manner." When Mrs. McKinley failed to show up, the King ladies considered it their duty to leave cards at the St. Charles Hotel, but the first lady was indisposed. Grace King's satisfaction for her part in such a function was evident. Certainly she liked to tire herself out doing such things if she felt demands put on her as an officer of the historical society, and especially as a citizen. The face of the city and the state in the national eye were a part of her own reason for being. And she experienced a certain amount of personal glory when so many people of importance congratulated her on the effect of the reception and on the president's own appreciation of the affair. She could congratulate herself that her taste in arranging the reception was many notches above the more usual New Orleans municipal reception, conceived by vulgar politicians—receptions of which she was mortally ashamed.[10]

*

10. *Ibid.*, May 5, 1901.

The public life was very different from the family's private life. Will King died at the Prytania Street house on July 16, 1901, after returning home in a state of illness the day before. It was a hot, sultry Sunday; Grace had been walking in the garden, looking at the plants that were dusty and drooping in the heat. Mrs. King came to her to talk about Will. She was, as usual, worried about him, afraid he might have had a sunstroke. But to Grace it was the same old weakness, not sunstroke. She was nevertheless somewhat alarmed this time. She wanted to telephone a doctor, but Mrs. King didn't think it necessary; she thought he needed something to calm his nerves. Grace went to Mr. Ammens, the pharmacist, who recommended diacodeine. She came back, gave a dose of it to Will, tried to calm him and said she would come back to give him another dose to help him get a good night's sleep and escape the demons produced by his overexcited brain. She came back at nine o'clock to give him the second dose. He was quiet then, his face very red, but he seemed to have no fever. He was quite himself at the time, and she was for the moment relieved.

In the evening there were sounds of a thunderstorm in the distance. She went about the house closing windows, all but the one in Will's room. She said she would come back and close it when the rain started. After the rain began, Nan came into the house and the women went to bed somewhat early, all of them with some kind of premonition weighing on them. The sultry weather, the coming storm, Will's illness—all these contributed to their depression. Grace went to bed miserable, feeling the need of tears to relieve her anxieties, but no tears came. She could only suffer in a dry, hard, silent way.

A loud clap of thunder with fearful lightning aroused them all from their beds. Grace ran to Will's room, but her mother was there before her, hurrying along the gallery, open to the rain, in her night clothes. She said Will was sleeping soundly. She had spoken to him, but he had not answered. She shut the window in his room. Grace told her she should not have exposed herself like that. Years later when she pondered the details of what happened that night, she wondered if it wouldn't have been better if her mother had trusted her more, confided in her more, and let her take over some of the care of Will; but she had hesitated to go too far, knowing that Mimi might suspect she was being supplanted. The household arrangements were largely taken over by the daughters as it was, and Mimi held on to the responsibility of Will, almost jealously.

There was little sleep for any of them that night. Grace was up by five o'clock; she made the coffee and then went to have her bath. Mimi was up early too, going, as she was accustomed, to Will's room. He wasn't in his bed, and the door of the adjoining water closet was bolted. She returned to her room and then came back a few minutes later, expecting to find him in his bed, but he still wasn't there. When she knocked on the closet door there was no answer. "Answer me, Will!" she said forcefully, but there was still no answer. Mimi then became frantic; she beat on the door with a wild energy. She called to Nan, who would never forget the terrible fear in her mother's face as she stood there beating on the door and calling on Will to open it.

When Nan called to Grace she joined them and in a loud voice ordered him to open the door at once or she would have it broken down. She was vexed at the moment, remembering the toll of this family problem on her mother's health. She was then determined that Will should go away, that he must not stay in the house to torment his mother in this way. Their brother Branch was away at the time, but when he returned she would tell him that Will should not stay there; it was too much for Mimi to endure. It seemed to Grace an age, although it was no more than five minutes from the time her mother began beating on the closet door until Nan had summoned Mr. Ammens the pharmacist, their neighbor. Mimi went out on the gallery and called for a policeman. By that time the women were the more fearful when the scent of gas came from under the door of the closet. The druggist and a watchman hurried upstairs, and with a hammer and the full strength of them both, they broke down the door.

"My God! he's dead," said the druggist.

Grace took her mother into Branch's bedroom and begged her to stay there with Nan; she watched as the two men brought Will's body from the closet, his legs and arms stiffly drawn up, his mouth open. She kept Mimi from the ghastly sight, then called Dr. Parham, who came and took charge of the distraught household. The men carried the stone-cold body into one of the bedrooms. Grace felt the stiffness of his arms as they tried to fold them down, and she bound a handkerchief around his face.

When the sisters began to discuss the death with Dr. Parham, they at first assumed that it was premeditated, a tragic suicide. Then as they pieced together the evidence they started to doubt such an explanation. Will had been dead at least four hours, possibly six or seven, but he had not closed the window himself when the rain came. Grace found a half-burned match on the floor, which might have been used to light the gas. Had he tried to light the gas and failed? There was only one small burner in the water closet. How could he have been asphyxiated by that? She concluded that Will had been overcome by weakness in the closet, dropped the match, and failed to light the burner. Overcome by gas, he had lain on the floor. Since he had been taking sulfonal as medication, which may have left him somewhat stupefied, he might have imagined that he was lying in bed. So Grace became convinced that it was not suicide, although Nina wrote in her diary that she believed it was.[11]

That night was a sleepless one for Grace, haunted as she was by the vision of Will being carried by the two men into the bedroom. After such an experience, she went over in her own mind, and later with Mimi and her sisters, each detail of the harrowing night. Unable to sleep, she jumped from bed and went to the gallery to watch the horsecars go by. Again at midnight she tried to sleep and, failing again, fled the darkness of her bedroom and sat until four o'clock on the doorsill leading into the back gallery, where she could hear the voices of Will's three male friends who were keeping vigil downstairs. During the day that passed before the funeral she spent much time sitting with her dead brother. Now it made her almost happy to sit by him, to look at his face, and to realize that the black horror that had enveloped him for as much as fifteen years had at last fallen away forever.

In the darkness before going to bed that night, she stumbled into Will's room, feeling like Dr. Johnson doing penance at Lichfield. This middle-aged, childless, unmarried woman, who so strongly wanted to see the King family restored to its original strength, felt deeply the failure here, where the male hope of the family lay on his bier. Now that the years of Will's torment were over and she could see him only as a handsomely dressed, gentlemanly corpse, she felt the pathos of his life, how he had made good resolutions to conquer his demon. She could not believe that she had ever been unkind or ungentle to him.

Will's funeral was held at 8:30 on Tuesday morning. The weather had changed from the sultriness of Sunday to a welcome coolness. She had never

11. *Ibid.*, July 17, 1901, and July 19, 1901.

seen Métairie Cemetery so beautiful; the rains had brightened and freshened the vegetation, and a mockingbird sang throughout the graveside service. Her mother stood silent and almost alone, her black veil thrown back, her hands clasped, tears running down her face. She looked calm, but Grace sensed that she had received her own death blow. "Like Mimi," she recalled a few years later, "we had each received a blow; it was not our death blow, but it mutilated life; it devastated our memory. We cannot look back without traversing a ruined space, haunted by hopeless despair."

The thought of Will's tragic death haunted her for years to come. An inveterate observer of yearly memorials, she found herself on later Julys reviewing the details of his death again and again:

The pity of it is we could only suffer & feel all the degradation & humility of his tragedy without doing any good. I would have gladly given my life to have saved his. I gave him indeed much of it—all the capacity I had for hope & pleasure—it seemed to me Will made me old. The trials & sorrows of home before that made me feel old, but Will literally made me old. Oh! the depths & the heights of life, the lights & shadows. How can one think of self instead of life? I feel every day more & more the immensity, the grandeur, the solemnity of it.[12]

In September her melancholy returned when she heard that her friend George C. Préot was dying. She now thought of him as "the truest, and the most unselfish friend I ever had." He had been her "mentor" when her first volumes of fiction were being written. His influence had been less conspicuous through the 1890s, but she met him occasionally—the last time on Canal Street on her way to a meeting of the historical society at Tulane. He told her she had grown much pleasanter and "more agreeable"; she had lost the nervousness, the striving of the years when she was grasping for recognition. He believed she had been unhappy then and not at peace with herself. But she answered him with the resignation she felt in 1901. "I told him," she wrote, "that I was happier, since I had got rid of all my hopes and had my future behind me—that I strive no more, for there was nothing now that could give me the pleasure." He took on some of the sadness she herself seemed to

---

12. Grace King's memorial journal, January 17, 1904, to January 29, 1905.

express and remarked that her most recent story ("Making Progress") was too sad. Why didn't she write more cheerful stories? She answered that she could only write of life as she knew it. She believed that "He was the only one who ever helped me in my writing—He was the first one who thought I could write." He had encouraged her to write for publication and had frequently sent her books of French literature to be used as models. The world felt empty of friends when he died, and she compared him with others who were not friends: "He alone was unselfish and disinterested."[13]

It was probably in November, 1901, when she reached the age of forty-nine, that she wrote May, "Birthdays come now to me with increasing forceful admonition to enjoy all the pretty things I have & get the most out of time. There is no use waiting for any more future—preparations are all done & over—the future has come, and if this present is the thing for which my whole past has been a preparation, then I had better take what I can get. It is true I feel sometimes as if I had taken a train to Europe and been shunted off at Osyka, but if Osyka is my destiny, I shall make my destiny Osyka."[14]

As 1901 came to an end the somber mood continued. Sitting comfortably by a fire burning in a little stove in her study, she was reading *War and Peace* again, hoping its vitality would revive in her some of the lost creative spirit. But it was Sunday and her thoughts were of her brother Will, whose death she knew would leave "a black mark all through our lives."[15]

Between the dates of the death of Will King in July, 1901, and that of her mother in December, 1903, Grace King produced seven relatively short works and she continued to write her novel for Macmillan. It is doubtful that the death of Will, for all the sorrow and stress, caused a serious diminishment of her energies. Although she was emotionally exhausted after his death, she was also relieved of the tension that distressed her during Will's final years. The seven works are all essays, indicating that she had almost ceased to write short stories.

13. Grace King Journal, September 22, 1901, quoted in Robert Bush (ed.), *Grace King of New Orleans* (Baton Rouge, 1973), 386.

14. Grace King to May McDowell, undated, c. November, 1901. Osyka is the small railroad station near the Mississippi border where Grace King got off on her visits to Charles Gayarré's country home.

15. Grace King to May McDowell, December 29, 1901.

"Fort Louis of Mobile: A Commemoration" appeared in *Outlook* in February, 1902. On January 23, 1902, Grace King had been invited to attend the bicentennial ceremony marking Bienville's moving of the first settlement on the Gulf Coast at Biloxi to Fort Louis of Mobile on the Mobile River and near the present city of Mobile, Alabama. The establishment of the fort, surrounded by protective squared log walls, constituted the first capital of the territory of Louisiana. The account of the ceremony is brief, but it is a superb example of how the born historian can resuscitate or resurrect the past and make it live in the imagination of the people of the present. She traveled with a large party aboard a revenue cutter up the Mobile River to the abandoned site of the eighteenth-century fort. Her description of the river, the people, and the surrounding natural world suggests in reverse the idea of Walt Whitman's "Crossing Brooklyn Ferry." Whitman looked forward to the people of the future who would cross from Brooklyn to Manhattan; Grace King looks back to the many loaded boats of Bienville, the soldiers, the priests, the Indians. Both authors feel sure that distance and time avail not. On the cutter, Grace King thinks of the bright blue January day and the dazzling sun as the same kind of day that flourished two hundred years before:

> The sun surely glistened on the water ahead of their prow as it did ahead of ours; the blue sky was as smiling and tender over them as over us. They passed through the same banks, the same trees, on one side and on the other; the same bayous poured their same floods through mouths fringed with grasses; that shallow marshy nook in the curve was there then as now, its tall reeds dry and golden in the sun and quivering in the fresh north breeze; their eyes noted the same patch of palmetto, the same cypress with their buttressed trunks standing in the same stretch of swamp; their boats went around the island in the river, as we did; they passed the first bluff and began to look for the second, as we did; hailed it when it came in sight, landed and climbed to the top, as we did, and stood upon a small tableland overlooking the river, covered with virginal forest.[16]

16. Grace King, "Fort Louis of Mobile: A Commemoration," *Outlook*, LXX (February 15, 1902), 433.

She described the little ceremony and compared the assembled crowd with those who were there two hundred years before. Then she remarked sadly that no vestige of the old fort was left, only the place where the plough had prepared a cotton field.

Also in 1902 Hamilton Mabie asked her for a brief article for *Outlook* on "The characteristic elements that American literature has contributed to the literature of the world." He wanted her to name in one of a series of articles he was publishing "ten books that are most characteristic of American genius and life, literature that could not have been written on any but American soil." Her answer tells us a good deal about her judgment of the national literature at the time. She begins by discounting the circumstance of birth in a particular place—something surprising from one of the more significant local colorists of the 1880s: "State and sectional demarcations seem very futile when applied to the republic of letters; in it a birthplace is of smallest consequence, as we know. A small jar, indeed, in which to hold a genius."

In putting together her genuine American list she starts with three historians for whom she had high respect—John Fiske, Francis Parkman, and Alfred Thayer Mahan, who "have contributed to the literature of the world histories that are characteristic of American genius and life." She then lists three poets—Poe, Longfellow, and Lanier—and to this group adds the authors of fiction—Cooper, Hawthorne, Mark Twain, and Joel Chandler Harris. She asserts that Twain and Harris have "contributed to the literature of the world new, original, and characteristic elements of American genius"; then she points out that "what they wrote could not have been produced on any but American soul." Her choice of the Georgian Sidney Lanier was made not solely out of sectional loyalty. She had early recognized his unique originality as a poet and as a theorizer about poetry. And her recognition of Mark Twain as a major American writer was hardly because he was her friend. She saw well beyond the popular conception of Mark Twain, who was not always accepted as a major writer in his own lifetime.[17]

In the first half of 1903 she published two short, minor works in the *Youth's Companion*—"The Flitting of Sister," a short story, and "New Orleans One

---

17. Grace King, "A Southern View," *Outlook*, LXXII (December 6, 1902), 786–87.

Hundred Years Ago," an account of the bright social life of the city at the time of the Louisiana Purchase. Also in 1903 appeared two relatively long biographical sketches that would serve as introductions. One was an account of the life and work of Prosper Mérimée in an anthology of his fiction translated by G. B. Ives.

For the new edition of Charles Gayarré's *History of Louisiana* Grace King wrote a long introduction, the longest account of Gayarré's life and work she was to produce. The work is a good beginning for a full biography, and it is a pity that she did not go on to complete a book about the man she knew so well. There is much to praise about the thirty-two pages of this introduction as an accurate account of the career of the major Creole scholar of his time; certain flaws of omission might also be charged against her.

On the good side, she sketches Gayarré's early history at the beginning of the century with skill and authority and continues throughout his productive career until the point of his triumph, the publication of his *History of Louisiana* (1851–1866). How beautifully she is able to reconstruct the life of the young Gayarré when he sat on the lap of Andrew Jackson in the plantation home of his maternal grandfather Étienne de Boré. And the information about that early career she got only in part from reading the historian's memoirs; most of it has the vitality of having been heard from the man himself. She is unusually honest in her treatment of the controversial point that the early Gayarré volumes are history spiked with fiction, almost comparable to the novels of Walter Scott. Gayarré himself had confessed "to an humble imitation of Sir Walter Scott, in this use of imagination as a bait to lure readers into knowledge of history." The wise Grace King comments, "Time abounds with such attempts, and the knowledge of history has lost, rather than gained from the concession of gilded facts to readers, these proving generally the most annoying errors to get rid of afterwards."

Then she proceeds to defend Gayarré's first volume *The Poetry of Romance of the History of Louisiana* (1848), believing that much good was achieved in the work. It is to her "the portal through which most readers enter the history of Louisiana." Like Gayarré she believed that in the history of the great territory "the things of the heart become confused with the things of the mind" and "there is not only a popular but a true poetic sentiment for it. . . . To withdraw its contributions . . . from the fiction and drama of the country since its publication, would produce indeed something like a collapse in our native pseudo-historical literature."[18]

In writing of his account of "New Orleans Bench and Bar of 1823" she points out that Gayarré is "the only one who has left a description of the men of that time that possesses the living quality of true history, the quality of transmitting the enthusiasm felt in one century to another; and . . . there is no test whose application so easily distinguishes the born from the self-made historian, as this one of the quality and vitality of the impressions he receives through life and the power of such impressions to evoke the enthusiasm of later and successive generations."[19] Having written a series of histories herself in the ten years that had just passed, Grace King showed that she had put a great deal of thought into what constituted the essential function of the historian. And through this statement we can conclude that she considered herself, as she considered Gayarré, a born historian.

In so brief an account of Gayarré's life as this we cannot expect a full portrait, and we hardly get one. Factually it is superb and well documented, answering our questions about a brilliant career that spanned most of the nineteenth century and touched the South, the national government, Philadelphia law study, and Paris from 1835 to 1843. Gayarré, who practiced law and wrote both history and fiction, was well known before the Civil War but, because of that conflict, became nationally forgotten. The missing element is the human quality. We never learn quite what kind of person Gayarré was from Grace King's account here, although she would be more personal about him in her memoirs, still many years in the future. There were matters, of course, that she was hardly aware of—Gayarré's fathering a son by a black woman in his youth, for example. This piece of information does humanize him, and the fact that he gave the son his own name is indeed admirable on the part of an upper-class Louisianian of antebellum times.[20] Grace King gives us the pathetic story of Gayarré's later years, when he was impoverished and

---

18. Grace King, "Charles Gayarré," introduction to Charles Gayarré, *History of Louisiana* (New Orleans, 1903), xix.

19. *Ibid.*, xiii.

20. Earl Noland Saucier, "Charles Gayarré, The Creole Historian" (Ph.D. dissertation, George Peabody College for Teachers, 1933), 43–44.

unable to win posts that he deserved, but here she is more than kind to the aging intellectual. She never breathes a word of his self-pity or his harebrained schemes to regain his lost wealth, schemes that tended to make her bored with him in later years. Of course she would not mention the pettiness of the quarrel that alienated them in his later years.

*

During the early years of the century the public image of Grace King as intellectual southern woman had not diminished, even if her literary production had begun to. Edwin Anderson Alderman (1861–1931) had become president of Tulane University in 1900. His appointment had signaled a rise in the national prestige of the university that was the intellectual center of New Orleans and the deep South. Alderman was a North Carolinian with a very liberal interpretation of the South. He became a friend of Grace King's and recognized her as a woman whose views on the region were important. When he was asked to deliver the commemoration day address at Johns Hopkins on February 23, 1903, he decided to write to over twenty important intellectuals in the country and ask them to contribute ideas on the South for his speech. Grace King was on the list of prestigious names whose opinions he asked. Others were Woodrow Wilson, Henry Adams, Frederick Jackson Turner, and Ellen Glasgow. He wanted to know the "contributions made by southern stock and southern civilization to our American character" and asked each of his correspondents to choose six or seven men who "typify the essential character contributions of the Southern states to the national life."

Grace King's answer to her friend was predictable, and it provides us with one of the more formal statements she made on a subject she felt most keenly about—the southern character. First she singled out individuality. The South had created, she wrote, "a standard of easy and luxurious living" that was the pattern of such refinement of social style throughout the country. She believed that if the southern influence were withdrawn, so much individuality would be lost that "we would see only business corporations and associations left." She was probably wrong about the first point. The isolation of the South in the antebellum period made its influence on social character in the country at large very slight. Where there was wealth in the United States the model for behavior was much more likely to be English or French.

She was on safer ground when she discussed individuality and the tendency of the southerner to avoid the reputation of being wealthy:

> The Southern man has begotten in the country a confidence in self as self, independent of any extraneous acquisitions. He stands for self against theories. I would venture to say that "I" and "We" are used a hundred times in the South—to once in the North. It is their own self esteem that makes Southerners careless of appearance. They would spend a million on any or every extravagance—but not a cent for the reputation of being wealthy.

When she came to list the southerners who typified the essential character contributions to the national life, she cited George Washington, Thomas Jefferson, John Marshall, Robert E. Lee, Sidney Lanier, Edgar Allan Poe, Zebulon Baird Vance, Ben Hill, L. Q. C. Lamar, Wade Hampton, Benjamin Tillman, Henry Clay, John Randolph, John C. Calhoun, and Andrew Jackson. Her concluding point indicates her own polarized notion of the national character: "Would it sound too aphoristic to say that if it were not for the South—the term gentleman and lady would fall out of our vocabulary, which would contain only man and woman—or that the South has prevented us from being a nation of Yankees, that the South stands out for the heroic against the successful?"[21]

Even if the statement was intentional exaggeration, it is quite true that outside the South today the words "lady" and "gentleman" are used hesitatingly as being elitist or even undemocratic. Grace King was somewhat prophetic here. The South itself had resisted becoming "a nation of Yankees" in her time, but she would no doubt agree that the southern centers of prosperity and progress in the latter part of this century—Atlanta, Birmingham, New Orleans, and Houston—have much of what she would call Yankee character about them.

*

On December 5, 1903, Sarah Ann King died in the Prytania Street house. Her death at the age of eighty-two held profound significance for her children

---

21. Grace King to Edwin Anderson Alderman, February 11, 1903, in Bush (ed.), *Grace King of New Orleans*, 386–88.

Sarah Ann Miller King, Grace King's mother, about 1895

Department of Archives and Manuscripts, Louisiana State University,
courtesy of John M. Coxe

because it had no doubt been hastened by the tragedy of their brother Will and also because the family saw itself as archetypal and heroic. Both Grace and Nina remembered and recorded the deathbed scene as a moment of high sentiment and even sanctity with overtones of Will's death still fresh in their memories. On the last day, when Mrs. King was given her medicine for the last time, her children drew around the bed and drank a solemn toast to her. She then asked for her music box, on which were played "Don't You Remember Sweet Alice, Ben Bolt?" and "The Last Rose of Summer." Details were recorded in the sisters' journals as if a woman of the highest importance had died.[22]

The event was the emotional crisis of Grace King's life. The grief she was to suffer was like no other she had known or would know. For well over a year it overwhelmed her and sapped her creative energy. Her suffering and her response to it were far more intense than most middle-aged daughters would show for their aged mothers. In part this is to be explained by the strong emotion she held for members of her own family, who had lived as a closely knit group through many years of struggle. She may also have suffered guilt: as much as she cared for her mother during her lifetime, the two women were quite different personalities whose attitudes on family matters had sometimes been at variance. Grace and her sister Nan observed mourning customs in the tradition of nineteenth-century Victorian sentiment, in a pattern long since established by the queen herself. From the attitudes of our own times we would say they nursed their grief and refused to let it die its own natural death.

Grace King entered a long period of despondency, during which she and Nan paid homage to their mother by weekly visits to Métairie Cemetery on Saturdays when the weather permitted it. The ride by streetcar was a long one; the sisters carried bouquets of flowers to decorate the grave, and they customarily sat and meditated or talked about their mother for some time before they left for home. Once home, Grace recorded each visit meticulously in a notebook, which she kept for the year beginning January 17, 1904, and ending January 29, 1905. The untitled work—a "Memorial Journal"—was written for personal reasons only, but in addition to being an invaluable

22. Grace King's Journal, December 12, 1903, and December 12, 1904; Nina Ansley King's Journal (1902–1904), December 4 and 5, 1903.

source of information about the character and inner feelings of the author and her interpretations of other members of her family, it has aesthetic qualities that make it quite unique. Her memoirs were to devote no more than a sentence to her mother's death, but the "Memorial Journal" reveals the profound effect of the event on her life. Its sustained tone of sorrow and grief and its probing of the meaning of life makes it comparable to Tennyson's *In Memoriam*, except that it is written in a spontaneous lyric prose produced always by the feeling of the moment. It reads like an extended prose elegy, the variety provided by the difference between one visit to the grave and the next, according to the weather, the birds, the flowers, or the conversation of the two sisters.

In her journal Grace King also included her private meditations and recollections in which her memory travels back to the days of L'Embarras Plantation, the privations of Delery and Erato streets, and the deaths of other members of the family. As she meditates upon all of these events she implies an attitude toward life that combines exaltation and despair. The nobility of life's drives are countered by the certainty of disappointment and the despondency associated with death. Mimi herself becomes exalted in her daughter's eyes to a point of veneration. The details of her daily life as they are remembered take on sacred significance and objects associated with her assume the dignity of relics: "Her little cheap trunk that she bought to go to Blowing Rock we opened as we open a chapel door." To Grace the most poignant of the details is the cup of coffee her mother brought her early in the morning. This was a small gesture that Mimi kept up as long as she was able; in the journal her daughter writes, "I make the coffee for myself now, & drink it, always with a sacramental feeling of remembrance."

In July of 1904 the suffering continued without change. Grace King spent a brief vacation with May McDowell at Crockett Springs, Virginia, in a small hotel, where the noisy activities of indifferent patrons were in ironic contrast to her interior suffering:

A wearying depressing day—the small hotel life, the meeting and talking with strangers & the tiresome hotel meals—the long stupid hours together. . . . & underneath it all clear & strong the day that I bear in my heart, the memories, the love, the longing & the wild despair that ebbs &

flows all through me. If I did not call to her, talk to her, if I did not feel her talking to me, helping me, I could not stand it. . . . Only the bare sad fact of grief, none of its beauties, heroisms calls to the heart, noble memories, inspiring thoughts, only the bare hard fact remains, rubbing into one, a secret hair cloth that mocks at all outward gladness. . . . This dreadful life, these dreadful people. Perhaps away from them in some future place of quiet & solitude I may find myself & the dear shades who accompany me through my days. I know they will be there, though I do not see them any more—or even feel them near. . . . Hell has no more painful torment than the deprivation of sight into & feeling of the higher atmosphere of sorrow in life.[23]

On a Sunday evening she attended service. Hymns were sung; then unexpectedly the sermon touched her. The Methodist minister, preaching on the text "For we are labourers together with God," raised her spirits because she could relate the idea to her mother's active life on behalf of others. She could not remember her mother idle; she saw her as one of the "Angels of God."

On another day she continued her meditation on the idea, conceiving of herself as only a part of the family whole—a part somewhat useless individually: "When one lives in such a broken world of thought, such as it is, bears the image or reflects the pure colour of her life, I seem indeed at times myself but a fragment broken out of her life, ugly & useless without the other fragments of the family, which pressed & formed all together should make such a fair mirror to show forth her face & heart."

This idealization of Mimi brought with it a debasement of herself and her brothers and sisters as lesser individuals than their parents. She became convinced that all of her ambition in life had come from her mother: "I know that I made no effort in life save what sprang from love of her. She must have known of my devotion, but what a poor demonstration I made of it! No, I cannot say that truthfully. Apart from some moments of impatience & fiery outbursts of temper, I did my best for her & for her alone—a poor awkward & shamefaced best."

It had been customary for her to attribute her accomplishment to her

23. Grace King's Memorial Journal, January 17, 1904, to January 29, 1905.

parents. She now meditated on the old head and heart question. Had she erred in following too much her father's intellectual bent rather than the more compassionate nature of her mother?

> Why did I want to work to accomplish anything? The barest and clearest truth that I see in my being—the one clear & undeniable fact in my life was my motive to work. It was to honour my father & mother—to show the world what their child could accomplish—to make demonstration of their values, their holy & divine parental love as I saw it & felt it. I had no thought of self as I have none now. But maybe it would have been better not to have striven for an intellectual demonstration. Ah! my father prized the intellect above the heart & my mother, all heart as she was, was proud of his intellect—so strangely unknown of the world.

She recorded the frequent dreams she had of her mother, in one of which she saw her venerated as a saint:

> She lay prepared for burial all in white with flowers over & about her, but death had had no power over her flesh. She was still in living warmth & suppleness & we lay by her & handled her & caressed her. She was dead but still a part of us. I said to myself in thought, "This is what is called a miracle. This is what happened to the old saints. It was her love that has preserved her." She was a saint, but how human & natural she was with us. But that is the way of saints. It is not their religion that made them saints, but their love & when I awoke I was struggling with the question—"Will she always remain thus with us? Shall we never have to give her up to the tomb?"

A few months later she was pondering the origin of her own religion and fantasized about a new one with motherhood at the center:

> I can imagine certain people transfering all this from their own to God the Saviour, the saints, the Virgin Mary. But who that has had a good mother, a self-sacrificing devoted mother, needs a Virgin Mary in their lives. God! yes, the Saviour! yes. They represent what the earthly father cannot—he would be God & Saviour to his children if he could answer their prayers, lay down his life for them. A child who has had a noble-minded father, a

1749 Coliseum Street, New Orleans, Grace King's home from 1904 to 1932,
photographed by David C. Coxe

hardworking father, can understand God & the Saviour through him. When I was a small child I had no doubt but that my father was worthy to be God if he could be God, but what can the idea of the Virgin Mary add to the idea of one's own mother? The Virgin Mary is the conception of a sensually minded man. No daughter could have conceived such a cult or a son who had had a good true mother. It is the counterpart of the disease in women who represent the Saviour as their heavenly bridegroom.[24]

The Kings frequently moved at times of family crisis or death. After the death of William Woodson King in 1881 they had moved from Terpsichore Street to South Rampart Street. Now after the death of the mother they left the large and stately Prytania Street house, which they had rented since 1896, for the first house they were to own since before the war. Branch King bought the Bradford House on Coliseum Street for $11,500 and deeded it to his three unmarried sisters. The house was less pretentious than the one they were leaving. Appropriately antebellum in style, it was a Greek Revival house near the street with Ionic and Corinthian orders for the front portico and the gallery, a brick house plastered with stucco. They entered through an iron gate from the street to a narrow hall; on the left was a double parlor with high ceilings, carved Corinthian columns, two mantels of tan and black marble. The windows were high, and the rooms when furnished were ablaze with crystal chandeliers and sconces. From a hallway behind the parlors they stepped into the garden, a feature that seems to have been always a part of the King homes, even in their poorest days.

Mrs. King had known of the probable purchase of the house on Coliseum Street; the grieving family took it over after her death when it seemed to Grace almost impossible to continue living in the house so closely associated with her. So Grace imagined that they brought their mother's love and spirit with them when they moved to the new house. She later realized that her brother Branch had indeed bought the house as a memorial to his mother, although he had never put it in words. He transferred the property to his three unmarried sisters as a way of assuring their security for life. The actual closing that took place in a lawyer's office in July, 1904, took on supreme

24. *Ibid.*

significance for Grace King; it was a King ceremony rather than a legal transaction:

> We went to the lawyer's office to accept the transfer of the house made by Branch to Nan, Nina & me, an act to me it was of solemn significance—the great landmark of our lives—the attainment of what our father worked so nobly for, the hope & prayer of Mimi—a permanent home for the family. What a track of life behind us since the day that the family quitted their home under the compulsion of Butler's orders, leaving their furniture—pictures, souvenirs, behind them. How we have struggled & worked, fallen down, gotten up again, to toil on, striving with others, striving with the villainous temper of one another, suffering what anguish of mind & heart, in the midnight hours of wakefulness, in consequence thereof—the home, we are where we were forty years ago! at the point from which the war drove us back.[25]

Branch King had not included himself as one of the owners of the house probably because of his thoughtfulness and generosity toward his sisters. He had not married and so had no plans for establishing a family. He had often been unwell since childhood, and he may have had some premonition about the brevity of his own life. His death of pneumonia on October 22, 1905, was a final blow to Grace King and her sisters in the series of personal tragedies that afflicted them since the turn of the century.[26]

Grace King seems not to have taken into account the fact that it was a middle-aged bachelor who had bought the Coliseum Street house for his three middle-aged maiden sisters. The very circumstance suggests the end of the family, although their brother Fred had sons and Will had left four children. It was an irony all too clear to Grace that the house itself was left without a head. She and Nan and Nina became more than grief-stricken after Branch's death since they were quite unprepared for it. They were now demoralized and frightened for their future.[27] The great family plan had been achieved after forty years of labor and waiting; now the very props were pulled from under its structure and the future held little hope.

25. Grace King Notebook, November 17, 1904, in Bush (ed.), *Grace King of New Orleans*, 6–7.
26. New Orleans *Times-Picayune*, October 23, 1905.
27. King, *Memories*, 237.

Three weeks after Branch's death Grace King described her state of emotional exhaustion, using not so much the idea that no man is an island as the idea that no one within a family is an island. We also die when a close member of our family dies:

> In a family we die with each one that dies & we bury with our loved ones so much of our own life that it seems to me in reality that it is we who die. There is hardly enough substance left to give it shape & form. But Branch drew not only from my heart, but from my strength. I am not only miserable but so weak, so depleted of vitality that I would not wonder if someone told me I was dying. People wasting away with disease must feel as I do, wasting away—from loss of heart. My heart has been amputated of two vital members. How can it live on?[28]

A week later she recalled her favorite brother coming into the house with baskets of fish he had caught. She missed the sound of his latchkey now. Within herself welled a protest, an outrage against his sudden loss: "I protest against the sudden deprivation of love, the slow storing of which in my heart during a lifetime had become a vital function." The month of December arrived and she was still pondering her loss: "How quickly & easily he slipped out of life! Just one week in October—it seemed as if he had come home only to meet that appointment with death, that I came back in August to get the house ready for it. Would it have been different had he stayed away longer? Could we have coaxed Death away, have wrestled one more respite from him?"[29]

On Christmas day, 1905, Grace and Nan had their coffee before dawn. From the gallery overlooking Coliseum Square they watched a red streak in the east grow wider. As the colors grew brighter and more distinct, the scene before them seemed like a pretty Christmas card: the trees in the square, the grass covered with white frost, a plume of black smoke rising from the river beyond the picturesque roofs of houses. But as bells began to ring from nearby churches proclaiming the joy of the day, the sounds and sights of Christmas became painfully ironic for them. Their only satisfaction was their trip to Métairie Cemetery later in the day and the bearing of bouquets of chrysanthe-

28. Grace King Journal, 1904–1906, November 14, 1905.
29. *Ibid.*, December 3, 1905.

The three King sisters, dressed in mourning about 1905: (left to right) Annie
(Nan), Nina, and Grace

mums and palms from their garden to decorate the graves of their dead. The sky was a serene blue as they walked about in the cemetery, arranging the flowers. They came away desolate and sad, as if they were the dead ones; and Christmas dinner was an ordeal in which the very food choked in their throats as tears were ready to roll from their eyes.[30]

In times of trouble the King family was always ready for a radical change. When the city fell in 1862 they moved to L'Embarras Plantation. After the death of each of the parents the family moved to a different house to escape painful associations. But now there was no question of losing the first house they had owned since before the war. The one way open to them was a trip to Europe. By Christmas, 1905, this was planned as their attempt to escape from the pains of grief. At Métairie Cemetery they had discussed it in the presence of their dead. It was the note of hope that would assure the continuity of their lives.

30. *Ibid.*, December 25, 1905.

Ten

The Second European Trip, 1906–1908

G race King would devote four chapters of her *Memories of a Southern Woman of Letters* to the events of her second visit to Europe. Such trips provided a great amount of variety to the story of her life, breaking up the account of routine activities in New Orleans. But it is also true that she valued her first two sojourns in Europe as among the most significant periods of her life. Many of the intellectual people whom she was close to on these visits are forgotten today, but her experiences provide us with a valuable picture of an intellectual southern woman in Europe during the late Victorian and Edwardian periods.

The immediate reasons for going to Europe in 1906 were emotional and economic. For all her mental strength and her ability to hold her own in a man's world, she seems to have needed the support of a brother in her household, and once the most responsible of her brothers was gone, she was left with little moral support within the family. Nan, who frequently echoed the emotional nature of her sister Grace, responded similarly and was ready for some radical departure from the home base. Nina, who was to be included, had wanted to have her first trip to Europe alone but willingly went along with her sisters' plans. They arranged to rent the Coliseum Street house for a year, expecting that the rental income of at least $1,000 would be the basis of support for their expenses in Europe.

In deep mourning for Branch, the three sisters sailed from New Orleans on the cotton freighter *Antietam* on January 23, 1906. They were accompanied by their ten-year-old nephew Carleton, son of their brother Will, whose guardianship they had assumed after Branch's death. The crossing was remarkably calm for winter weather. As the only passengers the Kings were pampered by the crew, and the long voyage of twenty-one days served as a period of emotional calm, a time during which they could realize the end of one period in their lives and the beginning of another. Grace read Edith Wharton's new novel *The House of Mirth*, which pleased her so much that she forgot her usual tendency to seasickness.[1]

Through an English friend the sisters learned of lodgings in the village of Newdigate, Surrey, where the simple country life was comforting. They made arrangements for Carleton to enter as a student at King's School, Canterbury, and in the process of accomplishing this, they familiarized themselves with the charms of the old city. They were entertained by the headmaster, who showed an interest in the South and asked questions about the racial situation there but was tactful enough not to offend them as Grace had been offended by Englishwomen on her earlier trip.

By early spring they were living at Finnsbury Park, London, where for three weeks they visited the usual London landmarks and museums. They attended a service held for victims of the San Francisco earthquake, at which the American ambassador Whitelaw Reid spoke. Grace King found him repellent. To her he was "what Chas. Dudley Warner & Mr Clemens & others of their kind had prepared me to expect—a mean-faced, insignificant looking Yankee with a weak uncertain voice & a manner that pretended but failed to be 'au fait.'"[2]

What she enjoyed most about London this time was "the freedom from responsibility & from the constant interruption of visitors. I believe we enjoy

---

1. Grace King to May McDowell, February 14, 1906, in the Grace King Papers, Department of Archives and Manuscripts, Louisiana State University, Baton Rouge. Unless otherwise noted, all quoted manuscript material is in this collection.
2. *Ibid.*, April 2, 1906.

this even more keenly than the novelty of our environment." The leisure and the escape from social pressures allowed her more time for work and for her customary reading. In her most recent list she recommended to May McDowell George Bernard Shaw's *Cashel Byron's Profession*: "It is ridiculous, but very amusing. Shaw is all the rage over here." She also read Olive Schreiner's *The Story of an African Farm*, Meredith's *Rhoda Fleming*, and Madame Blanc's *Constance*, which she called "the best story she has written."[3] Whether she was writing very much herself at the moment was unclear, but she was anxious to finish the as yet untitled "Macmillan novel" while she was in England," not only for the money I could get out of it but the prestige, which would be quite serviceable after my long absence from publication."[4]

In May they traveled to Oxford, planning to settle for a period of three months in the ancient village of Headington nearby. There they had lodgings in a small house in the garden of an old monastery with high brick walls overgrown with vines—a place with a tea table under the shade trees. This time letters of introduction which they had brought with them would be answered—it was not yet the summer holiday season as when Grace and Nan had last visited Oxford. Dr. William Walter Merry, rector of Lincoln College and vice chancellor of the university, was their best bet; he was an old schoolmate of a friend of theirs. They left their cards and were promptly invited to dinner. Nan was much taken with Dr. Merry, whose name was the more appropriate because "he talked and laughed in the most spontaneous way, asking questions and making reflexions on our replies." Because these were southern ladies and because the first thing an Englishman seemed to think about when he heard the word "South" was race, Merry brought up that ancient question—presumably in the most tactful way. "He has the right of the 'nigger' question," Nan wrote approvingly, "and does not believe in Booker Washington's experiment."[5] Other social pleasures followed in the Oxford area, developing in Grace and Nan greater respect for the English personality than they had had during their first trip of 1891–1892.

3. *Ibid.*, March 18, 1906.
4. *Ibid.*, April 2, 1906.
5. Annie Ragan King to May McDowell, May 15, 1906. Booker T. Washington's "experiment" was the serious industrial training of Negroes at Tuskegee Institute to develop in them both efficiency and independence.

When Nina suffered a nervous breakdown while they were at Oxford, they consulted the distinguished Dr. William Osler, Oxford professor and renowned brain specialist. He examined Nina, found her anemic and in need of nursing care. Osler was wise enough to see that she should be kept away from the society of her sisters, and she was sent to a nursing home in Eastbourne. Nina suffered intensely from what she considered the dominant personality of Grace. In her own diary she writes frequently about Grace's pride, and it had long become clear to them all that a strong irritation existed between the two. Part of Nina's unhappiness may have stemmed from her own failed aspirations in life; she had made sporadic attempts to become a writer but had failed to write anything publishable. Grace, on the other hand, had succeeded all too well. Nina probably resented comparison with Grace and also resented Grace's attempts to control the activities of the touring party. Osler was intelligent enough as a psychologist to perceive this at once.

Grace wrote frequently to May McDowell about Nina's condition, which as much as the grief for Branch dampened the joys of their tour. Still in England in November, she wrote, "I do sincerely believe that if I were out of her [Nina's] way, she will do much better than if I am there with her. I irritate her & keep her in a constant ill humour. It is merely a case of 'elective' antipathies for which we are hardly responsible. I shall do my best to turn my new experience to good account. I shall again set to work & again try to sew together what Fate has so often ripped apart."[6]

That she maintained a regular schedule of work while she was in England is evident from some of her letters, even though she makes no mention of this in her memoirs. At Headington she set to work on the "Macmillan novel" that would in time become *The Pleasant Ways of St. Médard*. The struggle she endured in the writing of it is evident in her comments at the time to her young friend Warrington Dawson: "I have gone to work at my sphynx-like undertaking. . . . How many times have I taken it up & had to throw it down again! Every sorrow that I have had for the past ten years has marked its notch on it—every worry and anxiety has left a scratch on it. I am almost super-stitious about going to it again, but I feel that if I do not finish it I shall never finish anything." She looked forward hopefully to the three months they were

6. Grace King to May McDowell, November 11, 1906.

to spend near Oxford, believing that a successful period of writing would uplift her low spirits. Her creative mind was working now with many "plans and projects." Once the Macmillan novel was completed she had "a new yarn to spin all ready—picked it up over here—a rather tantalising motif to me."[7] But she says no more about the new yarn, and there is no evidence that anything came of it.

The summer of 1906 passed; Grace and Nan had settled for some time at St. Leonard's, near Eastbourne on the south coast of England, to be near the place where Nina was recuperating. Then, convinced that they were in need of a visit to France, the three sisters crossed the channel from Dover to Calais. They went immediately to a hotel in Paris, where the first event of importance was meeting Warrington Dawson, whom Grace had not seen since he was a boy.

She had met him and his mother at Blowing Rock, the high mountain resort in North Carolina where she and the McDowells occasionally stayed in summer. She had always been fascinated by the tragic story of the elder Mrs. Dawson, who had fled from Baton Rouge to Charleston during the Civil War. She married Francis Warrington Dawson, an Englishman who had served in the Confederate army and later became editor of the Charleston *News and Courier*. After he was brutally murdered, Mrs. Dawson lived in Paris, where she educated her son, who would become a lifelong expatriate himself. To Grace King Mrs. Dawson's life was heroic: she was a southern aristocrat who had abandoned the United States for France when her native country had become unbearable during Reconstruction. Grace King had for some time corresponded with the young Warrington, who was beginning his career as a journalist and novelist. She would correspond with him to the end of her life, playing a role not unlike that played by Charles Gayarré in her own career. Dawson was the novice writer of fiction she hoped would become more distinguished than he actually did become.

In her letters she played the affectionate advisor to a man of the South whose ideals and background were similar to her own. In 1905 she had written him:

7. Grace King to Warrington Dawson, May 27, 1906, in the William R. Perkins Library, Duke University.

You must write (novels) I mean. You owe it to yourself, which means you owe it to your father and your mother and all the good ancestral blood that flows in their veins. You owe it to Charleston, and you owe it to the South. The now voiceless South. The South must *write* itself to the front of the nation, its old place. It has been written down until the young South is ashamed & is ready to flop into any section that is not the beaten one. You, with your dreams and aspirations can hardly figure in yourself the weakly, silly, practical, prosaic creature the Southern young man is of the present day, straining after football contests instead of political championship.[8]

She was surprised when he called at the Bradford Hotel. At twenty-eight, this tall, well dressed, distinguished-looking young man quite took her breath away with his polished manners and his protestations of friendship for the King family. She was impressed by the fact that his new novel, *The Scar*, was already a commercial success, and she had hopes that this young southerner would make his mark in the world.

But she did not stay long in Paris. Madame Blanc was expecting her at Meudon, the small town west of Paris where she was then living. Nan accompanied Grace in a taxi to the Gare Montparnasse for the short journey. It was their first ride through the city in fifteen years, an experience strangely familiar as they remembered the first impressions Paris had left on them in 1891. The city was as beautiful as it had been then, as they gazed at familiar buildings and rode down the Champs Elysées. Even the people at the station charmed them with their politeness, so different from the official character of the English whom they had just left.

Not having seen Madame Blanc since the time of her trip to the United States in 1894, Grace King was unprepared for the shock of finding her still gravely ill after an attack of double pneumonia.[9] Hearing that her friend Brunetière was dying, Madame Blanc had felt it necessary to go to him in cold

8. Grace King to Warrington Dawson, January 22, 1905, in the William R. Perkins Library, Duke University.

9. Grace King, *Memories of a Southern Woman of Letters* (New York, 1932), 275; see also Grace King to May McDowell, November 23, 1906.

and damp weather, and she suffered a relapse. Even so, she had arranged a room for Grace King on the third floor of the house she lived in—a country villa that adjoined a school for girls. Grace seems to have sensed that her friend was dying, and this awareness together with her own state of melancholy hardly made the weeks that passed joyful, yet the period seems to have been a moving and significant one for her. In giving her friend company and sometimes receiving her friends for her when she was too ill to do it, she felt that her presence was of some use in a time of illness.

In the morning they worked, Grace King in the upstairs room at a large table where she could spread out her manuscripts and pile up her letters in front of a huge inkstand. She had much work to do, presumably on the "Macmillan novel," but she found it difficult to concentrate on work and would often give it up, seize her hat and gloves and escape for a walk around Meudon, which she enjoyed. Her favorite walk was a long and interesting one to Bellevue, the ruined chateau where Madame de Pompadour had once lived. She was moved by the contrast between the decayed magnificence of the chateau and the splendid trees of the park that had flourished there since long before the Revolution of 1789.

After luncheon the two friends customarily sat together for conversation on literary subjects, Grace King speaking English, Madame Blanc French. The younger woman had long since been introduced to the joys of a controlled conversation with Charles Gayarré. Madame Blanc's conversation was almost entirely literary; that is, it concerned the lives and characters of writers she knew on both sides of the Atlantic. In nineteenth-century fashion she was more interested in the literary person than the literary work, and Grace King believed she "had never listened to a more charming conversationalist."

While she was at Meudon, Brunetière died, and the choice of his successor as editor of the *Revue des Deux Mondes* was made in part through discussions with Madame Blanc, who supported the pastoral poet Francis Jammes for the post. It was he who was chosen as the new editor. Other events made the stay at Meudon interesting and enriching, though they had little direct influence on the career of Grace King. She met the widow of Gustave Crauk, sculptor of the figure of Gaspard de Coligny, and became involved in Madame Crauk's attempt to promote the casting of a copy of the famous Paris statue for some city in the United States. Grace King thought of Charleston as the proper place for such a monument to the American Huguenot settlers, but nothing came of the plan. She might have met a greater sculptor than Gustave Crauk had she wished to. Auguste Rodin's studio and red brick villa were on a hill opposite Madame Blanc's quarters, and Madame Blanc would have introduced her, but she seems to have had little desire to present herself at the studio. Among the literary people who frequented Madame Blanc's salon, she met Édouard Rod, whom she admired as novelist and critic and whose introduction she had written for the *Library of the World's Best Literature*. The Baron de Pontalba visited her several times at Meudon, and their conversation centered almost entirely on Louisiana history.

Charles Wagner, her close friend of the "Union pour l'action morale," also visited her at Meudon. Wagner was about the same age as Grace King, and over the years she had helped publicize his career with a series of articles in American publications. Her admiration and affection for him were strong. After one of his visits, she realized his power to move his friends by his sincere approach to faith. Madame Blanc and Madame Coignet, a philosopher and translator of Kant, joined them; the discussion centered on death, immortality, and the problem of evil. He answered their questions simply, but with strong bursts of inspiration. God could only act on humanity through human beings, he said, and the best help we could get on earth was through one another, a kind of help we face unconsciously. When he was asked what demand he made on people who joined his church, he opened his hands and said, "I ask nothing, I only offer." Then he recited his beautiful confession of faith and so moved old Madame Coignet that tears ran down her face and Madame Blanc looked on happily. Grace King, too, was deeply moved by the visit and the hour's talk with the two elderly women who were themselves near death. She went downstairs with him and they agreed that she was doing the best thing she could in staying with her friend in her decline. When he left he said, "Mais il faut que je vous embrasse," and Grace kissed him on one cheek and then the other in good French style. She would have hugged him had he not been such a colossus. He had grown much older since she had seen him fourteen years ago, and he was most grateful to her for the articles she had written about him.[10]

10. *Ibid.*, December 16, 1906.

Grace King was highly selective in the literary people she approved of in France. She was a Francophile who could not condone laxity among French writers in their personal lives or in the sensuality of their novels. Early in 1907 she commented on Anatole France: "When I read through that vile book of Anatole France 'Le Lys Rouge' I am quite disgusted even with French morals & would just as soon leave this city of nasty women as not. No writer could write such a book about American women & not be horse-whipped; but here it is cited as a model of literary excellence."[11]

By this time she had become Madame Blanc's closest friend. Out of both pride and a sense of obligation she assumed the duty of caring for the dying woman in her final days. In her memoirs she recounts the details of her friend's death—the false alarm, the premature arrival of the priest to administer the last rites, the final moments some days later, the arrival of the family, the funeral at Meudon, and the mass at Montparnasse.

A few days after Madame Blanc's funeral Grace King moved into Paris to stay as the sole Protestant in the Couvent St. Maur, an exclusive place of residence which required of her the recommendations of her most distinguished French friends. The convent was a conservative institution founded by Madame de Maintenon, where the sisters wore long, trailing black silk gowns and black veils turned away from the face. The building was a seventeenth-century structure with a majestic portal, marble floor, and winding staircase. It had once been a refuge for young Protestant women who had returned to the Catholic fold; now it was an elegant boarding house for conservative ladies. Grace King remembered it well over twenty years later when she was writing her memoirs, filling several pages with the details that so impressed her—the routine of the day beginning with early coffee with croissants and ending with conversation in the drawing room, where the ladies sat in brocaded arm chairs that had been there since the days of Maintenon. These ladies were in a state of outrage against the anticlericalism of the Clemenceau government of 1907 and the laws being enforced to suppress religious institutions. Because Grace King had an historic respect for Catholicism, she sympathized with the plight of the convents in France.[12] She says nothing in her memoirs about the celebrated Dreyfus Affair, but the conservative ladies of

11. *Ibid.*, January 11, 1907.
12. King, *Memories*, 285.

the Couvent St. Maur probably opposed the Dreyfus exoneration of 1906 since they opposed the Clemenceau regime. Grace King seems to have associated with anti-Dreyfusards in France, although there is no evidence that she herself favored their position.

When the Baron de Pontalba visited her at the Couvent St. Maur, his conversation was steeped in his family's traditions in North America—so much so that it seemed to her the history of Louisiana was calling personally. Charles Wagner also came to see her. He was at the height of his popularity in Paris in 1907, and he had gained the friendship of Catholics by his support of their fight against anticlericalism. On one occasion Wagner took Grace King to a meeting of the *Union pour l'action morale*, the movement that had so fired her imagination fourteen years before. They slipped into the meeting unnoticed. Paul Desjardins was presiding. She noted that he had changed greatly from the man of "the pale, spiritualised face" that she remembered. He was now stronger looking and fuller faced. She listened to some of the speeches and reports, but found them "uninteresting, flat, and devoid of spirit." She told Wagner of her sense of the apathy of the meeting, but he was quick to try to convince her that the movement was indeed flourishing and had lost none of its spiritual vigor.[13] Wagner may also have told her about the beginning of the new phase of Desjardins' career—his restoration of the great Romanesque abbey at Pontigny and his expansion of his spiritual movement to what would become a major intellectual institution of twentieth-century France, the "Décades de Pontigny." From 1910 to 1939 writers as important as Gide, Malraux, Valéry, and Saint-Exupéry would meet in the ancient Burgundian village during the summer to participate in lively seminars over which Desjardins would preside.

Before setting out on a trip to Brittany, Grace King wrote an article on Madame Blanc which she called a "hard little job." Writing now did not come easily for her as it had in the past. Earlier that year she had confessed to May McDowell that "my mind has been so good for nothing in these last years, so tired & confused all the time, that I have not been able to write anything well & don't believe that I shall ever be able to write again. My mind has gone the way of my eyes & ears & legs."[14] What she was referring to did not indicate

13. *Ibid.*, 289.
14. Grace King to May McDowell, March 10, 1907.

any serious decline, but rather the regret of a woman of fifty-five that her faculties were not as sharp as they had been at thirty.

In the summer of 1907 Grace, Nan, and Nina journeyed to Rothéneuf on the Brittany coast for a stay on the sea near St. Malo. They were joined by Carleton, who took his vacation there from his school in Canterbury, and by May and Brevard McDowell, who were soon to begin a tour of the Continent. They could bathe in the bright sea in front of their hotel and go on walks to explore medieval St. Malo. The account of this time in *Memories of a Southern Woman of Letters* suggests that the weeks spent at Rothéneuf were happy ones. Over twenty years later Grace King remembered the details of their walks to St. Malo through prairies that were "a sheen of color, with thickly growing red and yellow poppies and thistles in bloom, and round tufted mulberry colored balls called 'serpelets' (wild thyme), growing everywhere." [15]

On her first trip to Mont St. Michel she exulted in the spiritual experience of that architectural miracle. The family party followed their guide up the high incline from the village below.

> What followed was not an earthly but a mystical experience too personal to be described. Out of the broad expanse of the quicksand left by the ocean at low tide rose the giant rock that bears the granite church of Saint Michel into the very heavens together with itself. The architects of the tenth and eleventh century structures attained what their imagination promised—"the substance of things hoped for, the evidence of things not seen." If art and architecture please God, then Mont-Saint-Michel must have been pronounced good by Him. Even the voluble tourists fell silent with wonder under the overwhelming impression made upon them. The nimble feet and tongue of the guide led us back to our car, a silent and a humbled crowd. [16]

As an American tourist she demonstrated her own competence as the one on whom nothing is lost, the fiction writer and historian who is constantly alert for the emotion of the moment and the sensuous details that convey the emotion. The three sisters traveled to Dinard, where she observed the minute

15. King, *Memories*, 293.
16. *Ibid.*, 296.

details of the funeral procession for a child. Her observation begins at a street doorway:

> A little bier stood in the entrance, with two tall candles at the head, a cruet of holy water with a sprinkler on a chair at the foot. Outside the door were hung elaborate bead wreaths, the official flowers of the French for the tomb. The little boy in the cassock looked very sad; his hair was rumpled. We asked if the one who had died was a relative. He nodded yes, and at the end of his pinning, he took up his silver censer and stationed himself at the door. The little coffin was brought down the stairs and placed on the bier and covered with a pretty white damask pall. A *bonne* in black, with a Breton cap, now became master of ceremonies. She it was who received the six little girls dressed in white dresses and black sashes who came to walk beside the coffin, all of them frightened and keeping their heads turned away from it, while their mothers or aunts straightened their sashes and buttoned their gloves for them. . . .
>
> One almost forgot to look at what followed, the mother weeping bitterly under her crepe veil, between, perhaps, her two sisters, in light mourning, walking beside her. After this group came the father, young and handsome, dressed in black broadcloth, with a deep band on his tall hat. With him were his brothers or brothers-in-law. The parents looked so young that the little one in the coffin must have been their first child, and the snowy linens with the fine stitching and richly embroidered monogram that served for draperies came doubtless from the trousseau.
>
> Down the street the little one went at the head of the procession to the church, leaving the great world of Dinard, entered hardly a year before, to judge by the size of her coffin. This, by a caprice of memory, is what Dinard gave us to remember her by for the years to come![17]

Grace King's memory of this scene after over twenty years is remarkable. It illustrates her power to observe as a romantic realist. The material was commonplace enough in Dinard in 1907, but to the American steeped in French tradition it was charged with emotion stirred by the picturesque

17. *Ibid.*, 299–301.

details. Had the scene taken place in New Orleans, it might well have inspired a story.

At the city of Tours the King sisters stayed at the Couvent St. Augustin. Such boarding houses were inexpensive and provided an atmosphere appropriate for unmarried ladies. They were also quiet places where one could read and meditate if one chose and avoid brushing elbows with the more hurried tourists of the hotels. As at St. Maur Grace King enjoyed the great halls and handsome furniture, the elegant dining room, where the table was set with heavy silver and fine linen. The other boarders were refined aristocrats "as firm in their old etiquette as in their faith and loyalty to monarchy." It was in fact a slightly different expression of the same values they were accustomed to at home.[18]

At Tours her memory went back to the days when Gayarré had lived there more than seventy years before and to the experiences he passed on to her of life in the 1830s. When she and her sisters sat in the public square to listen to the band music, they evoked the figure of the judge from the past and saw him as a young man. And from there they could go in thought to the Huguenot revolt in the late sixteenth century. Here Grace King the historian could touch the nerve of history, or, like Wordsworth on Westminster Bridge, she could see the city clothed in the beauty of nature:

> The great church of St. Martin was so near the convent that we could almost touch it, leaning out of our windows. Its great dome seemed to rest over it, and its sonorous bell roused us from sleep in the morning and timed our days for us. The Loire, flowing past the city in its perfect beauty, more perfect because it is indescribable, is beholden to no guide book as a creator of impressions. Before the days of guide books and even of printing she had flowed as she does now, between her soft green banks and around her willow-fringed islands, reflecting the blue sky and white clouds in her enigmatical waters that puzzle the beholder like eyes that are now gray, now black.[19]

The sisters toured the chateaux—Loches, Chenonceaux, Amboise, and Azay-le-Rideau; they visited a cemetery on All Saints' Day because it was an

18. *Ibid.*, 303.
19. *Ibid.*, 304.

old New Orleans custom. Then they traveled to Brussels, where they spent three months. The major event of that stay was the excursion to the battlefield of Waterloo, made on January 8, anniversary of the famous defeat of the British at New Orleans in the same year. The trip started in a rainstorm that changed to such a blinding snowstorm that they had to turn back to the famous inn, La Belle Alliance, where they sat around a fire and discussed the battle strategy in some comfort. Grace King provided a fact the others did not know—that after the battle of New Orleans the survivors of the British army were hurried from Louisiana to the field of Waterloo, where after their famous defeat they contributed to an even more famous victory.

Another memorable experience in Brussels was their coming to the Hotel de Ville in the evening at the moment the electric lights were turned on, illuminating the handsome Grand' Place with its ancient medieval buildings. As they stood there it seemed to Grace King that they were on "some theatrical stage, not in real life." She recalled the dramatic moment of the beheading of Counts Egmont and Hoorn by the Spanish rulers at that very spot in 1568 and, reliving the terror of that historic event, realized that her own view of the Grand' Place was those heroes' last sight on earth. Again she seemed to be saying that time and place availed not, that great events of the past were permanently recorded in the historic imagination.

They next spent four weeks in Bruges, a city that was understandably to Grace King's taste with its canals, its ancient buildings with tiled roofs, its Memlings and Van Eycks. She and her sisters spent many hours in the Belgian museums as her appreciation of painting increased with her greater exposure to it.

Antwerp, the final stop on this second tour of Europe, was "the most interesting city we had ever seen." But here the sisters learned that the economic prop for their trip was being pulled from under them: their tenants in New Orleans had abruptly left and the house on Coliseum Street was now empty. Other administrative problems had arisen concerning the estate of their brother Branch, and since Grace was the executor it was decided that she should return to New Orleans immediately, leaving her sisters to keep in touch with Carleton, who was to complete his year in the Canterbury school where he had started.

Grace King sailed alone on the *Kroonland* early in June, 1908. The voyage was a long bore, during which she was obliged to observe the kind of tourists she least admired. "Such people!" she wrote Nan and Nina, "such people! You don't know what the Americans are until you are thrown in with them on a sea trip. There was a ball last night. I saw only the flags & illumination for it on deck. I hear that the 'young people enjoyed themselves very much.' They would enjoy anything then." Of sea trips like this one she remarked, "Every effort has been made successfully to take from it every element of romance, adventure & novelty. I should call this vessel a floating 3d class N. Y. hotel. . . . The sense of the travelers aboard is that nothing in Europe is as good as we have at home & thank the Lord I am an American." [20]

She made use of the time to complete the four-volume history of the Thirty Years' War by Anton Gindely, she had a long time to prepare herself for an expected rejection of her Macmillan novel by George C. Brett, and she did a great deal of thinking about why she was returning before she had expected to—the possible sale of the house and the L'Embarras Plantation lands. She was opposed to the sale of the house; it might again be rented to help support her on a future trip to Europe. She was more likely to agree to the sale of the L'Embarras land, but not for the cheapest price they could get. She had earned little with her pen for a number of years. She and her sisters lived on minor dividends from securities inherited from their mother. Economically, the Macmillan novel was one hope for her, the L'Embarras Plantation lands the other. To sell or not to sell would be the question for years to come. They could sell the land at a low price now or await the possibility of the discovery of oil. For years the question would plague the Kings, until their land became like the Tennessee lands once owned by the Clemenses. Mark Twain's father had urged his family to hold on to the land; he believed it would make them rich.

Grace King's reception at the Macmillan Company was thoroughly cordial. Brett was charming and treated her with great kindness, but because the manuscript had not yet arrived she had to face another disappointment. She pointed out to May that "the devil shows a great variety of torment & versatility in his treatment against me." Brett assured her he would read the manuscript when it arrived and he felt sure it would prove to be all right.

20. Grace King to Annie Ragan King and Nina King, June 23, 1908.

Next she telephoned the *Outlook* to have a word with Hamilton Mabie, but he was out of town. So she indulged herself in sauntering down Fifth Avenue, allowing herself to be tempted by the fact that everything in the shops seemed both cheap and stylish. But the heat was dreadful and the city was dirty, the shop girls impudent and sly.

Returning to New Orleans late in June, 1908, she was invited to stay at the home of Mrs. T. G. Richardson, a doctor's widow who was the wealthiest and most philanthropic woman in the city. Both ladies were patronesses of Tulane University—Grace King intellectually, Ida Richardson financially. After enjoying the spacious Garden District home of her friend with its excellent library until October, she returned to her home on Coliseum Street and began to prepare it for her sisters, who would return from Europe early in the new year.[21] She published nothing in the year 1908 but resumed her duties as secretary of the Louisiana Historical Society, to which she devoted much time. During these months she may also have worked on the revision of the Macmillan novel, which had been returned to her with suggestions for that revision.

In November of 1908 she made a nostalgic visit to Mississippi to see her old friend Mrs. Gayarré, then living out her life at the plantation home of her nephew at Canton, northeast of Jackson. Grace King took the old train route she and her sister May had taken in the 1870s and 1880s on their way to Roncal to visit Judge Gayarré and his wife. As the train passed through the little towns on the Louisiana-Mississippi border, she felt all the associations of the past, especially the personality of the judge and her introduction to French culture and Louisiana history. She observed the changes—the formerly placid hamlets were now bustling towns. But as the train passed groves of sumac trees, she could almost see the old judge walking through them, peering through his glasses to find his way.

The train continued past Jackson to Canton, where she was met by young Vivian Ricks in his carriage. They drove nine miles through forests and old plantation country to the Ricks plantation, a very large one where the traditional rural life of the Deep South was still carried on. She was welcomed with old-fashioned hospitality and found that the elder Ricks, Mrs. Gayarré's

21. King, *Memories*, 325–31.

nephew, still employed many of the former family slaves and seemed to be as much the master of them as he had been as a young man before 1865. She found Mrs. Gayarré little changed in appearance after many years, but at eighty-eight so nearly blind that she could scarcely distinguish her friend. She was a most pathetic figure, with little to do with herself but sit all day and sing hymns or remember whatever she had once learned by heart. She was most excited and pleased to see her old friend, and the two women talked for a full day, reviewing all of the dead past.

Grace King described to May McDowell the prodigality of the rural household—enormous fires burning in the sitting room and in her large bedroom filled with fine old mahogany furniture. If the Kings were used to the refined Creole cooking of New Orleans, the Ricks were continuing the old southern country traditions—supper of huge hot biscuits, hot waffles, beef-steak, honey, hominy, corn bread, preserves, pickles, buttermilk, tea and coffee. "Such waste I have read about," she wrote her sister, "but I have never seen it before; the regular old Southern plantation prodigality."[22]

Her elderly Irish servant Mary Burke had prepared her for the journey and expected to meet her train when she returned. Grace King wrote her to postpone the meeting, but the letter never arrived and poor old Mary vainly went to the station and caught cold in the rain. Grace King arrived the next day and had to have a small boy carry her bags. Because she would be alone in the house and needed a servant to prepare her breakfast the next day, she first went to Mary's house near the station. Mary's daughter had given her mother a toddy and put her to bed after her exposure the night before in Miss Grace's behalf. But as soon as the elderly woman heard that her mistress was inquiring for her, she got up and came home with Grace. Kelly the night watchman was on the lookout for them, and they entered the dark and silent house together. By that time Grace King was very hungry. In her shawl bag she had brought from Mississippi a box of beaten biscuits and a cold partridge, remnants of the Ricks's hospitality. She sat down and ate the partridge with her fingers, judging it the most delicious one she had ever had. Then, tired after her long journey into the past, she went to bed, satisfied that Mary Burke was there to prepare a hot breakfast for her in the morning.[23]

22. Grace King to May McDowell, November 15, 1908.
23. *Ibid.*

Eleven

The Pleasant Ways of St. Médard, 1900–1916

G race King wrote three volumes that may be called novels, of which only one, the historical romance *La Dame de Sainte Hermine* (1924), is a conventional one. The other two—*Monsieur Motte* (1888) and *The Pleasant Ways of St. Médard* (1916)—are both episodic fictions divided into a series of sketches or stories with unifying elements of character, theme, and setting. There is of course no reason why such structures should not be called novels, and it is to the author's credit as a realist that in *The Pleasant Ways* she discarded the conventions of plot and suspense in favor of the plotless world of reality.

The episodic form of *Monsieur Motte*, as we have seen, formed an interesting four-movement work that could be compared to the sonata in music. Grace King had arrived at that original structure largely by chance, since she had begun with the first part as a short story unto itself. *The Pleasant Ways* has more contrast in its character range than the earlier work. Both, in content, are fiction produced by a genuine historian who wished to record the very tone and feeling of the Reconstruction era, which she herself had witnessed. The theme of the later work is much more varied and complicated than that of the life of the young Creole girl of *Monsieur Motte*; in it Grace King interpreted social history in an unspectacular way and with subtle ironies, as opposed to the conventional novels that exploited the violence of the period. To her that violence was atypical of the everyday life of New Orleanians in the years following the Civil War. The Ku Klux Klan was not an ever-present element in southern life. And even the romance that filled the best sellers about the era was, in her opinion, the stuff that editors sought to help sell their books. To her the romance of New Orleans life lay in the uncommon regional drama that manifested itself in the unstandardized life of the city. She observed little sentimentality in that life and very little romantic love.

At various times in her life she aspired to the writing of a full novel. She knew the international novel well when she wrote her first published essay, "Heroines of Novels." In 1892 during her first visit to Paris she wrote Charles Dudley Warner that she wished to try a full-length novel, but even at that time she had doubts as to whether she had the ability to produce a long novel with conventional plot. She had begun writing *The Pleasant Ways of St. Médard* on the suggestion of George C. Brett of the Macmillan Company after meeting him in New York in 1899. The novel seems not to have been named for years, indeed, probably not until it was accepted for publication in 1916. The name "St. Médard" resembles "St. Bernard," the name of the Louisiana parish immediately south of the city limits of New Orleans, and it may have been suggested by the Left Bank church of St. Médard in Paris.

Although *The Pleasant Ways* is a volume of only 338 pages, of all Grace King's work it took the longest to write and when completed waited longest to be accepted by a publisher. Research and writing began with vigor and enthusiasm in the fall of 1899 and continued to the end of that year, in spite of the family problems that had begun to dampen her spirits in the Prytania Street house.

At various times Grace King wrote that the series of deaths in her family following the turn of the century took their toll on her by exhausting her emotional energy. Thereafter long periods of time passed during which little or no progress was made on the ambitious work, and it was still incomplete when the King sisters sailed for Europe early in 1906.

The European trip of 1906–1908 was made more difficult by Nina's nervous breakdown, but Grace persisted in her attempt to finish the novel while she was in Europe. She wanted to reestablish herself in the literary world and she also needed the money a novel might be expected to earn. She had called it her "sphynx-like undertaking," meaning that the project posed a mysterious riddle as to its success and left that riddle unanswered for years.

Almost six years had passed since Brett had set her to work on what seemed an interminable task. Occasionally she wrote him of her progress and told him about the family illnesses and deaths that so affected her and hampered the novel's completion. He would then encourage her and suggest that her work might be serialized before it became a book.[1]

Although her reason for returning home from Europe without her sisters in June of 1908 was the settling of financial matters about the Coliseum Street house, the "Macmillan novel" was then complete and very much on Grace King's mind. From the *SS Kroonland* she wrote her sisters that she hoped to see George C. Brett when she arrived in New York and that she was quite prepared to hear him decline the novel with thanks. So many obstacles had kept this work from completion that she had steeled herself to its ultimate rejection by the publisher who had originally requested it.[2] Brett had written her from New York that he was pleased to hear that her health had improved and that he eagerly awaited the opportunity to read the completed manuscript. But although she had sent it separately, he had not yet received the manuscript when she arrived for her brief visit. It would require several months before a verdict could be sent her. Both Brett and his associate Edward C. Marsh read the novel and their eventual decision was to return it with suggestions for revision. They were still interested in the work but in another form.

In the spring of 1909 Grace King took seriously Brett's idea of publishing her work in a periodical. She wrote to Robert Underwood Johnson of *Century Magazine*, making this suggestion. Although nothing came of the idea, the letter itself is an interesting record of what the author intended to create in the novel:

I have a kind of story, written on the instigation of Mr. Brett about reconstruction. That is, I wanted it to be a story, & most of it is purely

1. George C. Brett to Grace King, August 22, 1906, in the Grace King Papers, Department of Archives and Manuscripts, Louisiana State University, Baton Rouge. Unless otherwise noted, all manuscript material is in this collection.
2. Grace King to Annie Ragan King, June 23, 1908.

fictitious; but it has unrolled itself in a most disgustingly real way, following life & nature instead of romance. I have my doubts about its being published first in book form—it seems to me to have dedicated itself *ab initio* to the service of a magazine—as serial. I am under contract for the book to the Macmillan Co, and—but—if—Are you filled up too far ahead to consider such a thing? The country seems to be turning in heart again toward the South. I should say that my wayward offspring is a light, humorous lady, looking at reconstruction more as a wife & mother than a politician—more moved by the slight than the grave troubles of it.[3]

The comment that "most of it is purely fictitious" is undoubtedly true, but quite obviously the setting, the tone, and many of the characters were adapted from the King family experience. It is a work very close to true history and it gives the impression of being authentic. If it is comparable to any other work of American fiction, it resembles Sarah Orne Jewett's *The Country of the Pointed Firs* (1896), also a series of sketches unified in theme, setting, and tone, and, like *The Pleasant Ways of St. Médard*, providing an illusion of reality. Both the Jewett and the King novels are devoid of any more plot than their commonplace characters generate in their commonplace lives. Critics and historians have usually used the term "sketch" or "series of sketches" to denigrate fictions which lack a full story. In both of these works the unity of the book is undeniable and the lack of a formal plot is the virtue that raises the fiction to a high point of realism. But Brett of Macmillan did not see it that way. In November, 1909, he wrote Grace King of her latest revision of the manuscript that he thought the construction of the story was its weakness, "the interest not culminating to a climax, and not being at any point very vivid from the plot standpoint."[4] Had he seen *The Country of the Pointed Firs* as a manuscript he would have made the same comment.

Years later Grace King wrote that she had revised *The Pleasant Ways* for Brett five times and that it cost her years of labor and energy. What she did not say is that she never really revised the book according to Brett's specific suggestions. There is no evidence that she ever rewrote the sketches as

---

3. Grace King to Robert Underwood Johnson, March 30, 1909, in the Century Collection, New York Public Library.
4. Brett to Grace King, November 19, 1909.

individual short stories. Her revisions were attempts to polish the work without compromising her own faith in the original idea of it or her own conception of its structure. Brett may have had a Reconstruction romance in mind like Thomas Nelson Page's *Red Rock* when he first suggested the idea to Miss King, but he never showed any disdain for her quiet, realistic material. He approved of that, but he may have feared that her failure to construct a story with a central plot would make the book a commercial failure.

Thomas Nelson Page himself was to sympathize with her when she met him in the 1920s and told him of her failure to produce the long novel she had always hoped to write. He assumed she meant that she had failed to accept the formula of the best seller and told her to open up the book and insert a love story into it: "Get a pretty girl and name her Jeanne, that name always takes! Make her fall in love with a Federal officer and your story will be printed at once! The publishers are right; the public wants love stories. Nothing easier than to write them. You can do it! . . . Don't let your story fail!"[5] Although Grace King in her *Memories* does not say so, she must have realized how completely vapid and meretricious the Page remark was, or else he was being inappropriately flippant at a time when she was discussing something very serious in her career. For she was certainly capable of writing a popular love story if she had wished to for the sake of making money. It did not take a Thomas Nelson Page to tell her how to compromise the integrity of her work by stooping to sentimentality. But as much as she wanted literary prestige and money from her writing, she knew better than he what constituted honest realism.

In September of 1910 Grace King made a trip north in which she first visited Heloise Cénas at Watch Hill, Rhode Island, and then continued on to Boston. "It feels funny to be here," she wrote Carleton from the New England hub. She had not visited Boston for many years and found it "very much like London." Visiting the town and battlefield of Lexington, she admitted that "Here I am filled with pride & patriotism & all sorts of commendable feelings. I hope it won't hurt your feelings to see the red coats killing the blue coats. I love to see it."[6] The remarks to her nephew were of course flippant and

5. Thomas Nelson Page to Grace King, in Grace King, *Memories of a Southern Woman of Letters* (New York, 1932), 378.
6. Grace King to Carleton King, September 9, 1910.

intended to continue her ancient feud with New England. But there is some question as to whether she meant that as an American she historically supported the Minutemen of Lexington or whether in a perverse way she was glad to see a battlefield where New Englanders were forced to withdraw and shed blood in the face of the colonial British enemy. We can probably interpret the remarks as meaning that although she was proud to be in the place where the redcoats were first resisted, she took some satisfaction in contemplating the suffering of soldiers who were the ancestors of those who invaded the South many years later.

Accompanied by her sisters, she continued by train to Halifax, Nova Scotia. Absorbing the history of the old port, she compared it later to "an old actress whose heroic role in a great play has become her permanent possession." She then traveled to the Evangeline country of Grand Pré, feeling there great sympathy for the Acadian legend and especially for the French exiles who were expelled by the British and who settled in Louisiana. The King sisters proceeded to Baddeck on Cape Breton Island, where Grace had pleasant recollections of Charles Dudley Warner, who had written a book about the area and had encouraged her to go there many years before.[7]

They next sailed on the Bras d'Or Lakes to Sydney for a brief trip to Newfoundland, returning to New York by way of Quebec and the Adirondacks. They were staying at the Hotel Manhattan on October 5, 1910. The one drama that Grace King attended was Maurice Maeterlinck's new symbolic play *The Blue Bird*, which she called "the most wonderful thing I have ever seen in a spectacular way." She saw Hamilton Mabie while she was in the city and also "the kindly despot" of the Macmillan Company, George C. Brett, with whom she must have discussed the perennial question of the book that was to be called *The Pleasant Ways of St. Médard*. But their talk brought the manuscript no closer to publication than it had been when she first submitted it. The Kings returned by steamer to New Orleans, "where loose threads of duties were lying to be taken up to weave into the work of life."[8]

Those loose threads continued to be woven without great variation of design through the next few years. In the spring of 1912 Grace King visited

7. King, *Memories*, 382–85.
8. Grace King to May McDowell, October 5, 1910; King, *Memories*, 385.

South Carolina, probably seeing for the first time Charleston and Columbia. She went by train to Charleston, which deeply impressed her as a city so beautiful there was "nothing finer in Europe." The exaggeration was understandable; she was seeing a great southern city for the first time and found it architecturally finer than she had expected. The visit to Columbia stirred her historic memories of the Civil War destruction of the city. She took some satisfaction in remembering that although Sherman had all but burned it to the ground, it was now bristling with a new energy and signs of the industrial revival of the South. It proved to her that "the race is not always to the swift nor the battle to the strong when the defeated ones lived long enough." The factories around Columbia, she thought, were fighting the Yankees with deadly sureness.[9]

The much read and much polished manuscript of her novel must have lain fallow for many months as the years passed to 1913. In May of that year Grace King planned what was to be her final trip to Europe. She had suffered a nervous collapse in the fall of 1912, and as she had recovered over the months that followed, she hoped to regain her strength through a vacation in the British Isles with Nan and Nina and her brother Judge Frederick King, who was now a widower. The trip was intended to restore their health and spirits by touring many of the places the ladies had not seen on their previous trips. She took the manuscript with her as a gesture of desperation, with the final hope that she might find a British publisher for the work. She had written Warrington Dawson in the spring of the year that her American publishers praised it highly, but they "demur as I am convinced from making public so Southern a version of Reconstruction." It is highly doubtful that the Macmillan rejection was on such grounds at all. Macmillan was a business enterprise and hardly a champion of Federal policies, and the book itself projects no more criticism of Federal policy than would be implied by the mildest story of Reconstruction in New Orleans. Grace King tended to feel somewhat paranoid about New York publishing houses. She asked Dawson for a note of introduction to Methuen in London in what she called her "effort to escape literary subjugation to Yankee publishers."[10]

9. Grace King to Annie Ragan King, March 19, 1912, and March 22, 1912.
10. Grace King to Warrington Dawson, May 15, 1913, in William R. Perkins Library, Duke University.

The several months of the European tour succeeded in giving the brother and three sisters the unexpected pleasures of travel and a renovation of spirit that they were all seeking. But the one literary achievement lay in that brown package, taking up some space in a trunk that accompanied them.

Grace King gives us the usual picture of her travels in her *Memories*, how the party left New Orleans by ship, how they watched the sight of the plantations and fields of sugar cane and corn as they descended the majestic river. It was like a panorama of history to her—"DeSoto's men, gaunt and weather-beaten, pushing on with sail and oar to get to the Gulf and on to Mexico; Iberville coming into the river from the Gulf, seeking traces of La Salle, and meeting Tonti; ships bringing in to new New Orleans timber which was needed for building the great city planned by France."[11]

The crossing was routine. The only event that caused her some irritation was the discovery that her brother's sons had supplied their father with a large jug of whiskey to fortify him on the long voyage with his maiden sisters. They were not out a day before the judge began to show the effects of it. The ladies put up with their tipsy brother until their collective pride could endure it no longer. Other passengers began to notice, and the humiliation was too great. As Grace pointed out to Carleton, "Like all men in such circumstances he was perfectly oblivious to the effect he was producing." Nan and Nina made a raid on the judge's state room, took the jug, and after dark Nina threw it over-board. Thereafter the ladies put Fred under the ship doctor's care and he remained reasonably sober for the remainder of the journey.[12]

The plague of a whiskey-drinking brother was nothing new to Grace, and it was particularly pathetic since she cared for her brothers, even though their habits vexed her. Fred, the surviving one, treated her with great affection and kindness; she thought of him as having the gentlemanly status of all the King men. When they reached London she took considerable pleasure in seeing this middle-aged man enjoy the mysterious grandeur of Westminster Abbey for the first time in his life. And since he was the most prosperous member of the party, the ladies were all willing to share his generosity, which often added to the luxury of the trip.

11. King, *Memories*, 339.
12. Grace King to Carleton King, August 15, 1913.

Arriving in England June 21, 1913, they had the distinction of being southerners in a London where Walter Hines Page was the Wilson-appointed ambassador. They knew Page, and after coming to their hotel he then invited them to the embassy. North Carolinian that he was, he could be proud of Grace King as a representative American southerner who had a distinguished career behind her as a delineator of southern life and as a well known regional historian.

Warrington Dawson visited them in their London hotel one day to invite them to hear him speak at some minor art society. He asked Grace about her novel and encouraged her to bring it to him; he would turn it over to James B. Pinker, an agent who had had success in finding publishers for rejected fictions. She turned the manuscript over to Pinker, hoping something might come of his efforts but hardly expecting very much.[13]

The tour continued with a dinner for them given by the youngest of the Macmillan family of publishers. He later entertained them at the theater, the play being Arnold Bennett's *Milestones*. After London the little quartet set off to the north, visiting Ely, Cambridge, Lincoln, York, Durham, and Edinburgh. Like good Victorians they all exulted in memories of their reading of Scottish history and Scottish fiction and poetry. Sterling, Loch Lomond, and the Rob Roy country all gave them the romantic thrill they had been expecting. Even Glasgow offered them much to enjoy, although in a letter to Carleton, Aunt Grace wrote, "We took train for Glasgow—a vile dirty town it was . . . without doubt the most repulsive city I have ever been in. In spite of handsome granite buildings & a general air of wealth, I just couldn't stand it."[14]

They traveled to Penrith and Carlisle in the Lake District, paying their respects to Wordsworth's spirit at Rydal Mount, and thence hurried on to their boat trip to Ireland. Fred took the ladies on a long drive around Dublin. Within the city Grace found little to delight her eye either in the architecture or in the everyday life of the people: "You can imagine what an Irish city would be. Well it is a thousand times worse here than any imagination could picture. Such filth, dirt, degradation, poverty & drunkenness!—No sense of decency either of body or conduct!—Why an Irishman should urge any one

13. King, *Memories*, 340–43.
14. Grace King to Carleton King, August 1, 1913.

to come here as McCloskey did your Uncle Fred is what I cannot under-stand." She was vexed with Fred for tearing them away from Edinburgh, where they were perfectly comfortable and happy. As for Dublin itself, she remarked, "I should as soon spend a week on Girod St. near the cemetery or amid the slums of Rampart St. And to make matters worse the weather is cold & rainy." All she could say of a positive nature was that she enjoyed the beautiful music at a service at St. Patrick's Cathedral.[15]

Her mood changed when they traveled by coach to Kilarney "over the most beautiful stretch of country we had seen in Europe. . . . It seemed indeed too beautiful for earth."[16] After a stay at Cork and a view of the Blarney Stone they returned by train to Dublin and took the boat to Liver-pool. A visit to Bath followed, where they settled for a pleasant rest of several weeks before their return home. From Bath they made several excursions to such memorable places as Wells, Glastonbury, Cheddar Gorge, Salisbury, and Stonehenge. But Bath itself made the best impression on Grace King, proba-bly because as a historian she was most at home in the eighteenth century and felt the sense of civilization and order that the old planned city still conveyed. Before they embarked for home they visited the walled city of Chester, a symbolic farewell to the Europe she would not see again.

It had been a pedestrian trip—several mean hotels and sometimes third class rail fare for the sake of economy. She might well have regretted some of it, though there had been many a glorious moment as well. Even if she no longer attempted to gain ingress to the intellectual circles of Europe as she had in the earlier stays in France, at least she had been entertained by the American ambassador. Her income was perilously low during these years, but even that didn't matter. "I don't care what the trip cost," she had written Carleton from Penrith, "We have already gained immense profit from it in health & spirits & general energy. There is nothing like travel for sharp[en]ing the spirits."[17] James B. Pinker would fail to sell any publisher her manuscript, but the fact that it had been turned over to him made it inevitable that it would one day be published. On November 4, 1913, the literary and dramatic agent reported his failure to interest a publisher in her book.

15. *Ibid.*, August 10, 1913.
16. King, *Memories*, 348.
17. Grace King to Carleton King, August 1, 1913.

Having left her manuscript to fend for itself in England, Grace King returned to the routine literary and social life of New Orleans. She had always had an eye for clothes and spent a certain amount of time getting together what she called her "toilette" as the seasons passed. Now she was beginning to feel old-fashioned as new styles began to be worn by the young. "Our clothes are as old-fashioned as we are," she wrote Carleton. "The tight skirts, loose waists & flat hair are all strange & foreign to me—but I must say the girls do look pretty in them." At a performance of *Il Trovatore* she was amazed to observe that the ladies were then wearing "their waists open in the back to the very waist—and to show it turn their backs to the audience." One day in November, 1913, she observed the hesitation waltz being performed at the Italian Gardens by exhibition dancers from New York. To her it looked "just like two engaged people sauntering around with an arm around each other's waist & neck—most lovingly."[18]

Time was changing the manners and style of the country and especially the position of women. Grace King had shown some interest in the radical position of nineteenth-century feminism when she met and talked with Isabella Beecher Hooker in Hartford in 1887. She writes in her *Memories* that she was converted to Mrs. Hooker's position on woman's rights, but she is no more specific than that. She never assumed a militant position on the subject of woman suffrage. Although in 1885, when she began to write for a living, she had been among southern women a shining example of the break with tradition, she was more a symbol of female independence than a propagandist for woman's rights. In 1913, when woman suffrage became a controversial issue in the United States and Great Britain, she made her position clear to Carleton, who seems to have thought she had become an advocate of radical feminist causes. She had made a speech before the Era Club, known in New Orleans for its advocacy of progressive legislation. No, she wrote him, her speech did not mean that she was a militant:

Nothing of the kind. They are an important & influential set of women & I needed them for, rather than against me, that is all. They were delighted to hear that in my opinion the Eng[lish] women deserved the vote & would

18. *Ibid.*, November 28, 1913.

get it. Their lawlessness consists of breaking a few windows & trying to horsewhip Asquith, who deserved it.

But to tell you the truth, I have lost confidence in the business & political efficiency of our men. . . . I don't think giving the vote to women will correct the depravity & extravagance of the men, but it will certainly not help them in their extravagance & depravity. Mannon [a lawyer friend] told us that the women would be given the vote by the next legislature & then you will hear our austere high-minded men howl about the degradation of women. "Degradation" Influence—It makes me sick to hear of such cant. But as I have always said, I am not a clamourer for the suffrage & not a militant.[19]

Her creative writing at this period had come to a standstill. She was going through that state of mind familiar to many authors, when they believe their creative powers have waned. She wrote in November, 1913, "I am keeping myself depressed trying to write when I feel that the gift of writing has been taken from me."[20]

Early in the spring of 1914 she invited Hamilton W. Mabie to stay with her and her sisters when he planned a three-day visit to New Orleans. She took upon herself these little traditional tasks of hospitality, making plans for her Quarante Club to meet him and expecting to ask him to speak to them. Her motives, as usual with northern literary figures, were mixed. She respected Mabie as a friend who had greatly helped her in the past and was doubtless capable of helping her in the future. Her comment to May McDowell was that Mabie was "a good literary business friend of mine & I am sure something profitable will come out of the visit. Besides," she added, "it is just as well for us to keep to the fore in society at the present crisis in our affairs particularly as you and your donations are always helping us out."[21] The crisis was financial. At that time in her life she and her two sisters' individual incomes for household expenses were a mere $400 and it was costing them $600 apiece to run the house. By the end of the year they were obliged to sell securities to pay their expenses, and Grace King was bemoaning the fact that they were

19. *Ibid.*, November 18, 1913.
20. *Ibid.*, November 13, 1913.
21. Grace King to May McDowell, March 13, 1914.

being "shoved slowly & surely to the wall." [22] The relatively wealthy brother-in-law, Brevard McDowell, contributed to the household whenever such contributions became necessary. We can probably interpret the comment about "keeping to the fore in society" as a face-saving activity, that is, to keep in society with some strength lest the social world begin to think the King family was in complete financial disarray.

During the years that passed before the publication of her novel, the Great War engulfed Europe and deeply distressed Americans like Grace King. The impact on her of the cataclysmic events of 1914 is suggested in her statement to Carleton that "the great war in Europe has at last driven our little Civil War & its losses from my mind & given us other news to think about." [23] A few weeks later she wrote similarly to Hamilton Mabie that "the war has weighed me down almost to illness, but . . . in its great cathedral shadow my own shadow has disappeared, my own past suffering from war is forgotten." [24]

The remarks suggest what was true—that she had suffered throughout her life as she relived the Confederate war, that the losses her family and her section had sustained were almost a continuing obsession. But now with an even greater war to occupy her mind, she could see the Civil War in perspective. Perhaps this meant that in her mind it was at last beginning to recede into the past, where it belonged. She and her sisters volunteered for wartime work in Queen Mary's Sewing Guild, promising to make six pajamas a month for wounded British soldiers.

In those early spring months of 1914 she read Edith Wharton's *The Custom of the Country*, which she considered the best novel of the past year, though she wearied of the perennial subject matter—"the struggle for money & social distinction"—which seemed to her to be the only drama for New York. She and Nan were reading in French Sainte-Beuve's *Port-Royal* in six volumes. The nights in June were delightful that year, and the two sisters spent them in their canvas cots on the open air gallery. Delighting in the "Perfect stillness & the constant soft breeze," they slept under sheets until dawn, when the chill forced them to put on cotton blankets. The experience was a pleasant change, so successful that during the day there was an almost morbid longing for night

22. Grace King to Carleton King, December 12, 1914.
23. *Ibid.*, November 16, 1914.
24. Grace King to Hamilton Mabie, January 1, 1915.

to come with the pleasure of sleeping on the gallery.[25] But in spite of such simple joys, Grace King's health was delicate. She suffered from high blood pressure, for which her doctor put her on a diet without meat, coffee, tea, fish, eggs, or oysters, and for a time he kept her from work and other kinds of exertion.[26]

*

The year 1915 was significant in her life. In that year came the breakthrough that would lead to the publication of *The Pleasant Ways of St. Médard*. Historically, it marked her participation in the celebration of the centenary of the Battle of New Orleans. In June Tulane would confer on her an honorary degree, perhaps the highest honor of her career. And she would meet George W. Cable, who, at the age of seventy, would make a trip to New Orleans in search of new material for a book.

The early weeks of 1915 were filled with the excitement of the ceremonies commemorating the centenary of the Battle of New Orleans, held under the auspices of the Louisiana Historical Society. As a historian and officer of the society, Grace King had the duty of speaking at the January 9, 1915, unveiling of a tablet placed at the old Ursuline Convent. And in the evening of that day she was an important guest at a banquet celebrating the centenary, held at the Hotel Grunewald.

In 1915 George W. Cable's attitudes toward the Creole and the Negro were less controversial than they had been in the 1880s. People who had opposed him in New Orleans then were either dead, like Charles Gayarré, or growing old, like Grace King. Cable was asked to address a meeting of the Louisiana Historical Society on the evening of March 17, 1915, in the large assembly room of the Cabildo. The hall was filled to overflowing, indicating a popular interest in this man, the most renowned author that New Orleans had ever produced. Did the large crowd come out of curiosity or pride, or did they come to pay a delayed homage to Cable to compensate for the treatment he had received in the 1880s? It was probably a combination of all of these elements that generated the excitement.

After the business meeting, Cable was introduced by the vice-president,

25. Grace King to May McDowell, June 17, 1914.
26. Grace King to Carleton King, April 2, 1914.

Mr. Dymond, "in most complimentary terms," according to the account of the meeting in the society's publication. Cable's remarks began "with expressions of affection and sentimental attachment to his native city, which he said had been his home during the precious years of childhood and youth, in whose public schools he had received his education, and among whose men and women he had gained his first friends and where he had also sought and found inspiration for his work." He had begun tactfully, speaking to an audience that must have held many besides Grace King who had misgivings about him. Then he read from an unpublished story called "The Maple Leaf," a true account of the adventures of a group of Confederate heroes who led a band of seventy-one captives in an escape from the Federal ship *Maple Leaf*. They endured many hardships in various southern states until they reached Confederate lines in Virginia.

Cable's choice of a story for the audience he was speaking to was another indication of his tact. And since he was an old professional on the lecture stage, he held them "with breathless interest." And they gave him a standing ovation because they recognized in him an old Confederate veteran who had shed blood for the old cause. His age had something to do with the emotional occasion. He was a frail, small, white-haired man, picturesquely bearded. His charm appealed to his audience, and he answered their applause with a recital that may have been the singing of one of the old Creole songs for which he was famous on the stage in years past. The author of the account concluded with the remark, "It was a unique and brilliant example of his genius, which also evoked enthusiastic plaudits." The official minutes of the meeting of the society were unsigned in publication, but the author was undoubtedly Grace King, the recording secretary.[27]

Eight years later, in 1923, she granted an interview to Louise Guyol, a correspondent for the Boston *Evening Transcript*, in which she gave an account of the Cable reading similar to the record that was published. She mentioned that "some of the members objected" to the invitation going to Cable while he was visiting New Orleans, without saying that she herself may well have been one of those dissenters. But if she was, she was completely caught up in the spirit of the occasion. Her personal response to Cable's reading of "The

27. Minutes of the meeting of the Louisiana Historical Society, March 17, 1915, *Louisiana Historical Quarterly*, VIII (1914–15), 24–26.

Maple Leaf" was that "it was beautifully written and really the most compelling little incident I have ever heard." Her conclusion was emotional and completely conciliatory in its attitude toward Cable. As she pointed out, "Many of us never dreamed the day would come when we would shake hands with Cable," yet "everyone rushed up and shook hands with him." She was glad that "at last he got that compliment from New Orleans. He deserved it, not only as tribute to his genius, but as compensation for the way we had treated him. I am glad. He is an old man, very picturesque, with beautiful manners." [28]

This account of Cable from the woman who had made a point of despising him throughout her career seems like an all-too-gracious burial of an old hatchet. And because the *Transcript* interview was reprinted in the *Louisiana Historical Quarterly* in 1923, we can be sure that Grace King approved of its contents. But, as both Edmund Wilson and Arlin Turner have pointed out, no mention of this reconciliation is made in *Memories of a Southern Woman of Letters.* In that last of Grace King's books she writes of her strong disapproval of Cable's position on Creoles and blacks and reveals that her animus against him had in fact been part of the drive that spurred her early career. Why, then, does she ignore the reconciliation in her memoirs? The tone of the Guyol interview is one of joy, and in it Grace King admits that "we" had treated Cable badly.

Certainly her attitude toward Cable had always been ambivalent. She had never hesitated to acknowledge what she called his "genius," and she must also have realized that her early fiction was partly in the Cable tradition. What he had started she had carried on with a greater loyalty to established attitudes. Cable and King were the two writers who more than any others made Americans aware of the character of New Orleans. But had Grace King included in her memoirs what she admitted in the Guyol interview, she would have betrayed a major principle of her career. For she would be saying that much of what her early writing stood for could now be repudiated. She was not going to say that because even at the end of her life she hardly believed it. The Guyol interview was an act of ladylike politeness to an elderly gentleman with whom she still disagreed. She was doubtless carried away with the emotional significance of that evening in the spring of 1915, but she had certainly

28. Louise Guyol, "A Southern Author in Her New Orleans Home," *Louisiana Historical Quarterly*, VI (July, 1923), 372

not changed her attitude toward the implications of Cable's fiction or his early essays on the Negro. To the end of her life her own attitudes on Creoles and blacks remained almost the same as they were in 1885 when she began to write.

In June of 1915 she achieved her highest academic honor—the honorary degree of doctor of letters from Tulane University. She had been a patroness of the university for many years; now the conferring of the degree at commencement would be one of the most satisfying events of her career. It was indeed a great day for her. She and her sisters were staying in Covington, the Coliseum Street house having been rented for the season. As she wrote the particulars to Carleton, they had to get up at six in the morning to take an early train to the city. It was a cool and beautiful day for them; everyone was in good spirits. By nine they were at the Coliseum Street house, where Maggie and Mary had a good breakfast prepared for them. They had the loan of their rooms for the day, so they dressed there and then took a taxi to the French Opera House, where Tulane commencements were held. Grace King was elated by the reception she received before the ceremony from both students and faculty of Tulane and of Newcomb College. They seemed to convey the idea that the main event of the day was her degree, making what she called a fuss over her. "If I had been younger & foolish," she wrote, "my head would have been turned. But I managed to keep it in the proper position on my shoulders—& answered compliments with compliments, & deftly turned the tables on the complimenters."

The other author there to receive a similar degree was her friend Ruth McEnery Stuart, but Mrs. Stuart was less well known to the Tulane family; she stood somewhat alone, while Grace King attracted the crowd. She walked in the procession just after the board of trustees and was given the place of honor on the stage. Nan and Nina sat in a box overlooking the stage, exchanging smiles of sisterly approval. The ceremony went on for ages—endless musical selections, announcements, long speeches. She grew childishly impatient for the moment when she would be given her degree. That moment came after Mrs. Stuart had received hers. Professor Peirce Butler of the English Department read the commendation in dignified prose that she took satisfaction in; then President Robert Sharp gave her the precious papers. Everyone on the stage stood while this was being done. And although she was most grateful, she pointed out to Carleton that she felt she had earned it. She and her sisters left the opera house full of the congratulations of the academic crowds, her arms full of flowers. When they descended the steps they could hardly move as the crowd waited to greet the literary ladies.[29]

They returned to Covington, and next morning Grace wrote to May McDowell, copying for her the charmed words of the commendation: "Be it known that in recognition of her exalted character, her eminent attainments in Arts & Letters, her constant devotion to the advancement of Truth & the Welfare of Society, the Administration of the Tulane University of Louisiana have this day conferred upon Grace King the degree of Doctor of Letters." Now indeed she felt as if goodness and mercy had followed her all the days of her life and that her cup was running over. After all the excitement she was glad to return to routine again. After the resurrection, she remarked, even the dead would want to get back to the repose of the grave.[30]

The degree from Tulane was one sign of the recognition she deserved for accomplishments, even though she had published little since the turn of the century. That summer, 1915, brought another, the turn of the tide in favor of *The Pleasant Ways of St. Médard*. A correspondence began between Grace King and the British critic Edward Garnett. He had happened to read the manuscript for a London publisher who wanted his opinion of it. His opinion was enthusiastic, and he urged publication of the novel in England, assuming that it had already been published in the United States. But the publisher refused on the grounds that he believed the book would not sell. Garnett wrote Grace King, asking her what the book's reception had been in America, adding, "It is a most exquisite achievement in its haunting sorrow & charm of atmosphere—a classic. I am saying so in a few clumsy lines in an article on 'criticism' for the *Atlantic Monthly*."[31] Curiously, his brief notice of *The Pleasant Ways* in the Issue of the *Atlantic* for February, 1916, also assumed that the manuscript was a book. After discussing Willa Cather's new book *O Pioneers!* he wrote:

Even higher, in its literary art, must we rank Grace King's *The Pleasant Ways of St. Médard*, a story rare in its historical significance. This poignant lament

29. Grace King to Carleton King, June 4, 1915, in Robert Bush (ed.), *Grace King of New Orleans* (Baton Rouge, 1973), 399–400.

30. Grace King to May McDowell, June 3, 1915.

31. Edward Garnett to Grace King, July 16, 1915.

for the South, at the close of the Civil War, rehearses a woman's lingering memories of the charm and grace of the New Orleans atmosphere, and of the poignant humiliation suffered by a ruined family. Will not its exquisite shades of feeling, delicate in vibrating sadness, give this novel a permanent place as an American literary classic?[32]

Grace King wrote Carleton about Garnett's letter and told him she intended to send it to Hamilton Mabie, who had also liked her novel. She hoped Mabie would advise her now as to what her next step should be: "Maybe my luck is going to turn enough to have my failure of a novel hatch into a success." She spent much time thereafter wondering whether that success would indeed come about after all the years of work on the manuscript. And she was inclined to think that most of her life had been passed in making ventures and then making herself miserable about them.[33]

She was greatly pleased with Garnett's notice and his letter. It seemed to compensate for the many years of waiting. She wrote him of her gratitude and told him his comments constituted the greatest compliment her writing had ever received. But the praise was not sufficient to move George C. Brett at Macmillan. She thought this might be attributed to his displeasure with Garnett's unfavorable comments in the same article on Ernest Poole's novel *The Harbor*, a Macmillan book.

Only a month after Garnett's article in the *Atlantic Monthly* Alfred Harcourt of Henry Holt and Company offered to publish *The Pleasant Ways* with the promise of a 10 percent royalty. "I have spent some very pleasant evenings with your little group of loving and lovable people," he wrote her. "At first, I didn't see the pattern, but I found its gradual unfolding very delightful; and thank heaven for the sense of humor that holds the balance all through." But even at this late date he wanted another revision. Certain passages of philosophizing, he suggested, could be cut because they were implicit in the story itself.[34] This time Grace King was probably quite willing to comply.

When *The Pleasant Ways of St. Médard* appeared in 1916 its reception was

32. Edward Garnett, "A Gossip on Criticism," *Atlantic Monthly*, CXVII (February, 1916), 174–85.
33. Grace King to Carleton King, August 3, 1915; Grace King to May McDowell, August 17, 1916.
34. Alfred Harcourt to Grace King, May 15, 1916.

almost entirely favorable. William Lyon Phelps admired the authenticity of the picture of New Orleans and wrote that the new book gave Grace King "a definite place as a literary artist." The reviewer for the *New Republic* wrote, "Something of the era hitherto unvoiced breathes in this exquisite memorial." The New York *Times* believed that the book restored Grace King to the reputation she had lost over the sixteen years since she had published an important work: "Her work, which is not nearly so widely known as it should be, is among the best, in some of its features, that American writers have produced. . . . She is contemptuous of the artful aid of dramatic situations, the reader's suspense, and cumulative interest. But she can make a character alive in a single sentence. . . . And equally subtle and effective is her pen when it is busied with a social order, a community, a regime." [35]

The reviewer for the Springfield *Republican* wrote that *The Pleasant Ways* was a book that "compelled the attention and excited the admiration. And if it was not an 'American classic' as Garnett had thought it was, perhaps it would be accepted as such in time." A writer for the Chicago *Dial* took issue with Garnett's calling the book a "lament"; the tone was, rather, a fully positive one: "These sketches have the charm of 'Il Penseroso' rather than the bitterness of woe. And out of the ruins of health, and wealth, and aristocratic assurance rises Character in these pages—indomitable, indestructible. Such a result is not a defeat, it is the highest victory attainable by humanity. I close this volume with a sense of elation—with that intellectual salute that moral victories receive." [36]

Of course Garnett had not said the book that he assumed had been published *was* a classic. He posed the possibility that it might become one and implied that it deserved to become one. But the three small printings that *The Pleasant Ways* went through were not enough to assure its permanence in the memory of either the critics or the reading public. The year 1916 may not have been a favorable one for the subject of Reconstruction; the Great War and our

35. William Lyon Phelps, review of Grace King's *The Pleasant Ways of St. Médard*, in *Dial*, LXI (September 21, 1916), 196; review of *The Pleasant Ways*, in *New Republic*, VIII (October 14, 1916), 278; review of *The Pleasant Ways*, in New York *Times*, XXI (August 27, 1916), 336.

36. Review of *The Pleasant Ways*, in Springfield *Republican*, September 10, 1916, p. 15; review of *The Pleasant Ways*, in *Dial* (Chicago), September 21, 1916.

involvement in it in 1917 were so much on people's minds that it may have diverted their attention from historic subject matter.

The sixteen years from 1899 when George C. Brett first asked Grace King for a novel until 1916 when Holt brought out the completed work spanned Grace King's life from the age of forty-seven to sixty-four. Although these years might have been the most productive ones of her life, during the period she produced no other book and relatively few articles and stories. She had always been the kind of writer who worked well on only one project at a time, and her difficulties in pleasing the Macmillan Company interfered with her completion of this particular project. But the numerous revisions doubtless made the novel a much better one than it would have been. And Alfred Harcourt's final insistence that she cut philosophical comment was the final stroke in the process of polishing. The book, consequently, speaks entirely through the simple drama of its story; the author herself is usually not a direct spokesman or interpreter of the action.

There were other reasons for her lack of productivity. When she first met George C. Brett in the late summer of 1899, she had told him that she believed she had come to the end of her little quiver. This was probably not just modesty; she no doubt had a sense that it was true, even though she hoped it was not. She felt that she had exploited her best ideas for books and stories, and those that were to come would be drawn with great labor from her brain. The three deaths in her family in the early years of the century had drained her emotionally, and this had affected her creative powers. So she implied to George W. Cable after he had written her a courteous note about *The Pleasant Ways of St. Médard*:

14 Oct. 1917

My dear Mr. Cable,

Your note is just what you meant it to be, graceful, agreeable, & warm hearted—just the note in fact to give me great pleasure & touch my heart.

St. Médard was written so long ago, during the golden age of my memory when my dear mother was still with us & my dear brother Branch. Life has been so dark without them that I have not written anything worth while since they left us. And I have had so much *business* to think about & attend to!

I hope that you are still as ever sturdily employed, giving us the stories that only you in all this great world can write.

Praise from you is indeed praise from "Sir Walter."

With many thanks
Cordially yours
Grace King[37]

The letter is a polite one to the one literary figure whom she had despised and still held in a kind of historic contempt. And the letter also suggests that no personal misgivings had ever been uttered between the two. Quite possibly Cable never knew of the original indignation against him that had set her pen in motion.

As she wrote him, it was true that the family deaths had drained much of her creative drive. She had once written that "Will made me old," referring to the tragedy of her younger brother, and indeed, over a period of a few years at the turn of the century and after, her hair had turned from a youthful reddish brown to white. In a snapshot taken early in the century with her two younger sisters she appeared in black silk mourning dress, standing straight as a ramrod with her hands clasped behind her and her firm chin jutting out, her head erect. The stance suggested an inner force of endurance that she could maintain even in the face of the deepest sorrow.[38]

She was possessed of a pertinacity about her works and a faith in them that made her persist until they were satisfactory. So it was that *The Pleasant Ways of St. Médard* had cost her sixteen years. The subject was the one closest to her heart because it involved the unsung heroism and endurance of her parents. Their loyalty to the old cause was also the story of hundreds of other families that had been involved in the Confederacy. The Kings were archetypal and their experience with variations was the experience of the South. *The Pleasant Ways* would be a kind of document; based on the everyday life of her own family, it is sound social history giving us a cross section of a humble quarter of the city after Appomattox. Several women told Grace King that it was their

---

37. Grace King to George W. Cable, October 14, 1917, in Bush (ed.), *Grace King of New Orleans*, 402. "Praise from 'Sir Walter'" is an echo of "praise from Sir Hubert," from the original "Approbation from Sir Hubert Stanley is praise indeed." Thomas Morton, *A Cure for the Heartache*, Act V, scene ii.

38. See p. 230.

own family story, so well did it depict the experience of the city from 1865 to 1870.

As Alfred Harcourt had written her, the pattern of the story does not appear in the early chapters and the unity of the work becomes clear only when the themes are gradually tied together. In the first chapter, "A Journey into a Far Country," the author introduces the Talbot family returning to the city, taking up residence in the poorest quarter, and being introduced to the French-speaking characters who are the permanent residents. Some of this material is reflected in the letters Grace King's father wrote her mother as he attempted to find a home for the family and bring them from the sugar plantation where they had spent the war years. Once the Talbots are settled the first real concern is the education of the children, who have had no more than family tutoring for three years. The chapter ends with the introduction of Mimi Pinseau, the Creole lady whose neighborhood school the Talbot children will attend. In the second chapter, then, we must be told the entire background of Mimi and her parents because, like the Talbots, they have had money but are now without it. The method is one of digression into the past in order to explain the present. For a woman, according to Grace King, is the accident or miracle of her past.

The third chapter, "Peace, Gentle Peace," takes the reader on Mrs. Talbot's first shopping expedition after her return and ends when she encounters Mademoiselle Coralie, her one time protégé, who snubs her. But the snub will not be explained until Chapter Twelve's full sketch of Mademoiselle Coralie reveals her unconscionable betrayal of her former patroness. Chapter Four, "Walking the Rainbow," concerns Mr. Talbot's legal career, and this is followed by "It Was a Famous Victory," in which a family Sunday walk on the levee near the site of the Battle of New Orleans becomes an eloquent statement about how it feels to be among the defeated. Each chapter dramatizes some aspect of Reconstruction life, the topsy-turvy life that contrasts so strongly with the world as it was before the war. "Tommy Cook" is about a young man who saved Mr. Talbot's law books for him. It is made clear that Tommy is not a gentleman, but in the new era such a young man can make his way without the old prerequisite of family background.

The ninth chapter deals with the essential question of Negroes and does so with a full knowledge and sympathy of the former slaves. At St. Médard Jerry and his wife Matilda are free, but there is no work for them in the community, and the Talbots have no money to pay them for their work. Even though the man and his wife are at first inclined to stay with their former owners, they gradually seek independence, which is at first a painful experience, even though it is of course inevitable. The connection with the Talbot family is not part of a plot but rather the customary experience of the separation of black and white families that followed the Emancipation Proclamation. That separation, in Grace King's eyes and from her memory, was the parting of the older generation of slaves from their masters with some feeling and even trepidation, but with absolutely none on the part of the younger generation of blacks.

The hero of *The Pleasant Ways* is the father, but the spiritual and emotional center of the family is the mother. From time to time her memory provides exposition for the action of the story; her consciousness delves into the past—back to the New Orleans she knew as opposed to the city she must now endure, then to the plantation life in war time, which was easier for her than facing poverty in the city. In the twelfth chapter we are given the full story of the betrayal of the family by Mademoiselle Coralie. The Talbots had left their home and most of their possessions in the hands of the Creole governess, who had always appeared to them to be modest and self-effacing. But as a poor girl who saw an opportunity to achieve affluence, she took to her own home as many of the Talbots' possessions as a wagon could hold, with the sole intention of dressing elegantly with her mistress's clothing and furnishing her tawdry home with the opulence of the Talbots' household. When Mrs. Talbot recognizes her in a shop, the younger woman pretends to be someone else and ignores her former patroness. And when Mrs. Talbot later goes to her home to see if by chance she has saved some of her silver, the governess has someone tell her at the door that the people she seeks have moved away long ago. This story has little to do with Mr. Talbot, but it is balanced by a similar betrayal he suffered when someone who owed him much in the law profession was able to seize the best law case dealing with riparian claims, the field of law in which he is the specialist. The balance between the two betrayals is an intentional structural device.

So also is the contrast between the Talbot and San Antonio families. The San Antonios are the richest people in St. Médard. Tony San Antonio is the saloon keeper who bought great quantities of cotton before the occupation of the city by Federal troops. He then hoarded this wealth so as to sell it to the Union and amass profits while other men of greater conscience were fighting for the Confederacy. Although the San Antonios have no connection with the Talbots, they are well known in the community since they occupy the best old plantation house in the area. It is Tony's sudden death that provides the first opportunity for the Talbots to lift themselves from poverty; Mr. Talbot will become the widow's lawyer and protect her immense wealth for her. So the book ends with the suggestion that after much endurance of betrayal and poverty and illness, the fortunes of the Talbots will change for the better. As the reviewer for the *Dial* had said, the book thus becomes not a lament at all but rather a celebration of character.

The tone of *The Pleasant Ways* in its total effect is therefore indeed "pleasant." The ordinary people of the community do not suffer from their poverty; it is the Talbots who suffer because they have been accustomed to the better life in years past. And as the book ends there is hope that they will again be on the road to affluence. But the life of St. Médard presents a variety of opportunities for the author to exhibit her own sense of the ironies of the time. The contrast between the San Antonios and the Talbots is one: Tony the barkeeper is at the top of Fortune's wheel, the patrician lawyer at the bottom. The San Antonio daughters are being educated like princesses at the Ursuline Convent, reared to move in a world completely foreign to their ignorant parents. Grace King's attitude toward the Talbot family does not imply that they should necessarily be above their neighbors, but that they should at least have the economic opportunity that the selfish San Antonios have. Mr. Talbot is the man of education ready to sponsor the less privileged. He has taken Tommy Cook, a street urchin, and set him on the road to the law profession. And Talbot is the only person who can control the wayward foundling Cribiche, bringing him into his own home to study with his own sons.

In particular episodes of the novel Grace King's irony is frequently the power that conveys the meaning rather than the physical action. The chapter "It Was a Famous Victory" records the Sunday habits of the Talbot family, customs the King family probably enjoyed in that area after the war. In St. Médard the Talbots live opposite the Federal barracks, where Sunday, when the military reveille is not sounded, is a day of relief. Late in the afternoon the family goes for a walk along the Mississippi and comes to the site of the Battle of New Orleans. The occasion calls for a full explanation of the battle from the recollections of the parents, whose own parents had been alive in 1814. The heroism of the princely commoner Jackson, of the Kentuckians, and of the British themselves presents a picture of past warfare, a famous victory for the city comparable to Blenheim in Robert Southey's poem. At the time a British steamship is coming up the river. Recognized by one of the children as a ship of the old enemy beaten by the New Orleanians, the child plays with the idea of being "whipped," saying she wouldn't appear at a place where she had been whipped. Without authorial comment, a pathetic contrast then develops between the southerners who have been "whipped" and dominated by the Federal power and those of 1814 who had been the victors. No one takes the time to explain the feelings of the adults, but the mother is full of stories of the gallantry of the Kentuckians in the days of the famous victory, which the family can only enjoy now as part of their regional memory, completely dampened by the subjugation of 1865. The conversation ends with a colloquy between the unknowing child and the suffering adult:

> "I used to hate it when I was whipped."
> "Oh! I don't mean that! I mean in battle. If I were a man I would never be whipped."
> "What would you do if the other army were stronger?"
> "I don't care if it were stronger, I would whip it."

Then, again without comment, the author carries the reader in the line of sight of her Sunday walkers to a view of the sunset and the city, a scene encompassing the distant skyline in a kind of beautiful decline of their world. She ends the episode with the sounding gun at the Federal barracks symbolizing the misery of subjugation:

> The path on top of the levee following the bending and curving banks produced the effect of a meandering sunset. Now it shone full opposite, now it glowed obliquely behind a distant forest, now the burning disk touched the ripples of the current straight ahead, and the British vessel seemed to be steering into it. Another turn and it had sunken halfway down behind the distant city, whose roofs, steeples, chimneys, and the

masts of vessels, were transfigured into the semblance of a heavenly vision for a brief, a flitting moment. Further on the bank turned them out of sight of it all,—and shadows began to creep over the water,—and when next they saw the West, the sun had disappeared, and all its brilliant splendor with it. In the faint rose flush of twilight beamed the evening star . . . far away from the little church of St. Médard came the tinkling bell of the Angelus . . . the evening gun fired at the barracks.[39]

Thomas Nelson Page had told Grace King that her novel would succeed if she opened it up and inserted a love story with a girl named Jeanne. His tone was flippant, even a little cynical, since it was the way he had found that led to publishing success. But when he wrote her in 1920 his tone was quite serious. He admired the final product *The Pleasant Ways*, in which she had made no compromise for the sake of monetary success. He also recognized in it an essential truth to the atmosphere of a time in the South that he had known in his own youth. He despaired that now an author had to have the key to the movies to produce the successful novel, and he knew that books like Grace King's never captured the movie audience. "I prefer still the reflections of life as it was lived," he wrote her, "and I think that this is the true art that you have practised. Later on when the novelist tries to write of the time we knew with its ways pleasant and unpleasant, he will go to books like yours to find the atmosphere of that time, I feel as if I had been there."[40]

39. Grace King, *The Pleasant Ways of St. Médard* (New York, 1916), 144.
40. Thomas Nelson Page to Grace King, August 22, 1920.

Twelve

Later Years and Later Works, 1916–1932

The span of years from the publication of *The Pleasant Ways of St. Médard* in 1916 to the end of Grace King's life in 1932 was characterized by hard work and local recognition. She spent those years mainly in New Orleans with occasional trips to Charlotte and to historic places in Virginia. The period was one of drawing in and summing up, a time of good productivity against the odds of oncoming age and bouts of ill health. Grace King maintained with pride the title she would use in her memoirs, "a southern woman of letters," and kept very bright her reputation among her own people in New Orleans. More than at any time in her career the intellectuals of the city paid her court and realized that she was the brightest jewel in their less-than-dazzling regional crown.

As in earlier years her family life dominated her emotions. The deaths of her sister May, her brother Fred, and her niece Warrene would confront her, but these bereavements had far less impact on her ability to write than the deaths of her mother and two brothers in the earlier years of the century. There were the usual quarrels in the family among the temperamental sisters, but there was also the continuing affection she showed for Nan and Nina as her closest friends. Her nephew Carleton was now a young man who best represented the new generation of Kings, and she tended to look upon him almost as the son she never could claim. And as usual if he vexed her from time to time, she did love and respect him, and she hoped that he would carry on the family tradition that she had exalted throughout her career.

Her connections with old friends outside the city were gradually breaking. Hamilton Mabie died in 1916, Henry Mills Alden in 1919, leaving her with no close friends in New York. Both of these men, as editors of *Outlook* and *Harper's Magazine*, had given her genuine friendship and did whatever they could to advance her career. As editors of that genteel generation, they had been more than happy to befriend and sponsor writers who were ladies or gentlemen. Grace King missed Mabie especially. His advice for many years had been unselfish and trustworthy; he had been something of a friendly agent who directed her to the proper publisher for her work either in history or fiction. And she had entertained him frequently on his visits to New Orleans.

She enjoyed occasional letters from Warrington Dawson, who was still living and writing in Paris. As a fellow southerner, she could always express freely to him the old Confederate resentments, the sectional bias that was never to leave her. After the fatiguing experience of completing a particularly difficult task in the summer of 1925 (probably the new edition of *Balcony Stories* with its two additional stories to be published by Macmillan), she wrote him, "Strength failed me at the end & even the will to work. Nothing but the thought of the handsome compensation kept me at it. This is the work [in] my life of the dastardly Yankees—having to think & work for money!"[1] Her conclusion as to where the blame lay for the struggle for money that continued to the end of her life was not without logic. If there had been no invasion of the South, if Farragut had not taken New Orleans in 1862, her father might have remained prosperous and endowed his daughters with generous incomes for life. She and her sisters could have spent leisurely lives as sterile bluestockings. But without work there would have been no publications, no career, no personal independence, no cosmopolitan life, no recognition.

In 1917 she was deeply involved emotionally in the events of the Great

1. Grace King to Warrington Dawson, August 19, 1925, in the William R. Perkins Library, Duke University.

War. Although she was in her middle sixties when the United States entered the war, she wished she had had the youth to engage in it. She wrote Carleton, an aspiring pilot, that she would like to have been an aviator. Good lifelong Democrat that she was, she usually agreed with the policy of President Wilson. As the events of April, 1917, unfolded, she felt the impropriety of proceeding with her routine activities. Wilson's war message to Congress converted her fully to his point of view. She pronounced it "the finest document of the war, I think—decidedly the finest state document any president has ever written." She felt as if she were living during the time of the French Revolution. She foresaw the coming Russian Revolution, believing that in Russia the Czar and "his foolish wife" would be executed as fools—"they deserve to be." She would have liked to join in and contribute her services to Red Cross work in the city: "If I were not so used up physically," she wrote May, "I would go down there myself & offer my services." [2]

She was much exercised about the rumors rife in the great port city. There was talk about three Germans caught trying to blow up the water plant or, as some said, putting typhoid germs in the water. Germans were being watched, especially at their gathering place, the Kolb Restaurant. Frequent patrol boats were to be seen on the Mississippi and there was talk about the possibility that the river would be mined. All of this activity and rumor reminded her of 1862, when she was a child and when the city had indeed been subjected to invasion and occupation. She asked herself if she were not going to end her career as she had begun it—in time of war. She still had a good many years to live, but as she approached the age of seventy she had the sense of being old. And despite the years of productive work still within her, she was well aware that the best of her work had already been produced.

She corresponded regularly with Carleton, telling him the news of New Orleans and the family, especially the details of his own family. His sister Warrene had died in March; his sister Grace had stayed on with her aunts to help manage the household until she could join her brother Brevard in Texas, where she would marry and settle permanently.

As the war continued, the elder Grace, as a single woman, felt somewhat

2. Grace King to May McDowell, April 3, 1917, in the Grace King Papers, Department of Archives and Manuscripts, Louisiana State University, Baton Rouge. Unless otherwise noted, all manuscript material is in this collection.

put down by the mothers who had sons in France. Such women would begin conversations with her in the cars and tell her about their sons' years of service, to which the aunt with a nephew could say little, since nephews didn't seem to count. She had never regretted before that she did not have a son, but now she wrote Carleton that what she most needed was a man in the house. In the warm month of June when she and her sisters were sleeping in the open air on the gallery, a fierce squall arose, blowing their beds over and making the curtains flap wildly over the balustrade. Grace and Nan tried to hold them, but the strong gale lifted the women up like feathers and nearly pitched them over the gallery. Incidents like this made her wish for the old days when her brothers were a part of the household.[3]

His Aunt Grace played the role of surrogate parent for Carleton, following his military career in Omaha, in Florida, and Princeton and attempting to buoy his spirits in times of discouragement. She was the one, also, who kept the young man aware of the family history and mission. Before All Saints' Day in 1918 she wrote him of its great significance as the day of retrospection, in which she could look back on the family experience with pride and not altogether with sadness. She saw in the history of the Kings more successes than failures and always "an indomitable spirit in all of us determined to get the best out of work & more determined not to give up in discouragement." Recalling the tragedy of her brother Will, who had struggled to master his addiction to alcohol, she reminded the young Carleton that his father had died "flag in hand, charging forward against the black spirits that had tried to down him. He had just found a new situation & was working hard in it." Then she cautioned the nephew, "Don't think I am sermonizing or lecturing. I am only talking out of my experience to you & you know I am a veteran in the war of life."[4]

Will's alcoholism had tarnished the 1890s and early years of the century for the family. Again the black spirits haunted the Kings, this time in her brother Fred, who had become a distinguished judge. Grace feared that his career too was now threatened by his habits of intemperance. She wrote Carleton that she was "pursued by the demon of the family. I wish I could leave N. O. & get beyond even the name of King." She feared that Fred's drinking might lead to

3. Grace King to Carleton King, June 27, 1918.
4. *Ibid.*, October 31, 1918.

his disgrace, which would be the more painful because of his prominence in the legal profession. But she also knew that only death could stop the whiskey drinking in the family. She could only hope that that end would come for Fred before disgrace. As it seemed to her whiskey was one of the inbred weaknesses of southern males: "Slavery and whiskey have always been their moving inspiration." She had remonstrated with Fred that she was ashamed to go about New Orleans and that she "could not stand any more humiliation on account of the King men."[5] The sermonizing was intended to caution Carleton against going the way of his father, her brother Will.

The young Carleton saw his father's family now in perspective, and he criticized his aunts from afar, drawing in rebuttal the stern admonitions of his Aunt Grace, who loved him and wanted to convey to him the complicated feeling she had for her own family. "There is no family life," she wrote him, "that is not founded on self-sacrifice—the seed of family devotion. We can look back on much sorrow & grief since you came into the family, a little boy, misunderstanding, & misunderstood, but the truth is we have grown together so closely that if we were forced apart we could not enjoy life. We might just as well recognise that as the fact oftentimes most apparent that we cannot on account of our faults live together. . . . & whatever I am, you are just like me."[6] Like Lord Chesterfield she was determined that her young man should be drawn to her way of thinking, and her major theme for him was family solidarity. Frequently she interpreted this strange and gifted family to him to emphasize its superiority. The Kings, after all, were like the ancient gods in comparison with ordinary mortals. They were powerful and talented and given to intense passions, especially anger; but their main quality was the King ideal: "Unfortunately we Kings put our standard very high & suffer when we are disappointed to a degree that low standard people do not imagine. But we *never give up*, & no matter where we are found at the end of life—we are always found with our ideal leading us like a standard."[7]

Armistice Day 1918 brought high excitement to New Orleans from morning until midnight. Grace King spent most of the day in the street, watching the wild joy. She was only sorry that she was not "young enough to scream &

5. *Ibid.*, April 19, 1917.
6. *Ibid.*, July 20, 1918.
7. *Ibid.*, October 6, 1918.

Grace King, about 1918, wearing the medal given her by the French government
and looking out from the porch of her home

Department of Archives and Manuscripts, Louisiana State University,
courtesy of John M. Coxe

yell with the others. It marks the greatest day in my life."[8] There was every reason for an American citizen to exult on that day, but for a daughter of the old Confederacy was there not something of the joy of victory that had been missing in the southern consciousness since 1865? How different was the situation in New Orleans at the end of the Great War that one could spend all day in the streets watching the joy of a wildly rejoicing city. Without saying so, Grace King must have compared the two vastly different ends of war and enjoyed the satisfaction of military victory that she had so missed at the time of Appomattox and after.

In that very week of the Allied victory she was informed of a personal triumph of her own. The French government would decorate her with the gold palms of *Officier de l'Instruction Publique*. The ceremony was held in the Kings' Coliseum Street house, the three sisters having invited many of their friends to a reception on a warm day in late November. When Charles Barret, the consul general of France in New Orleans, arrived to make the presentation, the double parlor was aglow with its brilliant prisms and vases of flowers on the tables, the guests buzzing with excited conversation. Wearing a gray dress, Grace King greeted the consul general, who treated her like an old friend. After the small talk the Frenchman took his place with some formality under the arch that separated the parlors and spoke enthusiastically about the quality of Miss King's writings and the value of her total accomplishment. While her friends stood about in solemn and silent awareness of the importance of the occasion, Barret opened a small red leather case and took out the golden palms with their purple rosette and pinned the medal on Grace King's breast. She exhibited the decoration with pride and then invited the guests into the dining room for white wine punch and white cake and fruit cake.[9] Then it seemed with some suddenness they had all gone away and another little ceremony in her life had become a memory.

*

During the final years of her career Grace King continued to produce works of fiction and history as she had in the past. If we compare the years from 1903 to 1916 with those from 1917 to 1932, it is apparent that during the earlier years

8. *Ibid.*, November 12, 1918.
9. Grace King to May McDowell, undated, ca. November, 1918.

she was held back by the shock of family deaths and later by the energy spent rewriting *The Pleasant Ways of St. Médard*. But the years that followed 1916 gave her a new invigorating energy to complete the work of her career. Unfortunately she chose minor subjects for these works; none of the four ranks in imaginative appeal with *The Pleasant Ways*.

Some of her best work of this time was done for the Louisiana Historical Society and published in their quarterly. Typical of her scholarship is "The Real Philip Nolan," an article that deals with the historic figure, as opposed to the fictional hero of Edward Everett Hale's "The Man Without a Country" (1863). The real Nolan was a contraband horse trader who was killed in a skirmish resulting from his activities along the Mexican border.[10] Her scholarship in articles of this sort is thorough and sound. She writes interestingly about historical subjects within her local province, and as the series of her contributions to the *Louisiana Historical Quarterly* accumulated, it is easy to see how intense her devotion to regional American history was.

*

By January of 1919 she had started a new work that would eventually be titled *Creole Families of New Orleans*. Like most of her other books the impetus had come from a publisher's request, and again it was the Macmillan Company that had made her a complimentary offer. She was in a new and optimistic mood, full of the old energy, but probably with less than a first-rate inspiration. She didn't believe she was wise to attempt the task after the long experience of *The Pleasant Ways*: "One must lead an elated life to write a book," she wrote Carleton, "& I don't find much cause of inspiration in my life." But one kept on as the wells of the old spirit began to run dry, even in a period of enervation. It was not delights alone that enervated one, "a too long endurance of roughness can produce the same effect. I find that I myself do not fight against ill fortune as I once did. I just give in & exclaim with the French 'C'est la fatalité.'"

But old inspiration or not, elation or not, she knew no better feeling than the energy and wish to work. "I am working so hard that my eyes are beginning to rebel," she wrote him, "& in fact my whole head seems to be

10. Grace King, "The Real Philip Nolan," *Louisiana Historical Quarterly*, X (March, 1918), 87–112.

going on a strike. I am only collecting materials now. After Easter I shall begin to write & then look out!!"[11]

It was good for her to be at work in 1919. Now that the excitement of the war was over she was inclined to suffer a lull that led to boredom, even though the new era brought with it such volatile issues as woman's suffrage and prohibition. Understandably she favored woman's suffrage, but she opposed prohibition as a measure that could not be enforced, and she resented the fact that the "drunkards" had forced it on everyone else.[12]

Early one morning in December, 1919, Grace King and her sisters heard of the fire that had broken out in the French Opera House in the Vieux Carré and completely destroyed that venerable center of the city's musical culture. The fire had started in the restaurant underneath the opera house. This tragedy was almost a personal one to the Kings, so involved were they in the Creole traditions of the city. Uninsured costumes worth $200,000 were destroyed besides the charming old building that was such an asset to the Quarter. Grace King was heartbroken by the event, and she could only console herself in a letter to May McDowell by saying that she was most thankful that she had attended the last performance and that that had been her favorite opera, Meyerbeer's *Les Huguenots*. A friend, Miss Farwell, had invited her along with Nan and Nina and two gentlemen. Now she remembered the performance that so perfectly suited her taste. "I sat as in a dream," she wrote, "& did not take my eyes from the stage & I thought of you as much as of the opera. How many times we have listened to the Huguenots together." Now the three sisters went to see the destruction, and because they could not get near the smouldering ruin, they came away, full of sorrow for the building that had meant so much to them. Even at Holmes Department Store, where they next went, everyone was talking about the fire, calling it the greatest calamity that could happen to the city. For the rest of the day Grace felt almost immobilized, unable to work as she thought about the old opera house. So many of the other theaters in the city hardly mattered; she bemoaned the fact that it was this precious one that had to go.[13]

11. Grace King to Carleton King, April 19, 1919.
12. *Ibid.*, January 17, 1919.
13. Grace King to May McDowell, December 4, 1919.

A malaise followed the excitement of the war years. She wrote Warrington Dawson in 1920, "We are surprisingly despondent in N. O. Prices are so high, money so scarce. We have fallen to the ground flat after our climb to the top of the heroic during the war."[14]

Grace King spent much of the year 1920 writing of the backgrounds and contributions to the city of the major Creole families. Also in 1920 her sister May McDowell died at a resort town and was brought home to Charlotte, N.C., where her husband had been mayor. Grace King made the last of many trips to Charlotte to attend the funeral. It was the end of her life's closest friendship and the end of a correspondence that had lasted almost forty years since May's marriage in 1881. She had been more candid with May in her letters than with anyone else; she could always unburden herself to the woman who knew her best.

Creole Families of New Orleans (1921) is a curious book that takes its place logically in the later work of Grace King. She had begun her career in 1885 by defending the Creoles against what she saw as the misinterpretations of George W. Cable. She chose to defend them even though she belonged to the English-speaking Protestant group whose forebears had settled in New Orleans after the Louisiana Purchase. Then in the early twenties, as her career was on the wane, she wrote an entire book on the history of the Creole accomplishment. It was a summing up for posterity, almost a swan song devoted to Creole history as seen through the histories of individual families. The single statement of the book is that it was a series of families who made New Orleans New Orleans. The unstated implication is that these families had lost much of their precious identity as they entered the twentieth century in the largest of American southern cities, as they intermarried with non-Creole families and often lost their names, as their French language gave way to English. Grace King saw herself as the preserver of that historical identity.

The Creole identity of *Creole Families* is also a defense of the aristocratic ideal, southern style, written at a time in the twentieth century when that ideal was at bay and counted far less than it had in the nineteenth century. Grace King the historian implies that New Orleans was created by Creole

14. Grace King to Warrington Dawson, November 29, 1920.

families who were dominant in the nineteenth century and who, for the most part, descended from honorable and frequently noble origins in France and Spain. W. J. Cash, in *The Mind of the South* (1941), was to point out that the Virginia aristocracy developed in the eighteenth century in the colonies, with very few of the original settlers being related to nobility. Grace King, however, presents scholarly evidence for the distinguished Continental origins of many of the Creole families she discusses.

Creole Families has its origin in genealogy, but the author may have invented a new literary genre in raising a dry-as-dust method of ancestor tracing to the status of literature. The development of a great city is here attributed to the breeding of powerful families capable of contributing their best men to the city's improvement, often through more than one generation. To produce a good family you need good genes and good breeding or the nurturing of such ideals as civic pride, ambition, and leadership. To produce a good city you need good families. She had no doubts about her theory, whether it was applied to the Creole families or the King family in their contributions to the city. The origins of the figures of her municipal panorama are either Canadian, French, or Spanish, or in the curious case of d'Arensbourg, Swedish and German. Except for Charles Gayarré and Pierre Beauregard, the Civil War general, all of the Creoles are nationally obscure. And ironically, the greatest of the New Orleans heroes was neither Creole nor New Orleanian—Andrew Jackson.

To take Beauregard as an example, his family records can be traced to the year 1290, when a Welsh ancestor of the general unsuccessfully rebelled against Edward I, fled to the court of Philip the Fair of France, and married a maid of honor of the king's sister. He then was given a post in the British possessions in France and established his family there. The immigrant ancestor of Pierre Beauregard was the commandant of a flotilla under Louis XIV, who brought assistance to Louisiana and carried back timber for naval construction in France. He was the great-grandfather of the future general. The general's mother was a Reggio, descended from the Dukes of Reggio and Modena. Grace King sketches the complicated career of the general, satisfied that her city's hero has been properly rooted in the European past, his ancestors having descended from dukes and having brushed shoulders with royalty.

The Beauregard chapter is one of the shortest in the volume since the general's relatives were unimportant. More interesting as social history is the account of the Marigny family who, although little known beyond their locale, were little less than archetypal in that they reflect the essential personality of early Creole New Orleans. Grace King finds the first mention of a Marigny on a list of officers who accompanied Iberville on the voyage on which he discovered the mouth of the Mississippi. She points out that there is no proof that this officer was the ancestor of the family in Louisiana, but that the family is usually traced to Pierre Philippe, Sieur de Marigny de Mandeville, to whom were issued letters patent of nobility.[15] She thus establishes the noble origins of the Marigny family in the New World as members of the military aristocracy. In fact the underlying motive for the settlement of New Orleans is the long time presence of the garrison of the king's soldiers in the city. In the late eighteenth century the family produced Pierre Philippe de Marigny, the member of the family who built an enormous fortune of $7,000,000 largely through real estate and made himself the richest citizen and largest landowner of New Orleans. His princely plantation faced the river, and there he lived with his family and an entire village of slaves. The house, long since razed, was, according to Grace King, "a primitive sort of palace," where he entertained in 1798 the French royal princes—the Duc d'Orléans (later King Louis Philippe) and his brothers, the Duc de Montpensier and the Comte de Beaujolais. Marigny also entertained the princes at his country home across the lake, which later became the resort town of Mandeville.

It is now understandable, according to Grace King's theory of family, that a son like Bernard de Marigny, third child of Philippe, would almost predictably have issued from such a father. Aristocrats needed background—preferably a full combination of nobility, money, land, and style. Bernard was born to all of these worldly values, and he became *the* Creole of the nineteenth century—that is, the nonscholarly Creole. Grace King calls him "the hero *par excellence* of New Orleans' social traditions; who, we may say, was to the Marigny family what the final bouquet is to a pyrotechnic display." She calls him "the Creole type; originating the standard of fine living and generous spending, of lordly pleasure and haughty indifference to the cost; the standard which he maintained so brilliantly for half a century, until, even to-day, one

15. Grace King, *Creole Families of New Orleans* (Baton Rouge, 1971), 9.

receives, as an accepted fact, that not to be fond of good eating and drinking, of card playing and pretty ladies; not to be a *fin gourmet*, not to be sensitive about honor, and to possess courage beyond all need of proof is, in sober truth—not to be a Creole."[16]

Now the old Cable-King undeclared debate becomes clear: Grace King saw Bernard Marigny as a man to be admired. If Cable did not specifically write about him, it is likely that he drew from the character of such a man for his superb and often satirical pictures of Creoles in *The Grandissimes*. In that novel the Creoles are fascinating, as they were to Cable, but they are also inordinately proud and cruelly unjust to their slaves. Grace King made no bones about the fact that she admired such people as historic symbols of the New Orleans experience. Cable the moralist judged the early Creoles from the perspective of the 1880s, stressing their injustice as a ruling class to their slaves and to those of mixed blood. Grace King admired the good life of the Creoles and the brilliant social world they moved in, but it was neither in her nature nor in her background to criticize them. She saw the qualities of life of the Marigny family as admirable virtues, signs of cultural accomplishment, reflections of French court life of the eighteenth century. Here was a provincial culture built by sugar and cotton planters, descendants of military and administrative officers, a culture that determined the entire character of the nineteenth-century city.

Cable's Grandissimes are a clannish lot who live at the expense of others, but little in the novel suggests the charms of their way of life or their opulence. In her portrait of Marigny Grace King stressed that opulence as the source of his romantic appeal. We hear of French chefs working at Mandeville.

> [There were] *grassées* that fed on magnolia berries; turkeys fattened on pecans; papabotse and snipe kept until they ripened and fell from their hangings; terrapin from his own pens; soft-shell crabs from the beach; oysters fresh from his own beach; green trout and perch from the bayous; sheepheads and croakers from the lake; pompano, red fish, snappers from the gulf; vegetables from his own garden; cress from his own sparkling forest spring; fruit from his orchard; eggs, chickens, capons from his own

16. *Ibid.*, 23.

fowl yard. These, with sherry, madeira, champagne, and liqueurs, were the crude elements of repasts that he combined into menus that Brillat-Savarin would have been glad to have composed.[17]

The Creole code of the duel also differs appreciably in the interpretations of Cable and King. It is a custom of barbaric cruelty to Cable, an act of antique nobility to King, a key to the refined sense of honor among Creoles.

Most of the reviews of *Creole Families* were favorable, usually stressing Grace King's accuracy and the charm of her literary style. The *New York Times Book Review* for May 1, 1921, devoted a full page by Ben Ray Redman to the book. Redman found it surprising "that this book . . . which is genealogical in spirit and intent, if not strictly so in form, should exercise an appeal for one to whom all the dead . . . are distant and, for the most part, unheard of strangers."[18]

Grace King wrote Warrington Dawson that *Creole Families* was "creating quite an excitement in this 'Far from the Madding crowd of books' place. The price causes inevitable consternation. How capricious is the taste of extravagant people. Our rich ones who literally are casting money before swine, in the way of luncheons, teas, and country club frolics, are affrighted at the idea of paying six dollars for a book." This was an old theme—her lover's quarrel with New Orleans, whose affluent elite ranked their social pleasures above the intellectual status of their city.

*

In the summer of 1921 Helen McAfee of the *Yale Review* wrote Grace King, praising *The Pleasant Ways of St. Médard* and asking for a possible future article on a New Orleans subject. Pleased with the compliment, Grace King prepared a biographical sketch of "Madame Girard, An Old French Teacher of New Orleans." Madame M. D. Girard, born in Saint Lucia and educated in Paris, had settled in New Orleans, where in her widowhood she was for many years a tutor in French for Creole and American children. Over the years of the second half of the century she became a familiar figure, almost an

17. *Ibid.*, 36.
18. Ben Ray Redman, review of *Creole Families of New Orleans*, in *New York Times Book Review* (May 1, 1921), 14.

institution in the city. In the article on Madame Girard Grace King presented a symbol of private education after the war, as her 1909 article on Mrs. Stamps had presented a symbol of the development of public education. The theme of education was dear to Grace King's heart as part of the South's heroic attempts to revive its culture. Both *Monsieur Motte* and *The Pleasant Ways of St. Médard* add to this recording of the educational and social history of the city.

During the period when she was writing the article on Madame Girard Grace King corresponded frequently with Helen McAfee. All went well until she received the page proof for her article. Because the editors had to conserve space, they were obliged to limit the length of the article, which resulted in a series of cuts about which Grace King had not been consulted. She first wrote McAfee, saying that on reading the proof her first impulse was to forbid its publication in the *Yale Review*. But her sisters had convinced her that only the literary value had been lost in the emendation. She complained about various changes and then condemned the editor's changing of the final sentence: "What a commonplace, utterly ignoble last sentence. No wonder American literature is so much below the European. Our literature is *degraded* by just such treatment."[19]

After an exchange of telegrams between New Haven and New Orleans, Grace King wrote, in part, to the editors of the *Yale Review*:

> It was certainly an unwarrantable liberty to mutilate my ms. in the way your office did. I could and would have shortened the article as you wished, & have preserved its literary flavour. The person who did the cutting "bricked" up the gaps in a clumsy & awkward way. Many picturesque little details were sacrificed, details that I thought of artistic worth. . . .
>
> I would take it as a personal favour if you would send me my ms. I *must* satisfy my friends & Mme Girard's by printing the article as I wrote it.[20]

The *Yale Review* answered her indignation with an extremely polite letter on November 26, stating that she had exceeded the maximum limit of six

19. Grace King to Helen McAfee, November 22, 1921, in the Beinecke Library, Yale University.
20. Grace King to the editors of *Yale Review*, November 23, 1921, in the Beinecke Library, Yale University.

thousand words for articles in their Christmas issue. They referred to her article as a sketch rather than a biography, emphasizing that they did not publish biographies. Later they sent her a check for sixty dollars for the article. The little controversy was resolved, and when the article was published its reception was greater than Grace King had expected it to be. In an entirely different mood from that of her earlier letters, she wrote Helen McAfee on January 2, 1922, saying that the article "is exciting here the most enthusiastic admiration," and she added, "I am only too glad to confess that your judgment was better than mine when you shortened the article." [21] The little controversy shows her great sensitivity about her writing and her pride that was ready to assert itself indignantly against a northern publisher. Her final admission that McAfee was right in the first place shows her willingness to accept the fact that her judgment was not always infallible.

The Madame Girard article drew its ultimate compliment from Jean Jules Jusserand, the French ambassador, who wrote Grace King an appreciative letter. "You have traced of this brave French woman of the islands and of Louisiana," he wrote her, "a portrait so charming and so living, giving it as a frame the milieu in which she lived, that milieu of which your writings will preserve for future generations the exact and charming picture." [22]

Because they also felt that she had helped preserve their regional milieu for future generations, the Louisiana Historical Society organized a tribute to Grace King on the evening of April 27, 1923. It took place in the *sala capitulaire* of the Cabildo on Jackson Square—the old Spanish building next to the cathedral that she had been partly responsible for converting into an historical museum. It was said that nothing like it by way of celebration had taken place there since the signing of the Louisiana Purchase in 1803. Hundreds attended, and many were turned away to stand in the street. Spokesmen for the society praised her as "the greatest living author of Louisiana," which, because of its limitation, may have sounded less complimentary than was intended. Her competence as historian and fiction writer was evaluated by people who were in a position to know. Her friend Professor Reginald Somers-Cocks of Tulane must have pleased her most when he said, "Miss King is undoubtedly the

21. Grace King to McAfee, January 2, 1922, in the Beinecke Library, Yale University.
22. Jean Jules Jusserand to Grace King, June 3, 1922, in Grace King, *Memories of a Southern Woman of Letters* (New York, 1932), 379–80.

foremost authority on the past history of New Orleans and as the past is key to the present she understands her city and its people as no else can. . . . She sees their faults and weaknesses no less clearly than their virtues but she deals tenderly with them and we feel that she would hardly change them if she could."

Grace King herself spoke at some length about Colonel William Preston Johnston's refounding of the historical society after the Civil War. In the early days she served as vice-president and later as recording secretary. After her remarks she was presented with a silver loving cup, the doors at the end of the room were opened, and a procession of friends entered, bearing bouquets and baskets of flowers which were laid in front of her. At the end of the ceremony everyone stood as the band played "Dixie." Her elation was intense and, as she recorded the event, she was "as in a dream, feeling what the French writer said in his description of Judgment Day, 'Quand le livre de notre conscience sera lu devant la compagnie!'"[23] The tribute was even more overwhelming and satisfying than the conferring of the honorary degree by Tulane University in 1915, especially since the ceremony was for her alone.

After she had touched several of the better minds of Paris during the *belle époque*, she had privately sneered at the New Orleans intelligentsia. Thirty years had passed and New Orleans was still not a major intellectual center. But in 1923 few would remember the name of Grace King in Paris or in Hartford or New York. What she had written to Carleton years ago, in 1914, was clearly true in 1923: "People in N Y always seemed so detached from one another to me & I always felt such a mere insignificant scrap of humanity there, whereas here I am a personality."[24]

*

When the Macmillan Company failed to get from Grace King the novel about Reconstruction they wanted and rejected even her final version of *The Pleasant Ways of St. Médard*, she set out to write the kind of novel that would be acceptable to them. This was the historical romance *La Dame de Sainte Hermine*, which they published without any objections in 1924. It does contain a love

23. King, *Memories*, 396–97; Presentation Remarks of W. O. Hart, April 27, 1923.
24. Grace King to Carleton King, February 4, 1914.

story and a unified plot, both of which were missing in *The Pleasant Ways*. Only one edition of the novel was published; it has never been reprinted and today is relatively unknown.

Grace King's first and only other attempt at historical romance was the novella "The Chevalier Alain de Triton" (1891), which never achieved for her the recognition she enjoyed for her short stories of contemporary New Orleans life. In both "The Chevalier" and *La Dame* she drew on her profound knowledge of the period of Bienville—the second quarter of the eighteenth century when New Orleans was in its infancy. In both works one learns a great deal about the quality of life in those early times. Grace King is primarily interested in the Canadians. Bienville and the fictional Dame Catherine are colonists deeply serious about the purpose of their austere lives—Bienville as the historic founder of New Orleans and Dame Catherine as a symbolic Canadian woman who is the female counterpart of the *coureurs de bois*.

In a letter of 1915 Grace King had said she was "a realist à la mode de la Nlle Orléans." She saw heroism and even romanticism in everyday life. "I had a mind very sensitive to romantic impressions," she wrote, "but critical as to their expression."[25] She applied the same principle to her treatment of historical figures and fictional characters in *La Dame*: seek out the heroic in their lives, but present it within the limits of commonplace reality; never force the heroic or the sentimental on the reader. Using this guideline, she produced realism even in her two attempts at historical romance. Here she spurned the depiction of violent and suspenseful actions and centered on the domestic, the everyday, the commonplace. She avoided dramatizing melodramatic scenes probably because she looked upon them as the hackneyed subjects of old-fashioned romancers like Scott, Cooper, and Alexandre Dumas *père*. The result by intention is not a very exciting romance, but the delicate story of two genteel and dignified lovers. *La Dame de Sainte Hermine* reads a little like a modern love story set in the eighteenth-century frontier.

Marie Alorge, la Dame de Sainte Hermine, at the beginning is a pathetic lady, a fish out of water, who finds herself in primitive Louisiana when she should more appropriately grace the salons of a fine chateau in France. In the

---

25. Grace King to Fred Lewis Pattee, January 19, 1915, in Robert Bush (ed.), *Grace King of New Orleans* (Baton Rouge, 1973), 398.

first scene, having arrived by ship from France and swooning into the arms of the stalwart Dame Catherine, she is an isolated figure, almost friendless in a strange land, projecting some of the pathos that Hawthorne felt for Hester Prynne in the opening scenes of *The Scarlet Letter*.

We soon learn why so graceful a young woman should be forced against her will to sail into a lifetime of exile. She has been cruelly treated by her uncle and by her cousin, whom she has been forced to marry. Her properties have been wrested from her on the false pretext of her infidelity to the cousin-husband, and she has been sent into colonial exile by one of those arbitrary warrants known as a *lettre de cachet*. Such situations were not uncommon, so Grace King was dealing with historic truth, even though the injustice done her heroine partakes of the melodramatic. Marie Alorge is an anomaly in New Orleans, where most of the women are the casket girls, to each of whom the king has given a small hope chest and a free ride to Louisiana as an inducement to marry one of his soldiers and help populate the little settlement. She is a genteel aristocrat, full of fine sentiments from her convent education and ready to appreciate the finer qualities of the king's commandant, who happens to be young, handsome, and single. Part of the simple plot is the resolution of this love story; the participants enjoy a short, happy marriage, which ends with the death of the young husband after his encounter with an Indian arrow.

In the early days of the courtship of Marie Alorge by the Chevalier Henri de Loubois, he describes to the lady the honeymoon of the tall middle-aged widow Dame Catherine: "I would rather have had their honeymoon than the honeymoon of any bridal couple in romance. Imagine! Imagine, madame, what their life was in the wild forest, braving together there the pursuing savages, sharing together their crust of bread and handful of parched corn! I used to pray to God to send me such a honeymoon."[26] He is of course describing the kind of romance of the wilderness made famous by Chateaubriand, but a kind that could also be dramatized realistically. The chevalier and Marie Alorge in one scene plaintively discuss the difference between moonlight in Europe and moonlight in the American wilderness. He points out,

> The moon is even more beautiful here than in France! . . . and there it has
> such noble sites to fall upon—castles, palaces, beautiful fields of green,

26. Grace King, *La Dame de Sainte Hermine* (New York, 1924), 40.

and rivers with banks bordered with drooping willow, and ripples running under the arches of stone bridges. But no one cares to look at the moonlight there! . . . Too many fine things to look at. The king, the court, the beautiful women, the splendid men in their uniforms covered with gold stars and braid! Even love disdains the moonlight there; it can get along without it. Here we have only forests and the great river and the Indians. They make up our noble views here![27]

Annette, a good-hearted, commonplace woman, is Marie Alorge's neighbor who serves as the chief vehicle for commonplace details. She has been sent to the New World as one of the casket girls. Her story is a digression that makes one of the most interesting chapters because it involves the debunking of the much romanticized myth of the origin of a portion of the Creole population in New Orleans. In Grace King's view the casket girls were good young women with respectable backgrounds, but they were so ugly that the nuns escorting them found it necessary to cover their faces with veils until after the mass marriage they were to undergo with their future husbands.

After the ceremony, the disappointed husbands go off to drink, leaving their brides to themselves. Annette tells the story of the arrival of her drunken husband at his home, where she has spent the evening cleaning house. His fellow soldiers throw him in the door:

And there he lay. He could not move; his eyes were closed; he breathed like a tired dog. I brought the candle close and looked at him. I had not had time to look at him before. He was a short man but stout; and he was ugly, madame; all black. His hair, his beard, the hair on his hands! A drunken man, I said, and as ugly as the devil. So ugly that I trembled, but enfin! how could he help that? I was ugly, too. I knelt down by him and I unbuttoned his shirt, his dirty shirt, and I took off his shoes, and at last I made up my mind to put him to bed. . . . I dragged him to it and put my shoulder under his arm, and I strained and strained; and God helped me so that I could hoist him on to the bed, and I rolled him on to it; and then I undressed him and put him at his ease and covered him with a sheet. And then the sickness began, just like my father. He was sick, sick, and I was sick too. I gave him water . . . and I wiped his face with a wet towel, and then when it was midnight, he went off to sleep.[28]

Narrative of this sort reveals some of the mud and dirt of frontier life as it must have been, not as Cooper saw his clean and tidy wilderness. Grace King married history and realism in her novel, but she was unsure of her accomplishment, fearing that she had written the book too hurriedly. When the reviewer for a northern publication called the work "crude," she bristled and came to the conclusion that "Yankees . . . cannot tell crudity from simplicity."[29] The style of the novel is graceful and lucid, but the subject matter has not enough complication or depth to make the novel a full success. As a quiet, meditative novel of history, however, *La Dame de Sainte Hermine* anticipates the kind of novel Willa Cather would write in *Death Comes for the Archbishop* (1926) and *Shadows on the Rock* (1931). Both King and Cather were serious scholars who created beauty out of the truthful treatment of history.

*

In 1920 H. L. Mencken had published his landmark essay "The Sahara of the Bozart," pointing out the dearth of cultural life and creativity throughout the old Confederacy. Mencken was largely right in his criticism of the South; almost no nationally known writers or artists were flourishing at that time. Indeed, Grace King would have been the first to deplore New Orleans' lack of cultural life as the South's largest city. But, ironically, "The Sahara of the Bozart" appeared just before the beginning of the southern renaissance of the 1920s.

New Orleans was to become a relatively important center for writers in the twenties, and Grace King was aware of the new creativity, though she was then an aging symbol whose world was a different one from that of the new writers of the South. The genteel tradition was still flourishing when the French Quarter became the center for a new literary energy. She had in common with the young writers her enthusiasm for the French Quarter and her own espousal of realism. She was a cultural preservationist, active in

28. *Ibid.*, 103–104.
29. Grace King to Warrington Dawson, September 22, 1924, in the William R. Perkins Library, Duke University.

organizations that respected the architectural antiquity of the Quarter. The younger writers frequently lived there, however, enjoying its sordidness along with its charm. The Quarter became a kind of southern Greenwich Village, the center of a new bohemianism.

In the city of the 1920s Grace King's position is gently satirized in the volume of pictorial sketches prepared by William Faulkner and his friend William Spratling, *Sherwood Anderson and Other Famous Creoles* (1926). Faulkner wrote the introduction, in which he parodied the style of Anderson, who had lived in the city since 1922. Spratling, a teacher in the Tulane School of Architecture, drew the cartoons for the book, one of which was based on the Wayman Adams portrait of Grace King, painted in the winter of 1925–1926. The painting featured Miss King in her prism-lighted parlor flanked by her two sisters who were her companions and literary aides-de-camp. The parody of the painting gently satirizes the reigning queen of New Orleans letters with an implication of the stuffiness of the older generation. The book's major effect was that it estranged the former friends Faulkner and Anderson.[30] It is unlikely that Grace King took any offense. She took herself quite seriously, but she may have been more resilient to satire than Anderson was.

In 1919 one of the chief mourners after the burning of the French Opera House in the Quarter was Lyle Saxon, a native of Baton Rouge who had moved to Royal Street just before the modern revival of the Quarter began and well before the sojourns there of Anderson and Faulkner. Saxon and Roark Bradford were the members of the new literary movement who became friends of Grace King. Saxon, then in his twenties, was destined to write several well-known books on Louisiana and, as a journalist, would become a friend of the younger authors who would enliven the *Times-Picayune* or contribute to the *Double Dealer*.

Faulkner must have known who Grace King was, but there is no evidence that he ever met her. He was a promising novice at the time of *Sherwood Anderson and Other Famous Creoles*, but his reputation as a major writer would not come until after the death of Grace King. She did meet Sherwood Anderson and corresponded with him briefly when she invited him to attend a

---

30. William Faulkner and William Spratling, *Sherwood Anderson and Other Famous Creoles* (Austin, Tex., 1925).

Grace King flanked by her sisters Nan and Nina, about 1925, an oil portrait by
Wayman Adams

Drawing satirizing the Wayman Adams portrait of Grace King, first published in
William Faulkner and William Spratling, *Sherwood Anderson and Other Famous Creoles*
(Austin: Pelican Bookshop, 1925)

University of Texas Press

meeting of Le Petit Salon. The ladies' club had been organized in 1924 with Grace King as president, and weekly meetings were held in an old house in the French Quarter. In her invitation she wrote that she hoped he would not refuse the incense they were prepared to burn before him.

Anderson's answer was unexpectedly shy and polite: "I should have called upon you before but that I was somewhat afraid. You see I thought you might possibly think me terrible since I have often been pictured as being.

"On the other hand I have admired you as a sincere craftsman and have thought it too bad that people really interested in the same elusive crafts should not have met.

"The tea idea frightens me a little. Before I say anything definite about it may I not come to call on you." [31]

Let us assume that he did call and either then or later presented her with his current book—more than likely *A Story Teller's Story* (1924). In her acknowledgment she called the work "overwhelming." "You have a pen of iron," she wrote, "& you use it like a giant. The reviewers are right in their estimate of you. Poignantly sad & marvelously beautiful—I must read it over again. What a book! What a book!" [32] In thanking her for her praise, Anderson wrote, "We, of a younger generation of writers in America, have been such truculent fellows. There has been so much of meeting flair with flair.

"Always however I have known and loved a gentler tribe of the ink party here—of which you, in my mind, have always been one—and have hoped some day to merit what would make me acceptable to gentler people too." [33]

Two years later, in 1926, Grace King also met Edmund Wilson through Lyle Saxon. She invited them both for dinner, but Wilson declined since the proposed date was the day he planned to leave New Orleans. He wrote her of the great pleasure he took in reading *New Orleans, The Place and the People*. [34]

Joseph Hergesheimer visited Grace King at least twice during this period. He came first as early as 1919, when she was not at home and he was entertained by Nan and Professor Reginald Somers-Cocks of Tulane. Grace King

31. Sherwood Anderson to Grace King, November 24, 1924, in Bush (ed.), *Grace King of New Orleans*, 29.

32. Grace King to Anderson, undated, ca. December, 1924, in *ibid.*, 29.

33. Anderson to Grace King, December 11, 1924, in *ibid.*

34. Edmund Wilson to Grace King, April 11, 1926.

referred to Hergesheimer with some disdain as "a Saturday Evening Post author . . . who is proclaimed as 'the great American author.'" He and the professor locked horns over the subject of John Galsworthy. Hergesheimer took such offense during the argument that he left the house abruptly. Describing the incident to Carleton, she wrote that he was "here getting up atmosphere for a new novel." On another occasion, probably as late as 1926, according to a story remembered by Edmund Wilson, Hergesheimer admired the handsome Victorian furniture of the King drawing room and asked her where she "picked up all these beautiful old things."[35] She was doubtless taken aback by such an inquiry from a Philadelphian; the Kings had had much of their furniture since Reconstruction times. The popular reputation of Hergesheimer may have galled her—the frequent publications especially in magazines like the *Saturday Evening Post* and the filming of his well-known story "Tol'able David." Grace King, who had exploited only the regional experience of her own roots, held in suspicion a northern author who went from place to place to gather atmosphere for novels.

She continued to encourage Warrington Dawson in his writing, linking him with her own emotional origins: "Young Southern writers differ from the other variety by their higher standpoint. Patriotism & the most exalted love for our parents was our inspiration. We knew we cared for no other motive, & our books are a part of the history of the Confederacy, as our lives are." Again, almost agreeing with the thesis of Mencken's "The Sahara of the Bozart," she bemoaned the fact that "books are of no account in the South, I am sorry to say. The Macmillans do not count upon New Orleans at all in the . . . sale of my books. No *best* book has a chance here—only the flimsiest & the newest immoral best sellers. I am very much disgusted about it. But I still work on. Our reward will come one of these days in the future." She urged him not to work too hard. She herself had "worked & am working beyond my strength, but there is nothing else in life for me." Then she completed her letter with comments on the death of Joseph Conrad, whom she had never met, but who had been a close friend of Dawson's: "He was one of the great admirations of my life," she wrote. "I always hoped one day to know him. He cannot be

35. Grace King to Carleton King, March 20, 1919; Edmund Wilson to Robert Bush, July 20, 1970, in Bush (ed.), *Grace King of New Orleans*, 28.

replaced in literature." A few months later she was inveighing against the best sellers, calling such novels as Edna Ferber's *So Big* "Humiliating—nothing less—to people who love good literature." [36] She felt a bitterness that her own novel, *La Dame de Sainte Hermine*, had sold so poorly and such commercial works sold so well.

Although in New Orleans she was the grande dame of the genteel past, her response to younger authors in the 1920s, especially Sherwood Anderson, is an indication that she saw little conflict between her own world and that of the new southern fiction. She was always one to keep up with the latest trends and to be familiar with the latest books. When local-color fiction was fashionable and marketable in the 1880s, she had produced her volumes in that genre, but when local color faded she progressed to a new kind of short story in her *Balcony Stories*, following the more European style of Maupassant and Daudet. In the 1890s she exploited, in four different volumes, her talent for biography and history. Even in her seventies she produced four books that demanded the expense of heavy labor from her. Her energies were relatively prodigious in her final decade for three reasons. One was that she wished to keep her name bright both professionally and socially. Another was that she wanted to earn enough money to maintain her social position. And she reveals a third in her comment to Warrington Dawson about her work—"there is nothing else in life for me."

She would have liked producing drama, and as early as 1887 she had submitted her dramatic version of the story "Monsieur Motte" to Augustin Daly, though he did not find it producible. Through the years she had interested herself in the drama, especially when she was visiting New York, London, or Paris. In New Orleans she attended productions of Shakespeare at Tulane and occasional performances of traveling companies. She became a friend of Otis Skinner when he performed in the city, and when a play of his was ill attended she was quick to scorn her fellow citizens for not patronizing the arts sufficiently.

She herself experimented in the writing of two plays late in life. In 1926 she published in the theater magazine *Drama* a one-act comedy entitled "A Splendid Offer," the setting of which is so unlikely for Grace King that one

---

36. Grace King to Warrington Dawson, November 21, 1924, in the William R. Perkins Library, Duke University.

might doubt her authorship. Her comedy of manners has a background of the Northeast—either New York or Boston—one of the few times she wrote about characters other than Louisianians. The all-female cast represents three generations of the same family and possibly echoes the kind of comedy written by Rachel Crothers in *Mary the Third* (1923). The central character is a matriarch who unsuccessfully challenges the marriage choices of both her granddaughter and her greatniece. When she loses the struggle between the generations, she is the first to admit that she met the same resistance from her parents when she was young. She won her contest then as the young women will win theirs now. The play reflects how traditional standards are abandoned when young women choose their husbands. The dialogue is rapid and sprightly. When one woman remarks, "No lady enjoys employment for which she receives pecuniary remuneration," [37] Grace King is satirizing the old snobbery about working women.

She also wrote a three-act play about Jean Lafitte called *An Old Romance*. Although this was never published and is still in manuscript, it was presented at the Beauregard House in the French Quarter several months after her death. There were three performances in October, 1932.

*

Late in the summer of 1926 Grace, Nan, and Nina traveled to Virginia. Early in September Grace wrote Warrington Dawson that they were "enjoying the good historical provender to be found here. Williamsburg is a perfect old Southern place with its William & Mary College . . . & fine old Bruton Church & splendid private libraries. We are amply 'wading' in history." During a period of fine weather they drove to Jamestown and Yorktown, exulting in the "glorious episode" of the surrender of Cornwallis. Grace King the Francophile considered the battle of Yorktown a French victory because of the presence of Rochambeau, de Grasse, and Lafayette. And the monuments pleased her as well because they were not "offensively American." [38]

She and Dawson corresponded sporadically, mutually admiring each

37. Grace King, "A Splendid Offer, A Comedy for Women," *Drama* (Chicago), XVI (March, 1926), 213–15.
38. Grace King to Dawson, September 1, 1926, in the William R. Perkins Library, Duke University.

other's writings as they were published. Late in 1928 she wrote him in a shaky hand, admitting that she held her pen now with difficulty. The year had been a hard one, bringing her "to the limit of endurance. A long period of malaise culminated last summer in a cutaneous affection on body not on face. I had to go to the mountains (Tenn.) for a change of air. It did me no good. I had to come home & put myself under a Dr & I am just now beginning to feel well. And then you know that our life in the South is still fringed with financial anxieties. I am so tired of them!"[39]

Part of her illness and fatigue was probably due to her exertion on the long book she had completed. *Mount Vernon on the Potomac, History of the Mount Vernon Ladies' Association of the Union* was published in 1929 by Macmillan. Grace King wrote it in her later years at the suggestion of her sister Nan, who had been appointed vice-regent of the Ladies' Association in 1912, representing Louisiana. Commissioned by the association, the book brought Grace a set fee of $2,000.[40] Like her other volumes, this one originated with a request from an organization or a publisher. Although it is her longest book (491 pages), it is perhaps her least interesting one because of its specialized subject.

In American civilization few accomplishments carried out exclusively by women are more worthy of praise than the purchase and restoration of Mount Vernon. The book stresses this point in the author's comments and through the speeches and correspondence of the association. Indeed, the point is so well taken that the reader senses a naïve flavor of feminist chauvinism as well as southern aristocratic chauvinism. The "ladies" of the title of the association is intended to convey the idea of women of culture and breeding, and we are given a sketch of the life of the first regent of the group—Miss Ann Pamela Cunningham of South Carolina—with an unusual emphasis on her "aristocratic" background. In the 1850s, when the association was founded, this approach was very much in vogue, and the bias is another example of Grace King's aristocratic approach to American civilization.

Of considerable interest is the account of the origin of the restoration when Miss Cunningham's mother sailed past the decaying mansion and later suggested the idea to her invalid daughter. And the details of the maintenance

---

39. *Ibid.*, December 8, 1928.
40. John S. Kendall, "A New Orleans Lady of Letters," *Louisiana Historical Quarterly*, XIX (April, 1936), 9.

of a certain unity among the women of the organization during the Civil War are also interesting. But often *Mount Vernon on the Potomac* is the tedious record of the change from one regent to another or of one ceremonial speech after another. The style lacks objectivity, and we thus read such eulogistic passages as: "Every member of the Association is deeply imbued with the seriousness of the duty which she has undertaken. . . . It is the same high spirit in which the White Crusaders took arms and fared forth to banish the Saracens from the Holy Land; the same high spirit in which George Washington, with a ragged and starving army, waged war through eight bitter years against the tyranny and oppression of a powerful monarchy."[41]

Among surviving members of the King family there is a traditional belief that Annie Ragan King (Nan) was more than a companion and researcher for her sister Grace. She was a self-effacing lady who may have collaborated on portions of some of the later books, especially *Mount Vernon on the Potomac* and *Memories of a Southern Woman of Letters*. Grace King labored in the writing of both of these, but she was in her last years when she undoubtedly welcomed Nan's assistance and possibly her contributions. As vice-regent of the Mount Vernon Association, Nan probably knew as much about the history of the group as her sister. Whether or not she was responsible for parts of the book cannot be proved, but it may explain why *Mount Vernon* stands as less than an impressive work of history.

*

In November, 1930, when she had little more than a year to live, Grace King wrote her expatriate friend Warrington Dawson:

> As you see my hand is nervous, & it is a task to make it write a legible letter. In fact, I have about given up writing letters & working also. The doctor says I am suffering from a nervous affection. That, my dear Warrington, it is not that only. I am just reaching the end of my line. That is all. And it is time.
>
> I work a little every day. I will finish my interminable Memories this winter, unless they finish me first. Tell me what you are doing—how you

41. Grace King, *Mount Vernon on the Potomac, History of the Mount Vernon Ladies' Association of the Union* (New York, 1929), 110.

are feeling—"Watchman . . . what of the night?" as it says in the Old Testament.[42]

Grace King was mentally alert to the end of her life, and her attitudes and loyalties were then consistent with those of her long past. Perhaps the last book she would read was Edgar Lee Masters' *Lincoln the Man* (1931), in which the Illinois poet savagely attacked the Civil War president as the destroyer of American liberty. Nothing could have pleased her more; she wrote that this was the best book on Lincoln she had read. It buoyed her spirits as she neared her own end; in a book of northern origin she saw a degree of vindication of the Confederate cause.[43]

Her last days were described by Nan in a typescript which she left with her sister's own papers. Grace King, a social person to the end, attended a meeting of the *Causeries de Lundi* on Monday, January 4, 1932. This was followed by a long automobile ride with her friend Mrs. Chaffraix. Two days passed, when on Wednesday night she called to Nan, who was sleeping in the adjoining room, to help her get back into bed. She had lost strength and had either fallen or sat down on the floor out of weakness. Nan could not lift her, but called Nina from her room. Nina could not lift her either, and all three sisters sat on the floor and laughed about the predicament. When the doctor came in the morning, he implied that Grace had had a stroke but that she was not paralyzed: she must stay in bed and not try to get up again. By this time she felt quite well and protested but obeyed the doctor. Her appetite was normal, and she saw Carleton after supper when he brought her a customary dish of ice cream.

On the following Monday she remarked that she was very tired, and on Wednesday she asked to have Dr. Coupeland come to give her Holy Communion. She also asked to see Carleton and his wife, and the family group took communion together.

A nurse did not prove necessary; the sisters and two friends took care of her needs for the few days that were left to her. Nan stayed by her bedside, rubbing her arms and legs sometimes to stimulate the circulation and to soothe her. During the final illness she seems not to have suffered at all. On

42. Grace King to Dawson, November 4, 1930, in Bush (ed.), *Grace King of New Orleans*, 404.
43. New Orleans *Morning Tribune*, June 22, 1932.

Thursday morning, January 14, 1932, her breathing grew softer and softer, and at 9:30 she died. The self-effacing Nan was there with a friend, Emma Nixon. The two women saw a small light shining just above the bed, a mysterious light that Nan leaves unexplained in her account of the last days.

How the dead looked in their coffins always commanded a strange respect among the Kings. Grace King herself was dressed in "the pretty costume she had had made for the Petit Salon . . . with her decoration of 'Officer de l'Instruction Publique'" that the French government had given her.

The day of the funeral was dark and threatening, but, quite appropriately, when the cortege reached Trinity Church the clouds disappeared, and again with perfect appropriateness a beautiful burst of sunshine lighted the coffin as it rested before the altar. The church was filled to the doors; tributes of flowers were taken to Métairie Cemetery by the carload, and the newspapers of New Orleans gave as much publicity to Grace King as they might have to a popular political figure.[44]

Such recognition for an excellent minor author would have been unlikely in Boston or New York, where minor authors were not rare. But Grace King had fulfilled her career potential in a city where authors were relatively rare. Cable, who had died in 1925, was the more important New Orleans author and still nationally known as such, but he had left the fold, had chosen to be the apostate. Grace King had done so much for New Orleans as a public figure that she deserved all of the acclaim the city could give her. In the end the loyalty ideal had paid its dividends: stay faithful to the old city and the old class and the old section, and none of these will forget you.

She had had ample time to put her career in final order. She had completed a preface to a paper William Notts had done on Charles Gayarré. She had corrected the proof for her autobiography just before her death. *Memories of a Southern Woman of Letters* was published by Macmillan in 1932, just a few months after her death. It was quite widely reviewed in major publications, and the tendency was to pay compliment to a career that was finished, but not necessarily to praise the memoirs themselves. The book has value in that it tells us much about the period from the Civil War to 1930, but its tendency is anecdotal rather than genuinely historical, and it rarely becomes critical or

---

44. Annie Ragan King, account of Grace King's last days (typescript), undated, ca. 1932.

analytical. Grace King seems to have thought that her autobiographical legacy should be a polite account of all her public experiences, a complimentary description of the various people of importance she had known in a long life, and she also seems to have rejected the idea that memoirs should be in any sense confessional. They were intended to reveal no private thoughts or intimacies. The finished book is therefore somewhat sketchy and vapid. In making public statements about her contemporaries or herself, she was entrapped by her southern respectability and her sense of loyalty. *Memories of a Southern Woman of Letters* gives us the polite and public Grace King, but it has little to say about what Ellen Glasgow would have called the woman within. Years before, Grace King's youthful suitor Gary Walker had pointed out to her that she was a double person, a public and a private young lady. *Memories* exhibits the public lady but not the more sensitive and critical woman.

The startling conclusion one comes to in reading the *Memories* is that, nearing eighty, she should recall so many graphic details of the events of her career but forget at times the chronological order of those events. Most surprising is her remembering Edward Garnett's complimentary remarks about *The Pleasant Ways of St. Médard* as appearing in the *Atlantic Monthly* in 1910. The date was in fact 1916, some months before the actual publication of the book. She also dates her third and final trip to Europe as 1911, when in fact it was 1913. It was on that trip that she took the manuscript of the novel to England and left it with an agent who would eventually turn it over to Garnett. Indications are that, having gone to great pains throughout her life to preserve her correspondence, she failed to consult her vast collection of documents in writing her autobiography.

One cannot deny that the book abounds in interesting passages, especially at the beginning when she writes with intensity about her family's escape into the Confederacy after the capitulation of New Orleans in 1862. These were memories she recalled herself and elaborated upon with the help of the stories told her by her mother and grandmother. The story of the privations suffered by the King family as they traveled from New Orleans to l'Embarras Plantation and lived there for the duration of the war years is well narrated as it happened to this archetypal family. But in detailing her subsequent life story Grace King was less than selective. As one of her critics wrote, "All must go in." [45] And when so much was to be included, even details that the reader cares little about, there was not enough space for adequate handling of such interesting subjects as the Nook Farm community, the New York publishers, and even the significant writers she met in Paris in 1892. It is ironic that frequently her personal letters to members of her family give a clearer and more penetrating picture of some of the people she met than her memoirs. And the reason for this is also clear: the letters were written shortly after the various encounters, the memoirs long after most of them.

Her life had been a meaningful one on the symbolic level. She was a special person for New Orleans, where her kind was rarer than in other large American cities. So her faithful disciple Nan would look for evidences to make a legend of her, recording the light above her bed in her final hours and the light that shone on the coffin for all to see. And since her death Grace King has been a tutelary divinity of the city and the state as much for what she represented as for the thirteen books she produced.

In 1918 she had written Carleton during a period of financial worry that in spite of the problem of the moment they would somehow manage. "Adversity has always been better for us than prosperity," she wrote him, "morally I mean & we may grow our angels' wings out of this trial." [46] Now the words would shed light on much of her life.

After the services at Trinity Church [47] and after the burial at Métairie, Nan and Nina returned to 1749 Coliseum Street, where they would reside for the rest of their lives. When the faithful Nan died in 1933 a *Times-Picayune* editorial honored her for her patient contributions to her sister's career. Nina lived in the house until her death in 1942. The three sisters had followed the single life, the worst path of all for family continuity. And yet Grace had frequently said that her work was a selfless dedication to family, to her father and mother, and to the South. When he died in 1901, she was grieved that her younger brother

45. Agnes Repplier, review of Grace King's *Memories of a Southern Woman of Letters*, in *Commonweal*, XVII (November 16, 1932), 83.

46. Grace King to Carleton King, July 1, 1918.

47. Grace King was probably baptized as a child at the First Presbyterian Church in New Orleans; however, the church has no records to confirm this. She was baptized later in life at Trinity Episcopal Church, New Orleans, and confirmed there on the same day, January 22, 1904.

Will had failed as the bright hope of the family. She thought of herself as maintaining the family ideal more than anyone else, but Will's tragedy had retarded the grand plan and left her in hopeless despair. Unlike her, however, he had done something essential for the cause: he had produced four children. Who would now occupy the stately Greek Revival house on Coliseum Street after the three single women were gone—the antebellum house with its parlors sparkling with prisms, the permanent home that marked the path of forty years that brought the family back to the status they had enjoyed before the war? Ironically, it was Will's issue. Carleton and his wife Aline lived there, and the children of their daughter, another Grace King, live there still. "Poor dear Willie," as his sister called him, had made his contribution to the future of the Kings after all.

Index